End-to-End Quality of Service
Over Heterogeneous Networks

Torsten Braun • Michel Diaz •
José Enríquez-Gabeiras • Thomas Staub

End-to-End
Quality of Service Over
Heterogeneous Networks

Prof. Dr. Torsten Braun
Thomas Staub
Universität Bern
Institut für Informatik und
Angewandte Mathematik (IAM)
Neubrückstr. 10
3012 Bern
Switzerland
braun@iam.unibe.ch
staub@iam.unibe.ch

Michel Diaz
LAAS - CNRS
7 Avenue du Colonel Roche
31400 Toulouse
France
diaz@laas.fr

José Enríquez Gabeiras
Telefónica I+D
Emilio Vargas 6
28043 Madrid
Spain
jeg@tid.es

ISBN 978-3-642-09799-7   e-ISBN 978-3-540-79120-1

DOI 10.1007/978-3-540-79120-1

ACM Computing Classification (1998): C.2.2

Cover design: KünkelLopka GmbH, Heidelberg

Printed on acid-free paper

9 8 7 6 5 4 3 2 1

springer.com

Preface

The Internet has evolved from an academic network for data applications such as file transfer and net news, to a global general-purpose network used for a variety of different applications—electronic mail, voice over IP, television, peer-to-peer file sharing, video streaming and many more. The heterogeneity of applications results in rather different application requirements in terms of bandwidth, delay, loss, etc. Ideally, the underlying network supports Quality-of-Service parameters such that applications can request the desired services from the network and do not need to take actions by themselves to achieve the desired communication quality. Initially, the Internet was not designed to support Quality of Service, and only in the last decade have appropriate mechanisms been developed. Those mechanisms operate mainly on the Internet Protocol (IP) level, but also network-specific mechanisms—e.g., targeted to particular wired/wireless access network technologies—are required.

The goal of the European 6th Framework Programme (FP6) Integrated Project "End-to-end Quality of Service Support over Heterogeneous Networks" (EuQoS) was to develop, implement and evaluate concepts and mechanisms to support QoS end-to-end, meaning that QoS mechanisms in end systems, access networks, interdomain links and within domains must be supported. The EuQoS project developed an impressive set of innovative solutions and novel scientific ideas to support end-to-end QoS on the Internet. New mechanisms and concepts were designed and implemented in a European-wide distributed testbed. In addition to the rather technical design and implementation work, the project also developed training material introducing basic QoS mechanisms and techniques. Several e-learning modules were developed and are currently being used at several partner universities for teaching on MSc or PhD levels.

The significant technical and educational results achieved during the EuQoS project motivated us to use the gained knowledge and experiences of the project partners and write this book on end-to-end QoS in heterogeneous IP networks. The book basically consists of three parts. In Chaps. 1–4, we discuss QoS mechanisms and protocols such as scheduling schemes, QoS architectures, metrics and measurement techniques, traffic engineering and signalling protocols, and the latest standardisation activities. In Chap. 5, we describe related work and recent developments in the area of transport protocols, in particular how TCP can be optimised toward QoS support and fairness. The EuQoS system presented in Chap. 6 extends and combines the basic mechanisms discussed in the previous chapters. We show how a combination of different QoS-enabling mechanisms and protocols can be used and extended to build a comprehensive end-to-end QoS architecture over heterogeneous wired/wireless access networks. To evaluate QoS mechanisms and architectures, appropriate evaluation schemes are required. The two chapters in the appendix describe how simulation—in particular the well-known network simulator ns-2—as well as emulation techniques can be used for tests and evaluations.

This book, which is based on the achievements of the EuQoS project, would not have been possible without funding from the European Commission, as well as the tremendous efforts and enthusiasm of all the people involved in the project. Special thanks to Mark Günter for proofreading the text contributions to this book.

Torsten Braun
Michel Diaz
José Enríquez Gabeiras
Thomas Staub

Bern, Toulouse, Madrid. January 2008.

Acknowledgements

The book editors and authors thank all people who were involved in the EuQoS project:

- **Telefonica I+D:** José Enríquez Gabeiras, María Ángeles Callejo Rodríguez, Francisco Javier Ramón Salguero, Gerardo García de Blas, Jorge Andrés Colás, Francisco Romero Bueno, Jesús Bravo Álvarez, María Luisa García Osma, Antonio J. Elizondo Armengol
- **University of Pisa (CPR/UoPisa):** Enzo Mingozzi, Giovanni Stea, Luciano Lenzini, Luca Bisti, Claudio Cicconetti, Linda Martorini, Abraham Gebrehiwot, Simone Bisogni, Paolo Sozzi, Alessandro Spanò, Luca Luigetti
- **Elsag Datamat:** Enrico Angori, Giuseppe Martufi, Marco Carusio, Alessandro Giorgini, Andrea Paselli, Giovanni Saccomandi, Marco Mauro
- **CNRS (LAAS-CNRS, ENSICA):** Michel Diaz, Florin Racaru, Ernesto Exposito, Philippe Owezarski, Patrick Sénac, Christophe Chassot, Nicolas Larrieu, Laurent Dairaine, Mathieu Gineste, Nicolas Van Wambeke, Slim Abdellatif, Sébastien Ardon, Roberto Willrich, Guillaume Auriol, Silvia Farraposo
- **France Telecom R&D:** Olivier Dugeon, Walid Htira, Michel Bourbao, Pascal Le Guern, Jean-Louis Le Roux, Stéphane Statiotis, Régis Fréchin, Claire Teisseire
- **Polska Telefonia Cyfrowa (ERA):** Michal Obuchowicz, Robert Parzydo, Adam Flizikowski, Edyta Rafalska, Karol Jez, Krzysztof Horszczaruk, Krzysztof Bronarski, Krzysztof Samp, Maciej Rozowicz, Michal Dudzinski, Pawel Caban, Piotr Zadroga, Slawomir Tkacz
- **Martel:** Martin Potts, Mark Guenter, Sandra Wittwer
- **NICTA:** Emmanuel Lochin, Guillaume Jourjon, Sebastien Ardon, Ernesto Exposito, Feiselia Tan, Laurent Dairaine
- **PointerCom:** Roberto Marega, Stefano Salsano, Donald Papalilo, Gianluca Martiniello, Valeria Calcagni

- **Polish Telecom R&D:** Zbigniew Kopertowski, Jaroslaw Kowalczyk, Tomasz Ciszkowski
- **Portugal Telecom Inovação (PTIN):** Jorge Carapinha, Nuno Carapeto, Paulo Loureiro, Arnaldo Santos, Eduardo Silva, Fernando Santiago, Helena Paula Matos, Hugo Manaia, Isabel Borges, Jacinto Barbeira, Filipe Peixinho.
- **Red Zinc:** Donal Morris, Brian Widger, Diarmuid O Neill, Léa Compin, Oscar Cuidad
- **Silogic:** Laurent Baresse, Benoît Baurens, Jean-Philippe Darmet, Yannick Lizzi, François Meaude
- **INDRA (previously SOLUZIONA):** Ignacio Fresno, Jaime Orozco, Luis Collantes Abril, Pablo Vaquero Barbón, Rubén Romero San Martín, Jorge Alonso, Maria Lurdes Sousa, Raul Manzano Barroso
- **Telscom AG:** Sathya Rao, Marcin Michalak
- **Technical University of Catalonia (UPC):** Jordi Domingo-Pascual, Loránd Jakab, Marcelo Yannuzzi, René Serral-Gracià, Xavier Masip-Bruin
- **University of Bern:** Torsten Braun, Thomas Staub, Dragan Milić, Marc Brogle, Marc-Alain Steinemann, Thomas Bernoulli, Gerald Wagenknecht, Markus Wulff, Patrick Lauer, Markus Anwander, Matthias Scheidegger
- **University of Paderborn/C-LAB:** Isabell Jahnich, Achim Rettberg, Chris Loeser, Michael Ditze, Kay Klobedanz, Sebastian Seitz, Andreas König, Volker Spaarmann, Matthias Grawinkel
- **University of Rome:** Antonio Pietrabissa, Francesco Delli Priscoli, Sabrina Giampaoletti, Emiliano Guainella, Erasmo Di Santo, Gianfranco Santoro, Ilaria Marchetti, Massimiliano Rossi
- **Universidade de Coimbra:** Edmundo Monteiro, Luís Cordeiro, Bruno Carvalho, Fernando Boavida, Gabriela Batista Leão, Isidro Caramelo, Jian Zhang, Jorge Sá Silva, Marilia Curado, Maxwel Carmo, Paulo Simões, Romulo Ribeiro, Vitor Bernardo, David Palma, Rui Vilão, Luís Conceição
- **Warsaw University of Technology:** Wojciech Burakowski, Andrzej Beben, Halina Tarasiuk, Jaroslaw Sliwinski, Jordi Mongay Batalla, Marek Dabrowski, Piotr Krawiec, Robert Janowski
- **Ericsson:** Antoine de Poorter, Julio López Roldan, Miguel Angel Recio, Jesus Renero Quintero, José Luis Agundez
- **Hospital Divino Espirito Santo:** José Manuel Ponte, António Vasco Viveiros, Carlos P. Duarte, Paula Maciel, José M. Jesus Silva, Maura Medeiros, Maria Dulce Raposo

Contents

Acronyms

The following list contains acronyms used in the book and their explanation. Most acronyms can be found in the index as well together with a page reference.

ALM   Application layer multicast
API   Application programming interface
CIDR   Classless Internet domain routing
COPS   Common Open Policy Service
DVMRP   Distance-vector multicast routing protocol
IGMP   Internet group management protocol
IP   Internet protocol
IPTV   Internet Protocol Television
IPv4   Internet protocol version 4
IPv6   Internet protocol version 6
ISP   Internet service provider
MM   Multicast Middleware
MOSPF   Multicast open shortest path first
NSIS   Next Step In Signalling
P2P   Peer-to-peer
PDP   Policy Decision Point
PEP   Policy Enforcement Point
PIM   Protocol-independant multicast
QoS   Quality of Service
SDP   Session Description Protocol
SE   Signalling Entities
SIP   Session initiation Protocol
SSQ   Synchronize State Query
TCP   Transmission control protocol

TTL   Time-To-Live
UAC   User Agent Client
UAS   User Agent Server
UDP   User datagram protocol
VLSM   Variable length subnet mask
MPLS   Multi Protocol Label Switching
TE   Traffic Engineering
RIP   Routing Information Protocol
IGP   Interior Gateway Protocol
OSPF   Open Shortest Path First
IS-IS   Intermediate System-Intermediate System
RSVP   ReSerVation Protocol
IETF   Internet Engineering Task Force
FEC   Forwarding Equivalence Class
LSR   Label-Switching Router
LFIB   Label Forwarding Information Base
ATM   Asynchronous Transfer Mode
DLCI   Data-Link Connection Identifier
VPI   Virtual Path Identifier
VCI   Virtual Channel Identifier
BGP   Border Gateway Protocol
LDP   Label Distribution Protocol
LIB   Label Information Base
LSP   Label-Switched Path
CBR   Constraint-Based Routing
TED   Traffic Engineering Database
CSPF   Constrained Shortest Path First
SPF   Shortest Path First
CR-LDP   Constraint-based Routing Label Distribution Protocol
TSPEC   Traffic Specification
ERO   Explicit Route Object
BA   Behavior Aggregate
PHB   Per Hop Behavior
DSCP   Diff-Serv Codepoint
OA   Ordered Aggregate
PSC   PHB Scheduling Class
AF   Assured Forwarding
E-LSP   EXP-Inferred-PSC LSP
L-LSP   Label-Only-Inferred-PSC LSP
BE   Best Effort
DS-TE   Diff-Serv-aware Traffic Engineering
CT   Class Type
BC   Bandwidth Constraint
MAM   Maximum Allocation Bandwidth Constraints Model
RDM   Russian Doll Bandwidth Constraints Model

AC	Access Category
ADSL	Asymmetric DSL
AIFS	Arbitrary Inter-Frame Space
AP	Access Point
AS	Autonomous Systems
ASPB	AS Path Builder
ATM	Asynchronous Transfer Mode
BR	Border Router
BRAS	Broadband Remote Access Server
BRPC	Backward Recursive Path Computation
CAC	Connection Admission Control
CBR	Constant Bit Rate
CoS	Class of Service
CPE	Customer Premises Equipment
CRA	Continuous Rate Assignment
CW	Contention Window
DAMA	Demand Assignment Multiple Access
DCF	Distributed Coordination Function
DSL	Digital Subscriber Line
DSLAM	Digital Subscriber Line Access Multiplexer
DVB-S	Digital Video Broadcasting - Satellite
DVB-RCS	Digital Video Broadcasting - Reverse Channel Satellite
e2e CoS	End-to-end Class of Service
EDCA	Enhanced Distributed Coordination Access
ER	Edge Router
ES	Ethernet Switch
FCA	Free Capacity Assignment
FTP	File Transfer Protocol
GGSN	GPRS Gateway Support Node
HTD	High Throughput Data
IPLR	IP Packet Loss Ratio
IPTD	IP Packet Transfer Delay
IPDV	IP Packet Delay Variation
MAC	Medium Access Control
MT	Mobile Terminal
NCC	Network Control Centre
NRT	Non Real Time
OGGSN	Open GPRS Gateway Support Node
PCC	Path Computation Client
PCE	Path Computation Element
PCEP	PCE Protocol
PQ	Priority Queuing
PR	Peak Rate
RA	Resource Allocator
RBDC	Rate Based Dynamic Capacity

RM	Resource Manager
RNC	Radio Network Controller
RT	Real Time
SHDSL	Symmetrical High Bitrate DSL
SLA	Service Level Agreement
ST	Satellite Terminal
STD	Standard
TERO	Traffic Engineering and Resource Optimization
TOS	Type of Service
UTRAN	UMTS Terrestrial Radio Access Network
VBDC	Volume Based Dynamic Capacity
VBR	Variable Bit Rate
VDSL	Very High Bitrate DSL
VoD	Video on Demand
VoIP	Voice over IP
VTC	Video Teleconference
WFQ	Weighted Fair Queueing
WMM	WiFi Multi-Media
WRED	Weighted Random Early Detection
WRR	Weighted Round-Robin
CLI	Command Line Interface
EQ-BGP	Enhanced QoS Border Gateway Protocol
QoS NLRI	QoS Network Layer Reachability Information
DoP	Degree of Preference
SNMP	Simple Network Management Protocol
TMN	Telecommunications Management Network
SAAA	Security, Authentication, Authorization and Accounting
QoSR	Quality of Service Routing
xDSL	Digital Subscriber Line
UMTS	Universal Mobile Telecommunications System
LAN	Local Area Network
NREN	National REsearch Network
GEANT	Multi-gigabit pan-European data communications network
NTI	Network Technology Independent
NTD	Network Technology Dependent
AQ-SSN	Application Quality Signalling and Service Negotiation
CHAR	CHARging module QCM Quality Control Module
MMS	Monitoring and Measurement System
EQ-SAP	EQ-Service Access Point
PQ-WFQ	Priority Queueing - Weighted Fair Queueing
SCTP	Stream Control Transmission Protocol
DCCP	Datagram Congestion Control Protocol
ETP	Enhanced Transport Protocol
gTFRC	TCP-Friendly Rate Congestion Control
TC	Time Constraints

SACK	Selective ACKnowledgement
PCMA	Pulse Code Modulation a-law
PCMU	Pulse Code Modulation mu-law
CIF	Common Intermediate Format
QCIF	Quarter Common Intermediate Format
SQCIF	Sub Quarter Common Intermediate Format
e2e	end-to-end

1

Motivation and Basics

Torsten Braun and Thomas Staub

Summary. This chapter provides an introduction to the topic of Quality of Service and motivates the rest of the chapters in the book. The performance of network applications (e.g., video on demand, collaboration tools, voice over IP, Internet TV, video conferencing) depends on the quality of network connections. Parameters such as packet loss, delay, delay variation, and out-of-order delivery are important to describe network performance. Since applications differ in their Quality-of-Service (QoS) needs, this chapter provides a classification of some typical applications and sheds light on their requirements. It further illustrates the implementation and performance of QoS-aware applications, as well as the benefits of such QoS-aware applications, and concludes with a short overview of the following chapters.

1.1 Quality of Service and its Parameters

Quality of Service (QoS) is a measure of the ability of network and computing systems to provide different levels of services to selected applications and associated network flows. Since Internet Protocol (IP) based networks are expected to form the basis for all kinds of future communication services such as data transfer, telephony, television, etc., and users expect at least the same quality for those services such as when delivered over dedicated networks, QoS support for IP networks is urgently required. Currently, however, IP networks are Best-Effort networks. As the name suggests, packet forwarding is performed with the best effort, but without guaranteeing bandwidth, delay bounds etc.

Before going into more detail, the term QoS must be defined more accurately. [1] distinguishes perceptual, application, system, network and device QoS [2] for multimedia systems. The network QoS parameters are most important for this book. They may be specified in terms of the network load including packet interarrival times, burstiness and packet sizes, as well as the network performance describing network service guarantees. Network performance can be described in more detail by several parameters such as delay, delay variation, bandwidth, and packet loss rate. These are the basic QoS parameters discussed hereafter. QoS supporting systems try to guarantee QoS by not exceeding QoS parameter limits. QoS parameters are also called QoS metrics in relation to measurement, see Chap. 2.

1.1.1 Delay and Delay Variations in End-to-End Packet Delivery

As described more formally in Chap. 2, the one-way delay (only called delay in this chapter) normally describes the average delay that packets experience over a specific connection. Packet delays can be split into four components:

- *Processing delay* is the time needed by network elements such as routers or end systems to process a packet. It depends on the processing speed of the network element hardware and the complexity of the functions to perform. These range from simple packet classification for forwarding and fire-walling, to complex payload modifications for encryption and content adaptation.
- Network components normally have input and/or output queues. The time a packet resides in these queues is called *queuing delay*. Queues become larger when the network becomes congested, which results in a longer queuing delay.
- *Transmission delay* is the time needed to transmit a packet at a specific bit rate. It can be calculated as

$$\text{transmission delay} = \frac{\text{number of bits to transmit}}{\text{transmission rate}}.$$

- The *propagation delay* describes the time needed by the signals to travel (propagate) through the medium. It can be calculated as

$$\text{propagation delay} = \frac{\text{physical distance}}{\text{propagation velocity}}.$$

Propagation and queuing delay are the key contributors to delay as long as no heavy processing like encryption or packetisation by applications (cf. Sect. 1.2.2.1) is needed.

In real-world networks, packets experience a delay on their path from the sender to the receiver, which is not constant but rather varying over time, because conditions on a route and the involved systems change. This is a result of the fluctuation of Internet traffic and resulting queue sizes. The delay is bounded by a minimum and maximum delay. The difference between these bounds is called delay variation. In the remainder of the section we use the same definition for the delay variation as the ITU-T for the IPDV as outlined in Chap. 2. The typical behaviour for the delay of packets of a single flow in the Internet is depicted in Fig. 1.1. Since processing, transmission, and propagation delay normally do not change for a given route, the delay variation has its source in the varying queuing delay.

The delay variation can be compensated by buffering packets, either within the network elements (routers) or the receiving end systems. Since end-system memory is much cheaper than router memory, buffering in the end system is usually preferred. Figure 1.2 shows the concept of play-out buffering. In this example, we assume that a continuous stream of packets is sent with a difference of 160 ms between each packet. Each packet has a timestamp indicating its transmission time. The delay of

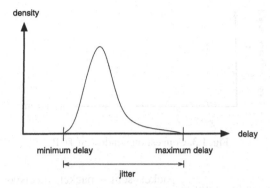

Fig. 1.1. Delay variation

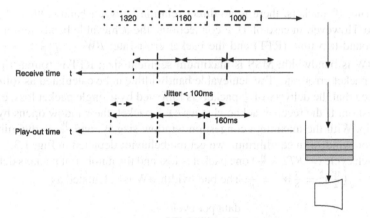

Fig. 1.2. Play-out buffer

the first and third packet is rather low (minimum delay), while the second packet experienced maximum delay. Assuming that the difference between the minimum and the maximum delay (delay variation) is not more than 100 ms, it is sufficient to delay each packet by 100 ms at the receiver. In this case, the first packet is delayed by additional 100 ms after reception and the second one arrives just in time so that the two packets can be played out with the original difference of 160 ms. The example shows that play-out buffering only works if the delay variation is bounded.

1.1.2 Bandwidth and Packet Loss Ratio

The bandwidth describes the capacity of a link or end-to-end path. It is measured in bits per second. The packet loss rate indicates the number of packets that do not reach the destination in relation to all sent packets. Packet loss has mainly two causes— packet errors, e.g. due to bad link quality (especially on wireless links) and packet drops, e.g. due to congestion. It can be calculated as

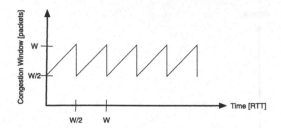

Fig. 1.3. Congestion window in TCP

$$\text{Packet loss ratio} = \frac{\text{packets sent} - \text{packets received}}{\text{packets sent}}.$$

Considering IP packets, there is no direct relation between bandwidth and packet loss ratio. However, in case of TCP connections, the achievable bandwidth depends on the round-trip time (RTT) and the packet error rate: $BW < \frac{MSS}{RTT} \times \frac{1}{\sqrt{p}}$ [3, 4] where BW is bandwidth; MSS is maximum segment size; RTT is round-trip time; and p is packet error rate. The achievable bandwidth can be calculated as follows. It is assumed that the delivery of $\frac{1}{p}$ packets is followed by a single packet loss, e.g. due to congestion. If the receiver acknowledges each packet, the window opens by 1 per round trip. With the maximum congestion window size W, and $\frac{W}{2}$ as the minimum congestion window in equilibrium, we get the behavior depicted in Fig. 1.3.

In each cycle ($= RTT \times \frac{W}{2}$) one packet is lost and the number of packets delivered is $(\frac{W}{2})^2 + \frac{1}{2}(\frac{W}{2})^2 = \frac{3}{8}W^2 = \frac{1}{p}$. The bandwidth BW is calculated as

$$BW = \frac{\text{data per cycle}}{\text{time per cycle}}$$

$$= \frac{MSS \times \frac{3}{8}W^2}{RTT \times \frac{W}{2}}$$

$$= \frac{\frac{MSS}{p}}{RTT \times \sqrt{\frac{2}{3}p}}$$

$$= \frac{MSS \times C}{RTT \times \sqrt{p}}, \quad C = \sqrt{1.5}.$$

We conclude that the achievable bandwidth for a TCP connection depends on the round-trip time, as well as on the error rate.

1.2 Applications' QoS Requirements

Many network applications work fine with Best-Effort services, while others have strong QoS requirements and only work with guaranteed QoS, or at least benefit significantly if QoS guarantees are possible. After describing two classification schemes of network applications, we give an overview of application requirements for audio, video and data applications.

1.2.1 Types of Network Applications

Each application probably has individual QoS requirements. However, they can be classified using different classification schemes. In the following we discuss two classification schemes for network applications, namely (in)elastic applications as well as (non-)interactive applications.

1.2.1.1 Elastic and Inelastic Applications

First, we distinguish between elastic and inelastic applications. An elastic application is able to adapt to changing QoS parameters and does not fail in that case. Elastic applications are also called Best-Effort applications. File transfer and e-mail are examples of elastic applications, because they do not require guaranteed bandwidth or delay bounds. In case of low bandwidth, the file or e-mail transfer just takes somewhat longer.

In contrast to elastic applications, inelastic applications need strict QoS guarantees. Real-time applications by nature are mostly inelastic, but may have some ability to adapt to certain QoS parameter changes. For example, audio/video conferencing can adapt to less bandwidth by using more efficient video codecs. A codec (derived from "coder/decoder") is a software or hardware device able to encode and decode a digital data stream. However, a minimum bandwidth is required to run the most efficient codec. Moreover, the delay requirements are quite stringent in such cases.

1.2.1.2 Interactive and Noninteractive Applications

Another classification scheme distinguishes interactive and noninteractive applications. Interactive applications include human interaction. Typically, a human user interacts remotely with another end system and expects a quick reaction to the performed action. The reaction should normally be as quick as possible with hard bounds of low delay. Due to the strict delay bounds, the error rate is quite important, because retransmissions are not possible without exceeding the tolerable delay if round-trip times are rather high. Forward error correction is a means to reduce delays in such a case, but additional processing is required by the end systems. Figure 1.4 shows the delay and error rate requirements for real-time voice transmissions. Interactive applications can also be categorised as real-time applications. In most cases, they are inelastic too.

Examples of interactive applications are voice over IP (VoIP), audio/video conferencing, collaborative online applications, and online games. Examples of noninteractive applications are Web browsing, file transfer, chats and multimedia streaming. For multimedia streaming a server begins to send a continuous stream of multimedia data to be played out at the receiver. In theory, insufficient bandwidth and

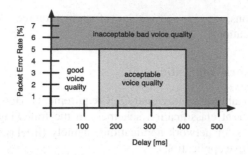

Fig. 1.4. Delay and error rate requirements for voice transmissions according to one-way values of [5]

delay variation can be compensated by buffering. If the bandwidth requirements are not met, the stream can only be played out after a significant delay introduced by buffering a huge amount of data, which can easily exceed available buffer space. As discussed in Sect. 1.1.1, large delay variation also has an impact on the required buffer size.

1.2.2 QoS Requirements of Applications

1.2.2.1 Audio Applications

Audio transmissions normally have widely varying bandwidth requirements, depending on whether telephony or high-fidelity music is being transferred. In addition to the encoded audio data, protocol overhead by IP, User Data Datagram (UDP), and Real-Time Transport Protocol (RTP) headers must be considered. Larger packets can reduce this overhead. In this case, several audio samples are collected and put together into a single packet, but longer packetisation intervals increase the delay. Moreover, sensitivity to packet loss is increased, since a single packet includes a rather long sequence of consecutive audio samples.

In particular, in case of interactive audio such as telephony, strong delay requirements exist. The recommended maximum tolerable delay for telephony is 150 ms [6]. This includes the four delay components described in Sect. 1.1.1 as well as packetisation delay. The delay variation should be limited too, since high delay variation increases the required size of play-out buffers at the receiver. Moreover, interactive audio applications are quite sensitive to packet loss. Thus, they require (very) low loss rates. The concrete numbers depend on the type of the audio application. Telephony using mother language requires less stringent error bounds than telephony using a foreign language or even high-fidelity music. Moreover, less efficient encodings have some degree of redundancy and can therefore tolerate higher packet loss.

In the case of streamed audio where a single user receives and listens to an audio stream without having interaction, the delay, bandwidth and error rate requirements can be relaxed. However, due to buffer limitations, guaranteeing QoS parameters might be desirable as well.

1.2.2.2 Video Applications

Many statements for audio apply to video transmissions as well. Audio and video transmissions have much in common. If interactive, both are sensitive to delay, delay variation and packet loss. However, there are several differences between audio and video. Most importantly, the required bandwidth for video is much higher, which depends highly on the quality level desired by the user or supported by the video equipment. While PC- or mobile hand-held-based video conferencing systems work with even a few tens of kbps, high-definition television demands several Mbps. The bandwidth requirements depend on several system parameters such as colour depth, screen size and resolution, frame rate and acceptable quality degradation by compression.

Another observation is that video traffic is usually burstier than audio traffic due to the used encoding schemes. Schemes like MPEG periodically send a so-called intracoded frame, which does not have any reference to other preceding or succeeding frames. Frames that are sent between these intracoded frames, so-called intercoded frames, can have a reference to other frames and only encode the difference (in terms of movement vectors, colour differences etc.) compared to the referred frames. This results in so-called weakly regular traffic for video, while audio often is strongly regular as depicted in Fig. 1.5. Weakly regular traffic creates some short-term bursts. The first option to handle such bursts is to provide sufficient resources (in particular bandwidth and buffer memory) in the network elements. The other option is to smooth out the traffic at the sender's end in order to produce rather constant traffic. However, this can again can lead to additional delays.

As for audio, the required video quality heavily depends on the type of the application scenario. A simple video conference with some known colleagues might have less stringent quality requirements than a movie or telemedicine applications. There is also a difference between stored and real-time video. If the video has been recorded in advance, video encoding can be more efficient resulting in higher burstiness, while live video compression may be less bursty due to the lack of processing time required for highly efficient interframe coding. The same as discussed for streamed audio applies to streamed video, but again, due to the higher bandwidth, buffer size requirements are much higher.

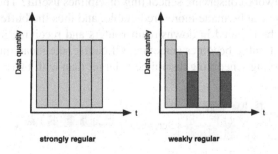

Fig. 1.5. Strongly and weakly regular traffic according to [1]

1.2.2.3 Data Traffic

Although nonaudio and nonvideo traffic is summarised as data traffic it must be kept in mind that there are many different data traffic classes. File transfers of multi-megabyte files as well as interactive console traffic is part of the data traffic category. The term transactional traffic is often used for interactive data traffic. Since there are thousands of data applications, it is impossible to discuss them all. Every application potentially has a unique traffic pattern and network requirements. Even different versions of the same application may result in very different traffic patterns [7].

1.3 Packet Scheduling in Network Elements

Sharing of network resources automatically introduces the problem of contention. Applications need QoS guarantees and congestion in networks is still common. Thus, scheduling disciplines implemented in network elements such as routers and switches are important so that network resources are shared fairly and performance guarantees for performance-critical applications. A scheduling discipline has to achieve two main tasks, as indicated by Fig. 1.6.

- First, it has to decide the order in which requests are serviced (packet selection).
- Second, it has to manage the service queue of requests awaiting service (packet dropping).

This section describes the concepts and requirements of a scheduling discipline and introduces some of the most important scheduling algorithms.

1.3.1 (Non)Work-Conserving Scheduling Disciplines

The most simple scheduling discipline is First Come First Serve (FCFS), also known as First In First Out. In this case, all arriving packets are served according to their arrival sequence. A scheduling discipline like FCFS is idle only if its queue is empty. Such schedulers are also called work-conserving [8]. On the other hand, a nonwork-conserving scheduling discipline may be idle even if it has packets to serve. A packet is sent only if it is eligible, otherwise it is delayed until it becomes eligible. However, why are nonwork-conserving scheduling disciplines useful? The reason is that downstream traffic can be made more predictable, and thus the buffer sizes and delay variation can be reduced in downstream routers and receiving systems. Bursts are eliminated and traffic becomes smoother. Of course, the mean queuing delay of a nonwork-conserving scheduling discipline is larger than with FCFS.

Fig. 1.6. Scheduling

The Conservation Law states that a work-conserving scheduling discipline can reduce a connection's mean delay, compared with FCFS, only at the expense of another connection. Thus, if a particular connection receives a lower delay than with FCFS, at least one other connection gets a higher delay. For that reason, the sum of delays with FCFS is a tight lower bound for the sum of delays for every scheduling discipline, whether it is work-conserving or not. The Conservation Law is as follows: $\sum \rho_i q_i = const$, with ρ_i as the mean utilisation of a link due to connection i and q_i as connection i's mean waiting time at the scheduler.

1.3.2 Fairness

Another important issue is fairness. A scheduling discipline should divide resources fairly among a set of users. A problem to be solved is when some users demand fewer resources than others do. So how can the resources left by these users be divided? The Max-Min Fair Share approach solves this problem by maximising the minimum share of a source whose demand is not fully satisfied. In this case, resources are allocated in the order of increasing demands. No user gets a resource share larger than its demand and sources with unsatisfied demand get an equal share of the resource. The resource allocation algorithm is as follows:

1. Divide capacity C by n: $\frac{C}{n}$ resources for each connection.
2. Connection 1 needs x_1 resources ($x_1 < \frac{C}{n}$).
3. Distribute exceeding resources $\frac{C}{n} - x_1$ equally among other connections, so that each connection gets $\frac{C}{n} + \frac{\frac{C}{n} - x_1}{(n-1)}$ resources allocated.
4. Continue the process if resource allocation is larger than x_2.

If we want to give a bigger share to some user than to others, we can use weights that reflect their relative resource share. The demands of the users are then normalised by the weight and sources with an unsatisfied demand get resource shares in proportion to their weights.

1.3.2.1 Requirements for Scheduling Disciplines

There are four (sometimes contradictory) requirements that a scheduling discipline must satisfy.

- Ease of implementation: In a high-speed network, once every few microseconds a server has to decide on which packet to pick for transmission. Therefore, a scheduling discipline should require only a few simple operations. Preferably, they should be implementable inexpensively in terms of hardware. Furthermore, the number of operations should be as independent of the number of scheduled connections as possible.
- Fairness and protection: An allocation at a network element can be considered as fair if it satisfies the max-min fair share criterion. For Best-Effort connections fairness is an intuitively desirable property. However, for guaranteed-service connections it is not a concern. A scheduling discipline provides protection if the

misbehaviour of one connection does not affect the performance of other connections.

- Performance bounds: A scheduling discipline should allow arbitrary connection performance bounds, limited by the conservation law only. Performance bounds can be defined in a deterministic or statistical way.
- Ease of efficiency and admission control: A scheduling discipline should be able to decide whether it is possible to meet the performance bounds of new connections or not. This decision is also called admission control. The decision should lead neither to network underutilisation, nor to jeopardising the performance of existing connections.

1.3.3 Scheduling Disciplines

In addition to FCFS, a variety of scheduling disciplines exist. An ideal and work-conserving scheduling discipline that provides a max-min fair allocation is Generalised Processor Sharing (GPS). Unfortunately, GPS cannot be implemented. GPS serves packets as if they are in separate logical queues. Each nonempty queue is visited in turn and an infinitesimally small amount of data in each queue is served. Thus, the scheduler can visit each queue at least once in any finite time interval. We assume N connections with equal weights send data to the scheduler infinitely fast. The GPS scheduler serves an infinitesimally small amount from each connection in turn. Therefore, each connection gets a share of $\frac{1}{N}$ of the bandwidth. If a connection sends less data than this share, the queue of this scheduler will occasionally be empty. Thus, the GPS scheduler skips empty queues, and because of its round-robin service the time saved is equally distributed to the other connections resulting in a new service rate. If another connection has a rate larger than $\frac{1}{N}$, but smaller than the new service rate, its queue will occasionally be empty too. Again, the remaining connections will receive a slightly larger share. Obviously, each connection with a rate smaller than its fair share gets its demand allocated, while each connection with a larger demand gets an equal share. Thus, we see that GPS service achieves the max-min fair share defined above.

A priority scheduler knows different priority levels, which have their own queue. Every incoming packet will be assigned to a priority level, depending on protocol type, application, IP addresses, etc. The packet with the highest priority will be processed. Packets with lower priority are selected only if there are no packets with higher priority available.

A (Weighted) Round-Robin scheduler has a queue for every service class and serves the packets from each nonempty buffer in turn. To obtain a service differentiation, service classes can have different weights so that the buffers will be served in proportion to their weight.

Weighted Fair Queuing is an emulation of GPS scheduling. For each incoming packet a finish number is calculated. The theoretical meaning of this finish number is the time the last bit of the packet should be transmitted if the GPS scheduler would be used. In practice, the finish number is only a service tag and does not stand for the actual time at which a packet is served. Packets are ordered by their finish number and serviced in that order. The finish number of a packet arriving at an inactive connection is the sum of the current round number and the packet size in bits. If the packet is arriving at an active connection, the finish number is the sum of the largest finish number in the queue, or of the packet last served and the packet size in bits. The finish number is calculated as [8]:

$$F(i, k, t) = \max\{F(i, k - 1, t), R(t)\} + P(i, k, t)/\phi(i), \quad \text{with}$$

$F(i, k, t)$: finish number of the kth packet of connection i with arriving time t
$P(i, k, t)$: packet length
$R(t)$: number of the round at time t
$\phi(i)$: weight of connection i.

The round number increases inversely proportional to the number of active connections. It indicates the number of rounds a bit-by-bit round robin scheduler has completed at a given time. A connection is active if the largest finish number in the connections queue or of the packet last served is bigger than the current round number.

Rate-controlled scheduling consists of two components: a regulator and a scheduler. The regulator determines the packets eligibility time and forwards only eligible packets to the scheduler. The scheduler uses an arbitrary algorithm (FIFO, Priority, Round Robin etc.) to schedule the packets.

1.3.4 Packet Dropping

The limited length of the various queues in a scheduler requires dropping packets in overload conditions. In order to avoid that important packets are dropped while less-important packets are not dropped, packets can be marked by applications or routers with a packet-drop priority. Packets with high drop priorities are dropped first. One approach could be to assign a low dropping priority to packets that have been travelling for a very long time. This avoids dropping packets that have already consumed a large amount of network resources.

Another issue is whether a scheduler drops packets when there is absolutely no space in the queue, or somewhat earlier to always have some space for important packets to serve. Alternatives are early dropping schemes such as Random Early Detection (RED). In this case, packets can be dropped even if the queue is not full. This always keeps some space for important packets arriving later. Those packets would otherwise have to be dropped.

When packets must be dropped, we can drop them from the tail of the queue. This is easy to implement, but may be unfair if packets of well-behaving connections have just arrived. An alternative is random dropping, where packets to be dropped are selected randomly. Even packets at the head of the queue can be dropped. This scheme has the advantage that the receiver will notify a packet loss earlier than for dropping packets at the tail. In this case, the congestion control mechanisms as implemented in TCP will react earlier.

1.4 Quality-of-Service Architectures

It is not sufficient to deploy routers with advanced packet schedulers to guarantee QoS between two computers in the Internet. End-to-end quality of service requires a system that is able to coordinate the routers in the network according to the users' demands. Several architectures have been proposed in the past to solve this problem. The following sections present two important cases, the Integrated Services and Differentiated Services architectures. We further discuss pure end-to-end approaches.

1.4.1 Integrated Services

The IETF's Integrated Services (IntServ) architecture (RFC 1633 [9]) was designed to overcome the inability of the Internet to provide guaranteed end-to-end QoS. It is based on the reservation of network and system resources (bandwidth, buffer, CPU time) depending on application requirements. In addition to the traditional Best-Effort service, IntServ provides the two new service classes: Controlled Load Service and Guaranteed Service. In order to use these services, the affected network elements must be configured by means of a signalling protocol. The most popular IntServ signalling protocol is the Resource Reservation Setup Protocol (RSVP).

Integrated Services relies on flow descriptors to characterise network traffic and reservation requests. Flow descriptors consist of a filter specification (FilterSpec) for identifying source(s) and destination(s) of the flow as well as a flow specification (FlowSpec) with information about the flow's traffic characteristics and the requested reservation. The abstraction of token buckets (RFC 2215 [10]) is used to describe the traffic characteristics of a flow. Token buckets are defined by the token rate r (in bytes/second) and the bucket size b (in bytes). See Fig. 1.7 for illustration. Packets will be sent (or forwarded) only if there are enough tokens in the bucket, which is refilled with r tokens per second. Flows that follow a token bucket model are predictable enough to allow for traffic guarantees. At the same time, they are flexible enough to cover most types of Internet flows. Optionally, three additional parameters may be used to make a flow even more predictable: the peak rate p (in bytes/second), the minimum and maximum packet sizes, m and M. These five parameters (r, b, p, m and M) make up an IntServ Traffic Specification (TSpec).

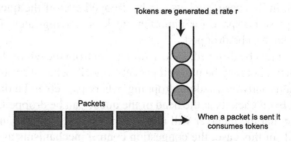

Fig. 1.7. The token bucket model

Most network applications can adapt to the relatively small variations in end-to-end latency and the occasional packet loss that occur when the network is not overloaded. However, when the network is congested their performance will degrade significantly. The Controlled Load service class (RFC 2211 [11]) aims to create such a congestion-less state. A flow can only enter the network if every network element on the flow's path has sufficient resources to satisfy the flow's traffic specification. Otherwise, the flow must be rejected. When a flow has been admitted, the network elements ensure that the flow complies with its traffic specification (this is called policing). The Controlled Load service only requires the basic token bucket parameters in traffic specifications. The Guaranteed Service class (RFC 2212 [12]) is aimed at applications with hard real-time requirements. It can provide a guaranteed upper bound for end-to-end latency, but it is also more expensive to implement. Each flow has to be handled separately and must be reshaped to maintain its characteristics.

The Resource Reservation Setup Protocol (RSVP) is the reservation protocol (RFC 2005 [13]) for IntServ architectures. It supports IP multicast and can be used without any changes to TCP and UDP. The two most important signalling messages in RSVP are PATH and RESV to establish sessions. The sender of a flow sends PATH messages along with the regular packets. This causes each router on the path to remember its previous hop, which allows any RESV messages travelling in the opposite direction to follow the same path. The RESV messages carry the actual reservation request (see Fig. 1.8). This approach has two advantages. First, each receiver can decide about the quality of service it wants to request. Second, reservations flowing upstream allow for elegant integration of multicast.

Another interesting aspect of RSVP is its use of soft states. Reservations must be refreshed in regular intervals to keep them active. This is done by resending the PATH and RESV messages, and reservation changes can be requested in the same manner. However, if a router does not receive any messages for a certain amount of time, the reservation will expire. This prevents "stale" entries in the routers' tables when end systems do not cancel their reservations. Nevertheless, reservations are made normally by the sender or by the receiver, using PATH_TEAR and RESV_TEAR messages, respectively.

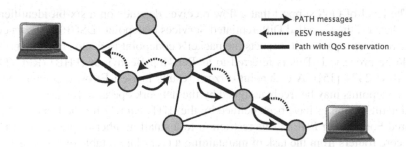

Fig. 1.8. Setting up a reservation with PATH and RESV messages

While RSVP has proved to be viable in small- to medium-sized networks, it has shown severe scalability problems in large-scale networks. The size of the flow state tables in RSVP routers tend to grow beyond manageable levels when faced with millions of users, each of which may have several active flows. Moreover, the overhead for a reservation may be too high for short-lived flows.

1.4.2 Differentiated Services

The Differentiated Services (DiffServ) approach aims to provide QoS support in large scale networks while avoiding the scalability problems of the Integrated Services (IntServ) concept. An Integrated Services router has to be able to distinguish between a potentially very large number of flows, resulting in very large flow state tables. The DiffServ architecture reduces this to a small number of aggregate flows. Furthermore, admission control or policing are no longer the responsibility of core routers. These changes make DiffServ much more scalable, but also less dynamic than IntServ.

Differentiated Services are built upon the concept of network domains. Usually, network domains correspond to a particular ISP network. Network operators negotiate contracts between each other, called Service Level Agreements (SLAs). SLAs contain Service Level Specifications (SLSs), which are the technical part of an SLA and define issues such as QoS parameters, encryption services, routing constraints etc. Several types of routers can be distinguished within a network:

- Core routers are inside a domain. They only forward packets according to the PHB (discussed later) are indicated in the packet headers.
- The responsibility of edge routers residing at the border to other domains is to police the incoming traffic (to control its conformance with the existing SLSs), and to make sure that the traffic leaving the domain does not violate the SLSs with the next ISP on the path. These routers are named ingress and egress router, respectively.
- First-hop routers are a special case of ingress routers. They are directly connected to an end user and mark the user's packets with codepoints according to the negotiated rules.

The level of QoS support that a flow receives depends on a six-bit identifier in the IP header; the so-called Differentiated Services codepoint (DSCP). When a core router receives a packet, it inspects the packet's codepoint to decide how the packet should be processed. This is referred to as Per Hop Behaviour (PHB) (RFC 2475 [14], RFC 2474 [15]). A codepoint of zero results in Best-Effort treatment, while other codepoints may be freely assigned by the network operator. Nevertheless, several default mappings have been defined by the IETF, namely for the Expedited and Assured Forwarding PHBs. This restriction to a small number of predefined PHBs frees core routers from the task of maintaining a (very large) table of flows. Instead, they only distinguish between a small number of macro-flows (or Behaviour Aggregates, BAs), i.e. the set of all flows that carry the same codepoint.

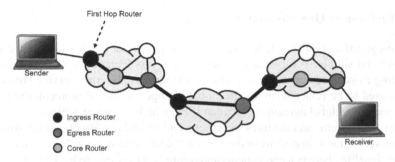

Fig. 1.9. The DiffServ view of the network

A customer would probably be interested in the end-to-end treatment of the packets, rather than in their hop-by-hop treatment. Per-domain behaviour (PDB) (RFC 3086 [16]) is the result of classification and traffic conditioning in edge routers, the PHB at interior routers, the traffic load and the network topology. A well-known example of a PDB is the "Virtual Wire" PDB [17], which is based on the "Expedited Forwarding" PHB (RFC 3246 [18]) and was intended as a circuit replacement over IP networks. PDBs can be used to implement different service classes. Creating such a service class (or Class of Service) requires conditioning the traffic aggregate so that its arrival rate at any node is always less than that node's configured minimum departure rate R. This is achieved by policing at the ingress and shaping at the egress router. The Expedited Forwarding PHB in interior routers must ensure that the traffic aggregate has a well-defined minimum departure rate R independent of the intensity of other traffic at the node. The Expedited Forwarding PHB can be implemented by priority or weighted round robin scheduling. The PDB for a given (aggregated) flow is defined in Service Level Specifications (SLSs).

In addition to the Expedited Forwarding PHB, the Assured Forwarding (AF) PHB group has been standardised (RFC2597 [19]). It provides delivery of IP packets based on four independent AF classes. Within each AF class, an IP packet can be assigned one of three different drop precedence levels. An IP packet belonging to AF class i with drop precedence j is marked with the AF codepoint AF_{ij}. A DiffServ node must allocate a minimum amount of forwarding resources to each AF class. Packets in one AF class must be forwarded independently from packets in another AF class. A DiffServ node does not reorder IP packets of the same flow if they belong to the same AF class.

PDBs and PHBs can be used to implement different service classes. A service class represents a set of traffic that requires specific delay, loss and jitter characteristics from the network (RFC 4594 [20]). A service class belongs to applications with similar characteristics and performance requirements, such as a non real-time service class for applications like file transfer, or a real-time service class for voice and other telephony services. Such a service class may be defined locally in a Differentiated Services domain, or across multiple DiffServ domains, possibly extending end-to-end.

1.4.3 End-to-End QoS Mechanisms

Both Integrated and Differentiated Services require special functionality in the network beyond simple IP forwarding. This is often problematic for several reasons. Replacing existing routers is expensive and, furthermore, Internet Service Providers have proved to be reluctant to accept global changes to the IP protocol since this would require a global agreement between ISPs, which is hard to achieve.

There are several architectures to achieve end-to-end quality of service without any—or very little—support from the network. They commonly rely on implicit or explicit signalling between end systems and require end systems to back off if there is any risk of congestion in the network. Unfortunately, this usually cannot be enforced, which makes these approaches viable only in controlled environments.

1.4.3.1 Endpoint Admission Control

Many of the end-to-end QoS architectures belong to the group of Endpoint Admission Control schemes. The basic idea of these schemes is simple: Before a new flow can enter the network, it must send a stream of probing packets to the flow's destination. The rate of the stream should be equal to the peak rate of the flow. If the number of successfully received probes is sufficiently high (e.g., ≥99%), the flow may enter the network—otherwise, it must back off. The streams probe packets thus serve as an admission control mechanism that is able to work without any support from the underlying network. This approach results in a service similar to the Controlled Load service from the Integrated Services architecture. The system cannot guarantee that a specific packet reaches its destination. However, the admission control mechanism ensures that virtually all packets of accepted flows do reach their destination.

Several variants of this scheme have been proposed. They can be categorised by two criteria [21]:

First, the admission control procedure can either simply rely on the probing stream's loss ratio, or it can require a marking mechanism in the network (e.g., based on the explicit congestion notification (ECN) bit in the IP header (RFC 2481 [22]). Marking approaches are generally more accurate.

Second, probing traffic can be either transmitted with the same priority or service class as regular data traffic (this is called in-band probing), or it can be transmitted with a different one (out-of-band probing). For example, if the network supports two levels of service, already accepted flows can be sent with high priority in order to protect them from low-priority probing traffic.

These criteria sort into four categories: in-band dropping, out-of-band dropping, in-band marking, and out-of-band marking (RFC 2481 [22]). In all these variants, the user data transmission is admitted only if the fraction of lost/marked packets stays below a certain threshold.

Unfortunately, all these approaches share a common problem: The measurement phase before a flow can enter the network may take several seconds, which is clearly too long for most applications.

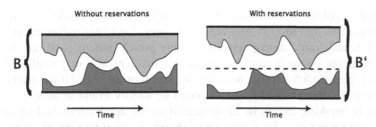

Fig. 1.10. The effect of statistical multiplexing: B is the link capacity, B' is the link capacity necessary with peak rate reservations

1.4.3.2 Statistical Multiplexing and Egress Admission Control

A major advantage of measurement-based end-to-end schemes, as compared to reservation-based systems like Integrated Services, is an effect called statistical multiplexing. Many flows have varying bandwidth usage over time. For example, the bandwidth used by video transmissions often depends on the amount of movement in the encoded video. As a result, two flows may use the same link without packet loss even if the sum of their peak rates is larger than the available bandwidth on the link, and if their bursts (short intervals at which a flow sends at its peak rate) do not occur at the same time (see Fig. 1.10). Accordingly, the QoS experienced by a number of flows sharing the same link may be very good even if the sum of their peak rates far exceeds the link's capacity. In contrast, reservation-based architectures usually allocate bandwidth at the peak bandwidth for every flow, which can result in very poor utilisation of the available link capacity.

1.4.3.3 Other End-to-End Approaches

A related approach without the need for active measurements is Egress Admission Control [23] that requires the edge routers of the network to perform admission control. They keep track of the amount of traffic leaving the network through them, and before a flow can enter the network, its traffic specification must be sent to its egress router. Based on this specification and the current traffic, the egress router will then make the admission control decision. In contrast to the endpoint admission control approaches, egress admission control requires ISPs to deploy new hardware in their network. Nevertheless, the necessary changes are kept to a minimum.

1.5 Implementation and Performance of QoS-aware Applications

1.5.1 Prerequisites for Successful QoS Applications

To support end-to-end QoS for network applications, the complete chain of involved systems and networks have to support it. Assuming that appropriate mechanisms exist on the network level, applications and the end system have to support QoS as well. Ideally, applications make use of end-to-end signalling in order to signal QoS requirements and agreed QoS between each other. Signalling information should include flow and traffic descriptions, describing which packets shall receive what kind of treatment by the network elements. Applications also may explicitly mark packets to receive QoS support accordingly. Appropriate scheduling mechanisms in operating systems and end systems should be ideally available as well. If such signalling or marking cannot be implemented in the applications and on the end systems, corresponding policies might be defined and used by network elements to enforce proper packet treatment.

1.5.2 Media Scaling

An important concept usually implemented in multimedia applications is media scaling. This is particularly valuable when the underlying network cannot deliver the full load generated by the application. Media scaling can be realised in both transparent and nontransparent ways.

1.5.2.1 Transparent Scaling

In case of transparent media scaling, network elements drop packets from the media stream and deliver only those packets for which there is sufficient capacity in the network. Excess traffic will be dropped. Preferably, less-important packets are dropped and the most-important packets are delivered to achieve good perception quality at the user. Ideally, those important packets are marked by the application to allow the network to select those packets. Packet selection and dropping is performed in a transparent way for the application. A sophisticated example for media scaling is Receiver-Driven Layered Multicast (RLM) [24], where different layers of a media stream are split over different multicast groups. Receivers join the multicast groups as long as packet loss is below a certain threshold. If only the base layer is received, the media stream can be decoded with a base quality. Any other received layer improves the perception quality accordingly.

1.5.2.2 Nontransparent Scaling

Nontransparent scaling is not transparent to the application. Receivers or network elements return feedback about packet loss and delivery. The sender reacts to high packet loss by choosing more efficient media encodings, e.g. by using higher compression and/or lower media quality. In case packet loss is low, the media quality can be increased again. For example, for still image transfer a JPEG picture can be encoded with high-quality (1.638 bit per pixel, 96 KB, Fig. 1.11(a)) and significant low-quality settings (0.137 bit per pixel, 8 KB, Fig. 1.11(b)) for high and low network capacity, respectively.

       (a) high quality   (b) low quality

Fig. 1.11. JPEG pictures with different quality settings

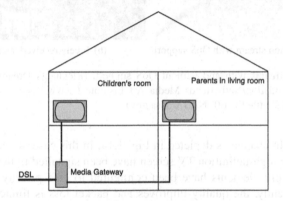

Fig. 1.12. QoS scenario

1.5.3 Applications' Performance Gain Due to QoS

The need for QoS in a scenario that is quite relevant for today is depicted in Fig. 1.12. Several persons living in a household share a single IP connection to an Internet Service Provider (ISP). The parents have subscribed to a high-definition TV service with additional monthly fees, while the children are enjoying Web 2.0 or Peer-to-Peer applications and are freely receiving streamed videos from some servers or peers. Unfortunately, the capacity of the access link is not sufficient for the simultaneous transfer of both video streams, see Fig. 1.13. However, if the video application displaying the high-definition TV program is linked with an end-to-end QoS system,

(a) High-definition stream   (b) Freely received stream

Fig. 1.13. Two simultaneously received video streams without QoS support. (Elephants Dream, (c) copyright 2006, Blender Foundation/Netherlands Media Art Institute/www.elephantsdream.org, CC Attribution 2.5 and shuttle lift-off, NASA/nasa.gov)

(a) High-definition stream with QoS support   (b) Freely received stream

Fig. 1.14. Video streams with and without QoS support. (Elephants Dream, (c) copyright 2006, Blender Foundation/Netherlands Media Art Institute / www.elephantsdream.org, CC Attribution 2.5 and shuttle lift-off, NASA/nasa.gov)

the situation might change as depicted in Fig. 1.14. In this case, the application requirements of the high-definition TV screen have been signalled to the QoS support system and network elements have been configured to give priority to this video stream. Consequently, the quality improves and packet loss is limited only to the freely received video stream, while the paying customers enjoy the QoS they expect for a pay service.

1.5.4 Summary

Despite high bandwidth availability in today's IP networks and techniques like adaptive applications, there is a strong demand for QoS support in IP-based communication systems. This demand is mainly coming from the fact that more and more applications have been moved from dedicated networks to IP based networks, in particular telephony and television. Important QoS parameters to be considered are bandwidth, delay, delay variation and error rates. Communication systems and networks must be designed to support QoS for certain network applications, in particular those where users are used to high quality and/or paying fees.

1.6 Structure of the Book

The following chapters introduce and explain mechanisms needed to design and implement a comprehensive QoS architecture for network applications running over IP networks. Chapter 2 presents methods for monitoring and measurement in IP-based networks. They are required for correct configuration of the network components and for traffic engineering (TE), which is the topic of Chapter 3. TE represents an important tool for providers to keep pace with the increasing traffic volume. Different TE techniques as well as the combination of TE and QoS are discussed. Chapter 4 covers signalling. The support of QoS over heterogeneous networks usually requires the establishment of sessions for the applications, e.g. video conferencing or video on demand. The sessions are set up using signalling and resource management. This book describes the signalling protocols Session Initiation Protocol (SIP), Next Steps In Signalling (NSIS) and Common Open Policy Service (COPS). They are used for application and network signalling. Chapter 5 is devoted to enhancements of transport protocols. Existing transport protocols offer only a limited set of services for the support of QoS. Enhanced transport protocols provide an adequate solution for providing soft QoS guarantees. The chapter shows the different mechanisms and their possibilities. Chapter 6 on the EuQoS system provides a case study based on the developments in the EuQoS project (End-to-End Quality of Service over Heterogeneous Networks) from the European Commission's Sixth Framework Programme. It shows the EuQoS architecture as one solution for providing end-to-end QoS. In the appendix, network simulation and emulation are introduced as two important techniques for network development and research.

2

QoS Measurements in IP-based Networks

René Serral-Gracià, Jordi Domingo-Pascual, Andrzej Bęben, and Philippe
Owezarski

Summary. In order to support multimedia applications, a variety of QoS parameters
must be supported for the respective data flows. These might include parameters such
as delay, delay variation, bandwidth, jitter, packet loss etc., on the network level.
Parameters can be defined on call (blocking probabilities, set-up latencies etc.) and
user level (e.g., mean opinion scores) as well. The parameters must be well defined
and appropriate measurement techniques are required to test whether the parameters
are met by the selected network services. In particular, many approaches for passive
and active measurements have been developed.

2.1 Introduction

The growth of the Internet came with the introduction of new services, imposing new
requirements on the network and demanding that operators monitor the behaviour
of the network, usually with parameters such as latency, bandwidth or reliability.
Hence, new techniques and metrics emerged to measure the quality of these services,
applications and the network performance, giving a quantitative view of its internal
status and performance. As the network kept growing, different requirements arose
and the metrics evolved toward more specific goals, such as QoS measurement.

Since acquiring the network (and QoS) metrics requires a structured methodology [25], a lack of this methodology might lead to unexpected or incorrect results in
the measurements.

This chapter is devoted to the review and analysis of the most relevant metrics
existing in QoS environments, as well as their applicability and significance. Along
with the metric description, this chapter discusses the different possible approaches
and caveats of applying such metrics in the real Internet measurement world.

Even if the metrics deliver a quantification of a specific component, often the
meaning of a metric is not always straightforward. Moreover, having accurate results
is not always feasible in the experimental field. In order to address this issue, a section
is devoted to the most frequently applied technologies and analytical tools in the area.

2.2 Measurement Metrics

A metric is a unit of measurement that coincides with a specific method or analysis. In the context of this chapter, metrics refer to the networking area, specifically to QoS, where a metric is defined as a quantitative value about any network aspect that permits studying its behaviour. Depending on how and where a metric is computed, it is possible to study different aspects of the same data.

The communication protocols are layered into what is known as the protocol stack. Depending on the layer, different information is available for measurement. Hence, at the physical level only wavelengths or electrical impulses are observed. At the link level, depending on the network technology packet, frames are assembled. While at the network level detailed information about individual IP packets is gathered, the transport level introduces services and the concept of connection that can be associated to a flow. A flow of packets at the transport layer can be defined by the 5-tuple source and destination address, source and destination port and protocol identifier.

The application level has knowledge about higher level information specific to the service (i.e., codecs of a voice transmission or frame rates for video streams). Finally, going one step further to the human level, it is possible to acquire subjective information about users' satisfaction with the offered services.

The call level refers to application level, specifically to voice transmissions. Subjective metrics, such as Mean Opinion Score (MOS), quantify the human perception of the measurement.

This section discusses the different metrics on the network (and transport) level, call level and subjective metrics.

2.2.1 Network Level

Most of the research efforts are centered on network and on transport, specifically on IP and TCP/UDP.

There are two main working groups standardising QoS measurement metrics, *IP Performance Metrics* (IPPM) and *International Telecommunication Union* (ITU).

IPPM is a working group of the *Internet Engineering Task Force* (IETF), and its task is to develop solid criteria for defining all the concepts related to performance metrics. This working group focuses on developing a set of standard metrics, which could be applied to measure the quality, the performance and the reliability of Internet communications. The metrics are not centered on providing a subjective result, but objective data that will highlight an unbiased quantitative measure of performance.

ITU, as a more general institution, focuses on the standardisation of QoS metrics on its ITU-T section. Contrary to IPPM, their approach uses a more generic theoretical description. The following sections describe the set of important measurement metrics. The basis of the definitions are based on IPPM's approach, but ITU's definition is provided when it differs or introduces interesting details related with QoS.

In order to understand the metrics, it is necessary to first introduce some concepts on which those metrics are based:

- *Wire-time:* Wire-time is the time that a packet takes from its delivery on the physical wire of the first bit (out of the Network Interface Card (NIC)) until its last bit reaches its destination. It mainly consists of the propagation delay and the transmission delay introduced in Sect. 1.1.1.
- *Type-P packet:* Given a set of packets, a Type-P packet is a packet, which complies with certain specified criteria. A set of Type-P packets is chosen for computing the desired performance metrics. Type-P packet is a versatile concept that is instantiated as required by each metric. The basis of Type-P packets are defined in [26], where a framework for generic metric notation and concepts is introduced.

2.2.1.1 Connectivity

One of the simplest and most important metrics is the degree of connectivity between two points. Connectivity is defined in [27]; its aim is to determine whether there is connectivity between a source and a destination or not, either in one way or both ways. It is a property that depends on an instant T, referring to the instant when such connectivity is tested. Hence, unidirectional connectivity is accomplished when a packet sent from the source (A) at a time T is able to reach its destination (B). Therefore, bidirectional connectivity is achieved when there is unidirectional connectivity from point A to point B and from the point B to A at the same instant T. These metrics are called *Instantaneous One-Way/Two-Way connectivity*, respectively. Analytically, connectivity is considered a boolean variable on a given instant (T) for a given connection.

To be able to determine connectivity during a time interval, a new metric is defined: *One-Way/Two-Way Connectivity* (note the absence of the word "instantaneous"). The instantaneous connectivity is checked at time T during a ΔT interval.

2.2.1.2 One-Way Delay

One-Way Delay (OWD) is defined by [28] as the time elapsed since the first bit of the packet has been sent on the network until its last bit has reached its destination.

An assumption usually taken on this metric is to compute the end-to-end delay, which includes the *wire-time*, the overhead imposed by the application's packet generation time and its processing time at the destination.

This metric by default assumes just one packet and is called *Instantaneous One-Way Delay (OWD)*. When considering a set of Type-P packets (i.e., a flow), the OWD of each individual packet shows the time evolution of the delays. This is more useful than the single value provided by the metric.

Mathematically, the OWD is computed by subtracting to the reception time the sender's timestamp as shown in (2.1), where N is the number of *Type-P* packets within the interval. Since time is a monotonically increasing function, OWD is always a strictly positive real number

Table 2.1. IP network QoS class definitions and network performance objectives

Network	QoS Classes					
Parameter	Class 0	Class 1	Class 2	Class 3	Class 4	Class 5
IPTD	100 ms	400 ms	100 ms	400 ms	1 s	U
IPDV	50 ms	50 ms	U	U	U	U
IPLR			1×10^{-3}			U
IPER			1×10^{-4}			U

$$OWD_i = T_{\text{reception}_i} - T_{\text{sender}_i} \quad 1 \leq i \leq N. \tag{2.1}$$

A critical issue in this environment is that both endpoints, source and destination, must be synchronised for accurate OWD computation. Details about synchronisation are presented in Sect. 2.3.1.1.

ITU-T refers to this metric as *IP Transfer Delay* (IPTD) with the same semantics, but focusing on QoS analysis. In QoS environments, OWD is an important metric, because it describes the degree of interactivity and the lag of the communication. In [29] ITU defines five different CoS bounds for the OWD as shown in Table 2.1. These bounds refer to the mean OWD (or IPTD). They range from 100 ms for real-time high sensitivity traffic to 1 s for low loss, bulk streaming traffic.

Analogously to OWD, [30] defines Round-Trip Delay as the time elapsed since a source emits a packet to a destination, and this destination answers back by emitting a response packet as soon as possible. This metric is defined, because a very high percentage of the traffic uses bidirectional transport protocols.

Just as the OWD, the value obtained from *Instantaneous Round-trip Delay* is an strictly positive real number, and it is computed using (2.2) that is similar as OWD, but only using the timestamps from the source point. Again, N refers to the number of the considered Type-P packets.

$$RTD_i = T_{\text{response}_i} - T_{\text{send}_i} \quad 1 \leq i \leq N. \tag{2.2}$$

2.2.1.3 One-Way Packet Loss

One-Way Packet Loss (OWPL) over a Type-P packet, is the condition whether a packet was successfully received from a source to a destination or not. It is defined in [31] as one-way because of:

1. *Asymmetry over a path:* The response to a packet is not always sent over the same path back to the origin.
2. *One-Way traffic:* Real-time applications or UDP traffic are unidirectional.

OWPL is a boolean metric, where 0 means that the packet has been received properly, and 1 that the packet has been lost.

ITU-T refers to this metric as *IP Packet Loss Ratio* (IPLR) and it is defined as the number of lost packets out of the total sent during the measurement interval (see Sect. 1.1.2). While IPPM considers errored packets as lost, ITU defines another metric *IP Packet Errored Ratio* (IPER) to quantify errored packets.

In QoS environments OWPL is critical for the overall quality of the communication, [29] defines a upper bound of IPLR of 1×10^{-3} for all the classes.

Analogously to OWPL, [30] defines Round-Trip Packet Loss, where a packet is considered as lost either when the packet emitted by the source does not reach its destination or when the response is lost.

The last case for considering a packet lost is when its OWD is greater than a predefined value, which usually is 255 seconds according to the TTL.

2.2.1.4 IP Delay Variation

IP Delay Variation (IPDV) is defined in [32] as the difference in OWD of a pair of packets on a stream of Type-P packets. The RFC does not define which pair of packets are to be used, but usually consecutive packets are selected. Hence, IPDV is computed as

$$IPDV_i = OWD_{i-1} - OWD_i \quad 1 \le i \le N. \qquad (2.3)$$

IPDV is a real number, either positive or negative. It is defined when both of the selected packets exist. In case of packet losses, no IPDV value is defined.

It is important not to confuse IPDV with jitter. In this context jitter is defined as the difference between the OWD of the selected packet and the OWD average of the interval. This requires having the whole set of packets for obtaining the real value.

The same metric is defined differently by ITU-T as shown in the expression

$$IPDV = IPTD_{\text{upper}} - IPTD_{\text{min}}, \qquad (2.4)$$

where $IPTD_{\text{upper}}$ is the $1-10^{-3}$ quantile of the OWD, and $IPTD_{\text{min}}$ is the minimum OWD value of the measurement. This permits the detection of congestion in the network, analysis of the TCP window behaviour and effects on IPDV of routing updates.

In QoS environments IPDV limits the lower bounds of the reception buffers. This metric is important both for the interactivity (small buffers) and the quality (late packets are considered as lost) of the communication. ITU-T defines an upper bound of 50 ms for the real-time classes.

2.2.1.5 Bulk Transport Capacity

Bulk Transport Capacity (BTC), as defined in [33], is the maximum net transport capacity of a link using a single congestion-aware protocol connection (i.e., TCP). This highlights the maximum theoretical capacity of the links connecting two different end points.

The metric results refer to the net throughput, where all headers, retransmissions or losses are subtracted from the overall performance.

This metric gives us an idea of the maximum performance from a user point of view where big data transfers are involved (FTP, big HTTP downloads, etc.).

The unit for measuring the BTC are the bps (bits per second), as in kbps (Kilobit per second: 10^3 bps), Mbps (Megabit per second: 10^6 bps), Gbps (Gigabit per second: 10^9 bps), etc.

The final bandwidth is computed with (2.5), which refers to the whole transmission. In (2.5) B refers to the net number of bits transmitted, and T is the time in seconds since the start of the transfer until the end.

$$BTC = \frac{B}{T}. \tag{2.5}$$

2.2.2 Call level

In the following section we provide an overview of QoS metrics corresponding to the "call level". Those metrics refer to the performance of call/session set-up (establishment) or release process. Even if this process was not originally considered in the Internet, the evolution of IP networks toward multiservice networks creates a need for call/session processing. In particular, the call set-up/release process allows a user to express his or her demands related to the required service, QoS guarantees as well as the submitted traffic. On the other hand, it allows the network to decide whether a call can be accepted, reserve adequate resources and, if necessary, to perform configuration of devices. As a consequence, the QoS provided at the call level is one of the key factors influencing the QoS perceived by the users. In the following we provide a description of typical call level metrics such as: call blocking, call set-up and call release latencies.

2.2.2.1 Call Blocking

Call Blocking (P_{BLOCK}) is the ratio of the number of blocked calls ($L_{BLOCKED}$) to the total number of call attempts (succeed or blocked) ($S_{ATTEMPTS}$) measured on the entire path the calls come through in a given measurement interval. Formally, this metric can be defined as

$$P_{BLOCK} = \frac{L_{BLOCKED}}{S_{ATTEMPTS}}. \tag{2.6}$$

Note that a given call is considered as blocked only when the call set-up is unsuccessful due to network reasons, e.g. lack of resources, call misrouting, or expiration of call set-up timers. This metric does not consider connection set-up failures caused by the unavailability of the called user or their occupancy. The call-blocking metric is measured indirectly by counting the number of accepted calls and the number of lost calls in a given measurement interval. The typical value of P_{BLOCK} should be less than 10^{-2}.

2.2.2.2 Call Set-Up Latency

The call set-up latency T_{set-up} is defined as the time between the submission of the first bit of a *set-up* message sent to network from the user terminal initialising a call,

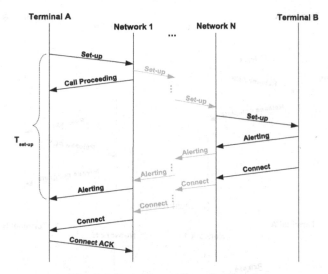

Fig. 2.1. Exemplary call set-up scenario

and the receiving of the last bit of the *alerting* message received from the network as presented in Fig. 2.1. Note that the time lost at the called side, while the destination was deciding whether to accept the call, is not included in call set-up latency. Values of call set-up latency should be reported as the mean and the 0.95 quantile of the call set-up latency distribution. The measurements should be performed under normal and heavy signalling load conditions.

2.2.2.3 Call Release Latency

The call release latency $T_{release}$ is defined as the time interval from the submission of the first bit of the *release* message to the network by the user terminal, which terminates the call until the last bit of the *release_ack* message is received by the same terminal. This event indicates that the terminal can initiate or receive a new call. Depending on the call scenario, the *release_ack* message may be sent locally or by the called side as presented in Fig. 2.2. Similarly, as for call set-up, the values of call release latency should be reported as the mean and the 0.95 quantile of call release latency distribution.

2.2.3 User Level

The user level metrics are related to QoS level experienced by a user. It is also called Perceived QOS (PQOS). This metric refers to the overall quality experienced by users. This quality is influenced by QoS assured at the network level, the quality of voice/video codecs, the effectiveness of supporting mechanisms in applications such as playback buffer, codec rate adapters, etc., as well as the quality provided at the call level as presented in Fig. 2.3.

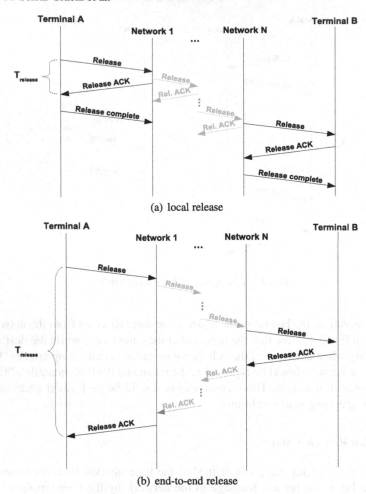

(a) local release

(b) end-to-end release

Fig. 2.2. Exemplary call release scenarios

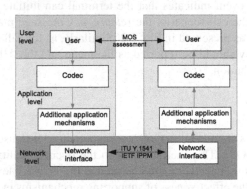

Fig. 2.3. The relation between QoS provided at the user level and the network level

Table 2.2. Types of MOS metric

	Listening-only	Conversational
Subjective	MOS-LQS	MOS-CQS
Objective	MOS-LQO	MOS-CQO
Estimated	MOS-LQE	MOS-CQE

Table 2.3. MOS values for typical voice codecs

Standard	Codec type	Rate [kbps]	Frame [ms]	Lookahead [ms]	MOS value
G.711	PCM	64	–	0	4.43
G.729	CS-ACELP	8	10	5	4.18
G.723.1	ACELP	5.3	30	7.5	3.83
G.723.1	MP-MLQ	6.3	30	7.5	4.00

The typical metric used to measure the QoS provided at the user level is Mean Opinion Score (MOS). According to ITU-T [34] the MOS is defined as:

The mean of opinion scores, i.e. of the values on predefined scale that subjects assign to their opinion on the performance of the telephone transmission system used either for conversation, or for listening to spoken material.

Originally, the MOS metric was only evaluated in a subjective way by the group of users that scores quality of voice transmission in the scale from 5 to 1, where the following scores are used: 5 = Excellent, 4 = Good, 3 = Fair, 2 = Poor, 1 = Bad quality. However, apart from the subjective approach, the MOS value can also be evaluated based on objective models or estimated models, see [34, 35]. As a consequence, we distinguish different types of MOS metrics as presented in Table 2.2, where LQ refers to Listening Quality, CQ to Conversational Quality, S to Subjective, O to Objective and E to Estimated.

In subjective methods, we calculate the MOS value as an arithmetic mean of subjective judgements of a group of users. The objective methods are performed, based on an objective model that allows assessing the perceived quality, e.g. by comparison of sent and received test signals. The estimated method allows calculating the MOS value based on a model of a communication system, e.g. E-model as proposed in [36]. As this approach does not require transmission of voice signals, it can be used for the network planning.

In Table 2.3 we present the exemplary MOS values for typical voice codecs. The MOS was measured in the reference network, where no packet transfer delay, delay variation nor packet losses were introduced. Note that even under such ideal network conditions, none of the codes offer MOS equal to 5. This is caused by quality degradation introduced by the particular voice codecs.

The MOS metric can also be used for evaluation of video quality. Its definition is similar to voice assessment. More details can be found in [37].

2.2.3.1 Subjective Assessment Method

The ITU-T in [34] recommends two methods for the subjective assessment of MOS that corresponds to conversation-opinion tests and listening-opinion tests.

Conversation-opinion tests require participation of a number of user pairs, who take part in a normal conversation using voice or video-conference applications. Every conversation should be purposeful and should have a natural beginning and a natural ending. The conversation must never be terminated in the middle of the test. After the test, each participant scores the perceived quality in the MOS scale. Conversation tests are intended to reproduce in the laboratory environment the conditions as close as possible to real life.

Listening-opinion tests require participation of a speaker and a number of listeners. The speaker reads a list of previously prepared sentences or phrases, while the listeners only listen and give opinions about the perceived voice quality. The speech material should consist of simple, meaningful and short sentences, chosen at random as being easy to understand. These sentences should be made up into lists in random order in such a way that there is no obvious connection of meaning between one sentence and the next. Very short and very long sentences should be avoided. The aim is that each sentence when spoken should fit into a time slot of 2–3 seconds. The sentences are organised in lists and after each list the listeners score the perceived quality in the MOS scale.

Another approach for MOS evaluation is based on the evaluation of logatom articulation that reflects the intelligibility of transmitted voice signals. The logatoms are meaningless words composed of a group of phonemes that are characteristic for a given language. In this test a speaker reads a list of logatoms, while listeners write them down exactly as they hear them. After the test, the lists written by the listeners are compared with the original one and then MOS value is evaluated based on the percentage of correctly written down logatoms. Note that logatoms were determined to be correctly written based on similar pronunciation, not on spelling. The logatom articulation test allows for eliminating the influence of human capabilities for guessing the meaning of words from the sentence context.

2.2.3.2 Objective Assessment Method

The objective methods are aimed at assessing the MOS value without users' participation. For this purpose, specialised models are defined that allow for the estimation of the perceived quality. This is based on the comparison of originally transmitted voice or video signal with the received one, but it can also be based on detailed characteristics of terminals and the network. In the following, we briefly present two objective methods that are standardised by ITU-T.

Perceptual evaluation of speech quality (PESQ) method [38] was designed to estimate the MOS value in an objective way. It requires transmission of the reference test voice signals that should be collected at the receiver side. Then, the original and the received voice signals are compared with the special PESQ algorithm. The key to this process is transformation of both the original and received signals into an internal representation that is analogous to the psychophysical representation of audio signals in the human auditory system, taking account of perceptual frequency and loudness. The internal representation is processed to take into account such effects as local gain variations and linear filtering that may—if they are not too severe—have little perceptual significance. Finally, the PESQ algorithm compares both signals and provides the MOS value on that basis. It should be noted that the PESQ does not provide a comprehensive evaluation of transmission quality. It only measures the effects of one-way speech distortion, such as degradation introduced by voice codes, channel errors, packet losses, delay variation, time wrapping of audio signals and noise on speech quality. On the other hand, the effects of loudness loss, delay, sidetone, echo, and other impairments related to two-way interaction are not reflected in the PESQ method. As a consequence, it is possible to have high PESQ scores, yet poor quality of the connection overall. The PESQ method can be applied for waveform codecs such as G.711; G.726; G.727 and for CELP and hybrid codecs e.g. G.728, G.729, G.723.1 as well as other codecs: GSM-FR, GSM-HR, GSM-EFR, GSM-AMR, CDMA-EVRC, TDMA ACELP, TDMA-VSELP, TETRA.

E-model method [36] was designed to estimate the value of MOS based on the set of parameters that represent the terminal, network and environmental quality factors. More precisely, it allows the computation of the MOS value based on 20 input parameters such as: voice codec distortion, quantisation, echo, room noise, SNR, loudness, sidetone, delay, loss factors, as well as the advantage factor reflecting human psychological aspects. Compared to other methods, the E-model does not require transmission of voice signals through the system under test. As a consequence, the E-model can be used as a planning tool that allows network designers to estimate the QoS level perceived by the users. It should be noted that E-model can only be used in case of telephony handsets that carry narrow-band voice signals (300–3400 Hz).

The important issue is that the E-model has not been fully verified by field surveys or laboratory tests for the very large number of possible combinations of input parameters. For many combinations of high importance to transmission planners, the E-model can be used with confidence, but for other parameter combinations, E-model predictions have been questioned and are currently under study.

2.3 Measurement Techniques

Metrics are the basis of any measurement system as they indicate *what* to measure. But knowing the important parameters on a network is not enough to fully study its behaviour. We also need to know *how* and *where* to measure. Hence, different techniques have been proposed to ease the measurement burden.

2.3.1 Previous Considerations

In general, measuring is not an easy task and QoS measurement is not an exception. In any measurement environment, before measuring any metric some issues have to be considered. This section highlights some typical problems found on network measurements such as clock synchronisation or analysis of the results, and points to some advice to avoid them.

2.3.1.1 Synchronisation

Measuring often uses delays as a performance metric (see Sect. 2.2.1). This process involves timestamping of the received packets at different measure points (OWD) where data are gathered. In order to have accurate one-way delays, all the involved clocks on the measurement have to be synchronised (e.g., indicate the same time value at the same instant). Besides the complexity of having accurate time sources, the main issue in this context is to verify that the computed metrics are correct. Hence, while measuring delays in a distributed scenario, it is important to keep track of the clock accuracy.

Synchronising clocks may seem straightforward using well-known protocols such as NTP. But, when working with microsecond resolutions (not untypical in current link speeds), the clocks must be very accurately synchronised in all the hosts involved in the timestamping.

Due to physical limitations, no clock is perfect; each clock has slightly different rates (*skew*) that are noticeable at small time scales. Moreover, the skew is not constant as it is affected by various external conditions (i.e., changes in temperature). These variations on the skew are known as *drift*. Besides, if the measurements do not include clock precision information, it is not possible to know whether the results are accurate enough.

Synchronisation must be maintained, and estimates about the error have to be known during the timestamping process. This can be achieved in different ways; the most relevant in network measurements are:

1. *Software Synchronisation* is the less precise form of clock synchronisation. This approach requires a daemon running on the host and an external time source that is used as a reference clock. The daemon instructs the system clock to converge toward the reference clock. The most-used protocol is the Network Time Protocol (NTP) as defined in [39].
2. *Hardware Synchronisation* is another approach using specific hardware connected directly to a reliable time source. The host using an external time source [e.g., a GPS antenna or a pulse per second source (PPS)], uses the precise time information delivered and performs the timestamp directly on the Network Interface Card (NIC), which forwards such information to the operating system.
   This mechanism guarantees precise timestamping, since no software is involved in the process. The drawback is the availability of NICs with such hardware capabilities.
3. *Mixed Software and Hardware Synchronisation:* In some environments having hardware timestamping is not possible or is too expensive. Hence, a common solution for synchronisation uses both software tools (NTP) with hardware time

sources (GPS antennas). This can be used in a LAN to broadcast time information to all the hosts in a more scalable way than using a pure hardware solution, achieving estimated errors within few microseconds precision.

Recently in [40], another trend in synchronisation was proposed. Instead of using remote clock sources, their solution is based on the use of the TSC (Time Stamp Counter) register found in modern microprocessors, which gives a higher accuracy on the local clock. The issue that remains to be solved is how to exploit this technique in a distributed environment with multiple clocks.

2.3.1.2 Data Collection, Storage and Analysis

Network measurement typically is composed of three different phases:

1. *Data gathering*, collecting of all the relevant data for the experiment.
2. *Data storage*, selecting which data to store and determining which analysis is possible to perform later on.
3. *Data analysis*, study and delivery of the results about the data acquired on previous phases.

Often, measuring network metrics requires the collection of existing traffic on the links. Such a collection is different depending on the layer where it is performed. Usually, the collection point is a station situated on the path of the traffic under study. Before performing any collection, one must answer these questions: (i) Where to collect data (e.g., in the border router, in the end point, etc.)? (ii) What to collect (e.g., all the packets, just one flow, one Class of Service, etc.)? Traffic Collection is presented in detail in Sect. 2.3.4.

Depending on what is collected and the traffic load, the data-collection task can be very resource consuming. Moreover, it can require using specific hardware equipment.

In order to decrease the required resources for such collection, different techniques have been proposed: (i) traffic aggregation (i.e., using protocols such as SNMP) and (ii) traffic sampling (i.e. as proposed in [41]). These techniques are detailed in Sect. 2.3.2.3.

After collecting all the required traffic, it needs to be stored (for later processing) or analysed (in case of real-time analysis). Storing the data is not straightforward, as the collection process can generate huge amounts of data per time unit. When measuring QoS parameters, the payload of the packets is often not relevant for the study, thus it is possible to store only the packet headers.

Besides, simply storing the traffic is not sufficient. Providing metadata along with the results permits one to understand how the measurements were taken to reduce the analysis complexity, in case the measurements are performed long before extracting the results, or to give other researchers better insights to the data. Such metadata is important as it describes how the measurements were taken, what the characteristics of the traffic are, what the reason for testing was, and explains the considerations taken to do the testing, etc. Work in this direction by the IETF's IP-

FIX working group in [42] defines a generic format designed specifically for storing networking information in a structured way. This format is based on XML in order to be extensible, and allows representing any kind of traffic along with its descriptive metadata.

The last phase of network measurement is analysis of the results. Such results may be processed online (i.e., for real-time QoS analysis), or processed offline (i.e., whether the QoS contract has been provided for a given test).

Online analysis has the limitation that not all the information is available, since it arrives during the study. Thus, concepts such as average one-way delay, or maximum jitter are limited to the already received set of data. Moreover, online analysis has to be efficient due to its real-time nature, limiting the amount of computations executed per time unit.

On the other hand, offline analysis does not have the time constraints and the whole data set is available. In this context, in order to analyse the data, statistics are used for summarising the obtained results. Not all the statistics are fit to describe all the measurements. More information about the most common statistics is provided in Sect. 2.3.2.1.

2.3.2 Base Techniques

Once the measurements have been performed, the next issue to solve is analysing and presenting the results rigorously. This can be achieved with the proper mathematical theory. There are statistical tools which help in this analysis. But even having the proper statistical tools, it can happen that the volume of data to manage is too big, or hardware limitations do not permit obtaining all the desired data. In this case we are required to use aggregation or sampling techniques, which help in reducing the information overhead of the system.

This section discusses some statistical principles that can help to represent the data meaningfully, along with the most basic aggregation and sampling techniques, which help to discard data of the measurement set without affecting negatively the final result.

2.3.2.1 Statistical Tools

QoS metric measurements deliver objective results about network performance, but depending on the objectives of the measurement, just having the metric values is not enough.

Statistics are a mathematical tool that permits summarising formally a set of results in order to look for some desirable properties and to obtain significant results. A full discussion about statistics is out of the scope of this book. Only basic statistics that help the QoS measurement are presented. Part of this section is based on [29] where a clear description about the useful statistics for the metrics is provided. Some hints are taken from [43], which provides a good overview on Internet Measurements in general.

Among all the estimators, the most used are the simple first-moment estimators, the average and the standard deviation, which are used to summarise the results from the experiments. It has to be noted that such estimators can often be misleading, depending on the size or the diversity of the samples.

Other broadly used values are the minimum and the maximum values. When using them one must care about the existence of outliers. For example, in Table 2.1 some upper bounds for the metrics are defined. Such upper bounds refer to average values (as an estimator of the mean) in case of IPTD (or OWD) and *maximum* values in case of IPDV and IPLR. In these QoS measurements, *maximum* values assume that no outliers are present on the set of results. In order to remove such outliers, the most common technique is to use the 99.9th percentile ($1-10^{-3}$ quantile) of the set. Obtaining this percentile needs a set of at least 1000 samples.

Different from upper bounds, lower bounds do not tend to have the outliers problem, since they usually are bound by physical constraints (distances, bandwidth, processing time, etc.). In the case of some metrics such as OWD, such lower bounds are rarely studied. Nevertheless, if needed, the 0.1th percentile can be used.

Besides the pure statistical analysis of the data, it is often useful to have a general overview on the results (i.e. graphically representing the data). One broadly used graphical representation is a histogram showing the percentage of values on the result set with a given property. In QoS measurements, this often means OWD or IPDV. These kinds of histograms are known as One-Way Delay Distribution (OWDD) and IP Delay Variation Distribution (IPDVD). This shows how the spectrum of OWD (or IPDV) is distributed.

Even though broadly used, histograms tend to aggregate the data into bins, with a consequent loss of information. In order to overcome this limitation, using Cumulative Distribution Functions (CDF) tend to be more understandable in general. Examples of these graphical representations can be found later in this chapter.

2.3.2.2 Aggregation

Aggregation is a technique that groups together a set of data with similar properties with the goal of reducing the data set, and speeding up the processing. In the field of networking, common examples of these properties include aggregating statistics per flow, per source address, destination port etc. In QoS, the most common example is the equal treatment of packets within the same Class of Service (CoS) in a DiffServ environment.

Aggregation is always tied to loss of information; if there is no loss, the process is called classification and its goal is to ease the further location of the data. However, the aggregation is irreversible and the aggregate always contains less information than the original set. Reducing the amount of data to process enables the required speeding up of the analysis, so that even hardware not designed for statistical analysis can deliver meaningful results without excessive computational needs.

Networking equipment (e.g., routers, switches, etc.) contains statistical information about the traffic on the network. In order to reduce the computational burden of those statistics, the reported is aggregated in packet counts per interface, number of flows etc. All these statistics can be queried using *SNMP* (Simple Network Management Protocol). SNMP is the standard protocol for querying networking equipment. It is currently at version 3 [44] and defines a structured query language for statistics retrieval, among other functionalities. Instead of keeping detailed information about the traffic profile, the networking equipment periodically updates the databases with the new data about the traffic, which permits reducing the memory requirements of the operation.

Another protocol that uses aggregation in order to deliver network statistics is Cisco Netflow. It provides statistics for network traffic accounting, usage-based network billing, network planning and security. Netflow, instead of the generic approach of SNMP, is designed specifically for flow-based statistics, and delivers more detailed information about the traffic. Netflow has per-flow statistics which include number of packets, protocol, amount of traffic, etc., with a versatile design that permits selecting which flows have to be monitored. Netflow exports the information using the new proposal from the IETF IPFIX presented previously. Lately, in the framework of the Lobster IST project [45], IPFIX has been extended with QoS reporting facilities. Such improvements include interpacket distance, distribution of packet sizes, maximum rate etc.

2.3.2.3 Sampling

Sampling is a technique broadly used for reducing the set of information. Opposed to aggregation, which clusters data with similar characteristics, traffic sampling chooses a subset of packets for analysis and ignores the rest. The selected packets are later analysed as if they were the full set. No statistical operations are performed before the analysis.

Selecting which packets to sample depends on the goal of the analysis. As presented by [43], sampling can be performed in three different ways:

- *Random sampling:* a packet is sampled with some fixed probability p.
- *Deterministic sampling:* using a deterministic function, for example sample one out of N packets.
- *Stratified sampling:* the set of packets is divided into subsets and the sampling is performed within the subsets. This technique is useful in the case that it is required to have at least one sample of each subset. The drawback is that the packet must be analysed before being selected.

All the above mechanisms are useful on generic networking measurements, but in QoS measurements it is not possible to use them, because in QoS OWD are involved and this requires a distributed infrastructure. Thus, it requires a deterministic selection of packets on all the measurement points. However, the deterministic sampling presented before is not an option, because the packet sets of each measurement point might be different (packet losses, route changes etc.). In order to overcome this, [46] proposes a distributed sampling algorithm, namely *Trajectory Sampling*, based on a hash function which guarantees that the same packet is sampled on all the measurement points. As detailed in Sect. 2.3.4 this, together with [47], permits QoS assessment of arbitrary flows.

2.3.3 Active Measurements

Active measurement is a technique used to perform measurements by inserting synthetic traffic into the network in order to analyse its performance. This controlled traffic is used to compare the results delivered by the network with what is expected from it, i.e. counting packet losses, computing OWD, etc. Depending on the traffic characteristics, different analyses can be conducted (i.e., network reliability, CoS compliance, etc.).

This measurement technique is used in several contexts with different goals. In QoS parameters analysis it is especially very useful, since it permits the study of QoS metrics presented before in a controlled manner, verifying whether a network fulfils the QoS constraints or not.

Usually, active measurements in QoS environments are used for assessing whether the QoS metrics are within specified thresholds. The usefulness of this technique relies on the fact that the generation is deterministic and known beforehand. Hence, the variation of the computed metrics at the reception point are due to the underlying network behaviour.

With active measurements the amount of generated traffic might vary, depending on the measurement goal. There are tests that require few packets, but sometimes in order to understand the dynamics of the network, long tests with high packet rates are needed. Precisely, the drawback of active measurements is the intrusive nature of the technique, as the synthetic traffic might affect the traffic already present on the network, but essentially the state of the network and its level of performance.

Here, the discussion focuses on the different usages and alternatives for QoS analysis. Some existing platforms and applications are also discussed for completeness.

2.3.3.1 Network Characteristics

In QoS environments one of the critical parameters to consider is network latency. Its definition is equivalent to OWD, described in Sect. 2.2.1. In order to acquire network latency with active measurements, at least two Active Measurement Points (AMP) have to be deployed on the edges of the networks under study. Figure 2.4 shows a simple scenario where the generated packets cross three different domains. Active measurements are useful in this scenario in order to acquire real values about the metrics offered by the network. Before testing, both AMP need to be synchronised to obtain a reliable timestamping of the packets. If the synchronisation is provided by NTP, it is advisable to have a dedicated link for the NTP traffic. In the case where AMPs are separated by several domains or by considerable geographical distance, the best option is to use different NTP servers—if possible stratum 1—that are close to each AMP.

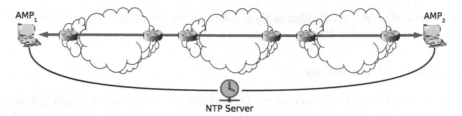

Fig. 2.4. Active measurement example scenario

This technique has the limitation that it is only possible to acquire information from end-to-end (at AMPs). Hence, specific events along the path of the packets are difficult to study (i.e., path of the traffic, load balancing, etc.).

Another time-related metric that is often studied is IPDV. Even if it uses time-stamps (specifically OWD) for obtaining its value, synchronisation among the hosts is not required, as it computes the differences of OWDs. The only requirement of this metric is that there is no skew on the clocks, or that the clocks' differences are kept constant [48].

As an example, Fig. 2.5 shows two different ways of representing OWD. The test was performed over a wireless testbed during two different Level 3 handovers. As it can be noted, there are two periods where packet losses are high (represented as 0 delay in Fig. 2.5(a)) during the handovers, and 95% of the traffic has a delay below $40ms$ (see CDF in Fig. 2.5(b)). This second representation helps us to understand the delay distribution in the tests, ignoring packet losses and easily detecting outliers (99.9th percentile).

Another network characteristic that determines the network's reliability is the packet loss ratio. The most used definition for this metric is the one proposed by ITU-T. With active measurements it is straightforward to compute the packet loss ratio, as the total number of generated packets is known in advance. Hence, active traffic tools usually use a sequence number on the generated packets in order to compute the number of packet losses and per packet OWDs at the destination.

2.3.3.2 Bandwidth Estimation

Bandwidth estimation is a set of techniques developed for estimating the available bandwidth between two end-hosts. The main difference of bandwidth estimation with Bulk Transfer Capacity is that with this approach the link is not overloaded for computing the bandwidth, but the packets are generated with specific character-istics (usually back-to-back) and the bandwidth is estimated depending on their delay variation. From the many existing methods for achieving this, the most used are:

1. The *Probe Gap Model* (PGM) exploits the information in the time gap between the arrivals of two successive probes at the receiver. This technique was proposed in [49], even if sometimes the algorithm tends to underestimate the available bandwidth in multihop paths [50].

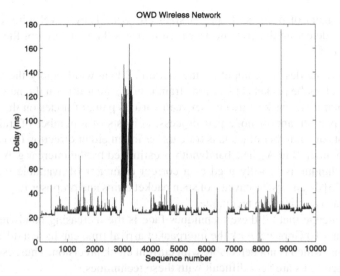

(a) Instantaneous OWD

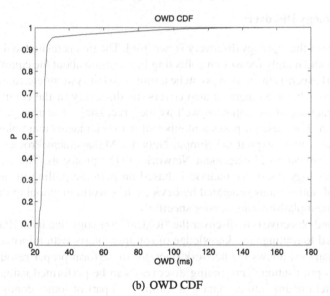

(b) OWD CDF

Fig. 2.5. Various representations of delay.

2. The *Probe Rate Model* is based on the concept of self-inducted congestion [51] and [52]. When there is no congestion on the path, the interarrivals of the packets should be the same at both ends. The differences indicate less available bandwidth.

3. *Packet quartets*, presented in [53], is a two-step method where at first linear regression is used to estimate the bandwidth, and in the second phase back-

to-back pairs of packets of special sizes are sent. They travel with a tweaked TTL for detecting the bottleneck, which narrows the real value of the available bandwidth.

All the above modes for computing the estimated bandwidth apply the technique called train of probe packets [54]. In the train model, the traffic on the network consists of a number of packet streams between various pairs of nodes on the network. Each node-pair stream, or node-pair process, consists of a number of trains. Each train consists of a number of packets (or cars) going in either direction (from node A to B or from node B to A). The bandwidth is estimated by the intercar gap.

This technique is broadly used as a correct estimator of available bandwidth. However, [55] discusses the caveats of such packet trains and proposes improvements using a capacity-estimation technique.

The challenge that all these techniques face is the increasing bandwidth of the networks. In a 10 Gbps network the interpacket arrival time can have a difference of less than 1 ns, which is not detectable with current clock precision. Thus, estimations on high-speed links are very difficult with these techniques.

2.3.3.3 Topology Discovery

The objective of the topology discovery is two-fold. The first is related to the network management and mainly focuses on collecting information about the equipment used in the network, such as the routers, switches, transmission systems etc., and the physical connections between them. It also covers the discovery of the equipment configuration, tracking of its status, as well as the processing of alarms generated by the equipment. For these purposes a number of network management platforms are proposed that usually exploit the Simple Network Management Protocol (SNMP) or Telecommunications Management Network (TMN) protocols. The basic principle of the topology discovery method is based on periodic polling of devices and processing of notifications generated by devices. It is worth mentioning that usually the management platforms are vendor specific.

The second objective is to discover the "logical" topology that in an IP network is mainly related to routing. The knowledge of routing, jointly with information about the traffic matrices, allows the network operator to perform proper resource provisioning and optimisation. The routing discovery can be performed using the management system taking into account that routing is a part of router configuration or by the routing monitors. The routing monitor is a "dummy" router that does not advertise any prefix, but only collects routing information. In case of distance vector protocols, as with Routing Information Protocol (RIP), the routing monitor has to receive routing information from all routers. On the other hand, in case of link state protocols such as Open Shortest Path First (OSPF), it is enough that the route monitor receives information only from one router. Then, the route monitor computes the routing based on information about the state of all links.

2.3.3.4 Platforms and Applications

Usually, active measurement platforms are based on a closed testbed and not on a production network. There are several research projects that provide a broader analysis of the Internet from an active point of view. The most important at this moment are:

- *PlanetLab:* is a collection of nodes (more than 800 at the time of writing) connected to the Internet, which form an overlay network that is used for researchers to test distributed applications, protocols etc. at the nodes. The tests include, among others, QoS overlays, scalable object location or content distribution networks [56].
- *Cooperative Association for Internet Data Analysis* (CAIDA) is one of the most active research branches on both active and passive measurement platforms. The use of innovative technologies for extracting diverse information from the Internet is being developed. Projects like Skitter (Internet Atlas Project), AS Mapping and many more, are in the active measurement part of this consortium [57].
  Active Measurement Project (AMP) was initially promoted by NLANR, but since June 2006 it belongs to CAIDA. It focuses on site-to-site active measurements and analyses conducted between campuses connected by high-performance networks. The data collected by AMP has proved to be a valuable resource for network analysis to study the network and to derive performance models for various aspects of Internet traffic [58].
- *Test Traffic Measurement Service* (TTM) [59] is part of RIPE. It measures key parameters of the connectivity between a given site and other measurement points. TTM allows a comprehensive and continuous monitoring of the connectivity of a network running an application to other parts of the Internet.
- *Etomic:* In order to visualise and to understand the dynamics of the Internet, its topology should be continuously monitored and the traffic of data packets should be measured with high temporal precision and good spatial resolution. This gives a nanosecond active measurement precision for inferring the Internet topology [60].
- *DIMES* is a distributed scientific research project aimed at studying the structure and topology of the Internet, with the help of a volunteer community (similar in spirit to projects such as SETI@Home) [61]. Both Dimes and Etomic belong to a greater consortium called Evergrow [62].

In order to generate traffic for active testing, there are many applications. The following list describes the more relevant for traffic generation, topology discovery and bandwidth estimation. The list is far from complete, since it only states representative applications of the most common active measurement fields.

- The *OWAMP* application follows the implementation of the OWAMP protocol [63]. This tool proposes a full new methodology for active testing, with time tracking and security issues. Moreover, it permits the generation of a broad range of traffic patterns.

- *MGEN* is one of the most used traffic generation tools in QoS environments. It provides programs for generating real-time multicast/unicast UDP/IP traffic flows with optional support for RSVP. The MGEN tools transmit and receive (and log) timestamped, sequence numbered packets. Offline analysis of the log files can be performed to assess network metrics such as Packet Loss, OWD, IPDV, etc.
- *Ping* is a classic tool for reachability/latency assessment. Measures hop-to-hop latency and packet loss.
- *Traceroute* is a TCP/IP utility, which allows the determination of the route taken by a packet to reach a particular host. Traceroute works by increasing the "time to live" value of each successive packet sent, and reporting each hop to the gateway that returned the expired packet. There are several versions of this tool. Some of them work with ICMP, others with TCP, but the standard advises using UDP packets.
- *pchar* is a reimplementation of Van Jacobson's pathchar utility for characterising the individual hops of a path between two network hosts. It works on both IPv4 and IPv6 networks and allows any user to find the bandwidth, delay, average queue and loss rate of every hop between any source and destination on the Internet.
- The *NetPerf* tool can be considered as performing bandwidth estimation, but in reality it calculates the Bulk data transfer. This application generates as much traffic as the network can handle in order to compute the goodput.

2.3.4 Passive Measurements

After presenting active measurements, this section focuses on the other main approach to traffic analysis, namely passive measurement. While active measurement uses an intrusive method for inferring network characteristics, passive measurements analyse already existing traffic without intruding on the network's normal operations.

Passive measurements are more suitable for analysing traffic generated by real protocols and applications, because with synthetic traffic it is very difficult to emulate real traffic, since not all the traffic properties are easy to model.

Even being the proper technique for traffic analysis, traffic collection has to face various challenges. On the one hand, accessing a vantage point in order to collect relevant traffic is often administratively and legally difficult, given that private data must not be sniffed out of the network. On the other hand, the required resources to perform the traffic collection (specially on backbone links) are often hard to obtain and require specific hardware.

Moreover, in QoS environments traffic collection is focused on analysing the network metrics of the relevant applications under QoS constraints (e.g., VoIP, Video Streaming, etc.) and to assess whether the QoS contracts are fulfilled or not. This requires using multiple measurement points with the added complexity of its management.

This section describes the usage of passive measurements in QoS environments, together with the possibilities and limitations for traffic collection. The section concludes with the list of the most relevant platforms and applications in the area.

2.3.4.1 Network Characteristics

The previous section presented how to apply active measurements in order to obtain various QoS metrics. Acquiring them using passive measurements is more challenging, because traffic monitoring assumes independent monitoring points. This requires using multiple collection points, which cooperate in a distributed infrastructure to detect and compute the network parameters of the traffic.

Computing QoS metrics requires matching the same packet on the various monitoring points. This is accomplished by generating a unique identifier for each collected packet (*packet identifier*). While various alternatives to do this exist, most of the contributions, as in [47], propose generating the packet identifier by a fast CRC computation obtained from fields of the packet's header and the first bytes of the payload:

- IP Source and Destination.
- Datagram Identifier.
- Protocol Identifier.
- 27 bytes of the packet's payload.

Optionally, the TCP window distinguishes among retransmissions when monitoring TCP flows. Using 27 bytes of the packet's payload overcomes potential identifier collision caused by some operating systems leaving a blank Datagram Identifier. Further discussion about the selected fields and CRC computation can be found at [47].

The per-packet information gathered on the measurement points has to be centralised to a processing station with the following information:

- *Packet identifier.*
- *Timestamp (64-bit):* Time when the packet was captured, required for OWD.
- *Size (16-bit):* Packet size, used for bandwidth measurement.

This processing station matches the CRC from the various collection points and computes all the QoS metrics. Since some metrics involve timestamps, the measurement points need to be synchronised.

With this approach, the packet loss ratio is computed by counting the packets without matches at the measurement points. Since passive measurements are not from end-to-end, the measurement points must be placed smartly, as load balanced links or route changes might affect the collection and consequently the metrics values.

Identifying such packets with a packet identifier is not enough, because in QoS environments traffic is aggregated (e.g., DiffServ), and usually the relevant statistics are presented per aggregate (e.g., mean per flow OWD). Hence, it is necessary to have an aggregate identifier (i.e., it can be per CoS, per flow, etc.) to compute the required metrics.

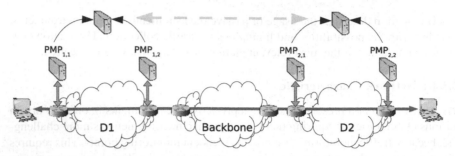

Fig. 2.6. Passive measurement example scenario

The described technique can be used for online QoS assessment. Figure 2.6 shows a simple scenario where each border router of Domain 1 (D1) and Domain 2 (D2) collects traffic and sends it to the processing node, which computes the QoS metrics. In a full-featured scenario such information is forwarded to the MMS (Monitoring and Measurement System) in order to assess whether the QoS is properly provided or not. If the analysis is conducted from end-to-end, each different domain needs to share the QoS parameters with the peer domains.

2.3.4.2 Traffic Collection

One challenging issue with passive measurements is the collection of the network traffic. The first concern is where to deploy the collection points, the second is how to collect the traffic (e.g., using specific network equipment or not).

Deployment of measurement points is an issue, because they need direct access to the traffic without interfering with the normal network operations. Usually, this is achieved by installing optical splitters on the monitored links and setting up the collection station there. Another alternative is to perform the collection directly on the networking equipment. Since the latter may interfere with the normal network operation, only general statistics are gathered using specific protocols for this purpose such as SMTP, NetFlow, etc.

Besides the deployment of the measurement points, the other important issue is how to acquire and analyse the traffic. Two different alternatives are available: software and hardware collection.

Software collection is used when the capture requirements are not high. The traffic collection is normally performed in the operating system kernel. This gives a powerful environment with the required access to the resources. The most used mechanism is the *BSD Packet Filter (BPF)* [64]. BPF provides a protocol independent interface to data link layers. All packets arriving on the network interface, regardless of their destination, are accessible through this mechanism. The specification defines a query language, which permits the selection of the desired traffic for analysis, efficiently discarding unwanted packets.

Software capturing has the advantage of versatility. But, on contemporary networks, problems arise when it is necessary to capture all the traffic on high-speed links with thousands of simultaneous flows traversing the collection point. In this situation, it is very important to have real-time packet capturing and processing. To accomplish this, there are the hardware solutions which, although they lack the flexibility of the software approach, enable wire speed capture with minimal software operation.

2.3.4.3 Platforms and Applications

There are several research groups that provide a broad analysis of the Internet from a passive point of view. The complexity of having access to vantage points make passive platforms more difficult to deploy. In any case, there are research groups aiming to deploy full-featured traffic monitoring platforms. The most relevant are:

- *PERFormance Service-Oriented Network monitoring ARchitecture* (PerfSONAR) is an infrastructure for network performance monitoring, making it easy to solve end-to-end performance problems on paths crossing several networks. It focuses on studying the capacity and availability of the links, specifically its perceived quality. PerfSONAR delivers a service-oriented interface to monitor the network status [65].
- The *InterMON* project focuses on data gathering, its automated access and database design for interdomain QoS analysis [66]. This infrastructure aims at delivering human-understandable information about traffic traces.
- The goal of the *Passive Measurement Analysis* (PMA) project is to deliver new insights into the operation, behaviour and health of the Internet for the benefit of network users and operators. Passive header trace data provides the means to study workload profiles for a number of strategically located measurement points in high-speed environments [67].
- As a successor of the SCAMPI project, *Lobster* is a pilot European infrastructure for accurate Internet traffic monitoring. Based on passive monitoring, their goal is to deploy an infrastructure that can efficiently monitor up to 10 Gbps of traffic in order to detect security attacks and test the performance of network services [45].
- *CoralReef* is the monitoring infrastructure proposed by CAIDA. It delivers a solid passive monitoring platform. Monitoring of optical networks is done with an optical splitter, which diverts a small fraction of the light from the optical fiber to the monitor device. Real-time monitoring support includes system network interfaces, FreeBSD drivers for Apptel POINT (OC12 and OC3 ATM) and FORE ATM (OC3 ATM) cards, and support for Linux drivers for Endace DAG (OC3 and OC12, POS and ATM) cards. The package also includes programming APIs for C and Perl, as well as applications for capture, analysis and Web report generation. The CoralReef software suite includes tools for analysis of traces collected by these type of monitors.

Besides the different platforms using passive measurements, there are software applications that implement the traffic collection. The most relevant are:

- *libpcap* is not really an application, but a library that implements the user interface with the BPF explained earlier. It is present in the most important platforms, and its broad adoption makes it a suitable candidate for any traffic collection needs.
- *tcpdump* is a console application that uses *libpcap* for capturing the packets. The application permits the specification of filters, full packet capture, header-based capture, protocol decoding etc. It is broadly used as it was the first implementation to fully use the *libpcap* functionalities.
- *Wireshark* is formerly known as Ethereal. It is a network protocol analyser for Unix and Windows, also based on *libpcap*. It allows the live experimentation of data from a network or from a capture file on disk. The user can interactively browse the capture data, viewing summary and detailed information for each packet. Wireshark has a more mature implementation than tcpdump, either because of its offline processing capabilities, or because of supporting the Product Data Markup Language (PDML), which is the XML-based file format for traces storage in a portable way.

2.4 Conclusions

Traffic measurements are an important issue in any QoS-aware environment. In this chapter we described the most important objective and subjective metrics, which report a value or set of values describing the perceived quality from the user or the network point of view. Obtaining such metrics is not straightforward, since it involves different distributed points with the consequent complexity of managing the infrastructure. Obtaining accurate results requires a tight control of the network set up. For example, in order to compute the one-way delays it is required to synchronise the systems' clocks involved in the measurement.

These metrics are computed by analysing packets in the network. Due to the required high volume of information and processing, we presented an overview of traffic sampling and aggregation techniques, which are two of the most commonly used mechanisms to smartly reduce the set of data for analysis with minimal loss in accuracy.

Finally, the chapter described two different ways of extracting the metrics. First, by actively generating traffic into the network it is possible to accurately analyse its behaviour, and since the traffic is controlled, any change in the original characteristics of the traffic can be studied.

The second approach is by passively monitoring the already existing traffic, which is a difficult task in a distributed scenario. Moreover, passive traffic analysis has to overcome confidentiality issues about the collected traffic, along with the administrative issues on having the collection point in vantage points with access to the traffic.

3

Traffic Engineering

Luciano Lenzini, Enzo Mingozzi, and Giovanni Stea

Summary. Traffic Engineering has become an extremely important tool for Internet Service Providers (ISPs) as they struggle to keep pace with the ever-increasing volume of Internet traffic. Through appropriate application of Traffic Engineering techniques, providers can offer better service to their customers, reduce congestion in the network, maximise bandwidth utilisation and, in general, enhance performance. In this chapter, after a brief introduction to the concept of Traffic Engineering, its implementation based on Multi Protocol Label Switching (MPLS) and Constraint-Based Routing is illustrated in detail. Moreover, the recently devised enhancements to MPLS-based Traffic Engineering solutions, aimed at explicitly supporting Quality of Service, are outlined.

3.1 Introduction

Traffic Engineering is the set of theories and techniques related to the performance optimisation of operational networks. More specifically, it "encompasses the application of technology and scientific principles to the measurement, modeling, characterisation, and control of Internet traffic, and the application of such knowledge and techniques to achieve specific performance objectives" [68]. Traffic Engineering has become a key tool for Internet Service Providers (ISPs) as they struggle to keep pace with the ever-increasing volume of Internet traffic. It is now well understood that the efficiency and costs of ISPs are directly related to how efficiently they exploit their network resources. Thus, good Traffic Engineering is of paramount importance in order to be able to offer competitive services to the customers. Through Traffic Engineering, ISPs can achieve many desirable goals:

- Minimising congestion and packet loss in the network.
- Improving link utilisation.
- Minimising the total delay experienced by packets.
- Increasing the number of customers with the current assets.
- Routing paths around known bottlenecks or points of congestion in the network.

- Using available aggregate bandwidth and long-haul fibre in a more efficient way by ensuring that subsets of the network do not become overused, while other subsets of the network along potential alternate paths do not become underused.
- Providing more options to differentiate the service offered to customers.

This chapter presents the general concepts of Traffic Engineering. First, in Sect. 3.2, it motivates the need for Traffic Engineering. More specifically, Multi-Protocol Label Switching (MPLS), currently the de-facto standard technology enabling Traffic Engineering, is described in detail in Sect. 3.3. Then, the specific aspects of MPLS-based Traffic Engineering, such as Constraint-Based Routing and Explicit Route Signalling, are presented in Sect. 3.4. This chapter ends with an overview of the recent techniques devised to incorporate Quality of Service (QoS) into Traffic Engineering in Sect. 3.5.

3.2 A Motivating Example

After the network is deployed, the ISP must map customer traffic flows onto the physical topology. Until the early 1990s, mapping traffic flows onto a physical topology was not approached in a really scientific way. Plain IP routing, based on shortest path computations, was considered to be enough to support the relatively low traffic volumes. Today, as ISP networks grow larger, as the circuits supporting IP grow faster, and as the demands of customers become greater, the mapping of traffic flows onto physical topologies needs to be approached in a radically different way, so that the offered load can be supported in a controlled and efficient manner. Traffic Engineering provides the ability to move traffic flows away from the shortest path selected by the Interior Gateway Protocol and onto a potentially less congested physical path across the service provider's network, thus improving performance.

In a "plain IP" network domain, there are two main factors that make efficient Traffic Engineering almost impossible. First, the routing algorithms run at each node only aim to compute the least-cost path to a destination. The cost can be represented either by the number of hops (as in the RIP protocol) or by the sum of advertised per-link costs (as in OSPF and IS-IS, both of which use Dijkstra's algorithm to compute the shortest path). Such routing algorithms, therefore, are completely oblivious of the actual available bandwidth on the links. Note that the available bandwidth is not an additive metric. This means that setting the link cost as a function of the link bandwidth (e.g., as the reciprocal of the link bandwidth) and then using Dijkstra would still not work. Thus, plain IP routing provides no guarantee that the selected path has enough bandwidth to support an expected traffic load.

Second, in a plain IP scenario, forwarding decisions are taken based on the IP destination address. In fact, the next hop for a packet is selected as the one corresponding to the longest-prefix matching entry of the forwarding table. Thus, a router will forward all the packets destined to the same egress router along the *same* path. Now, in a packet-switching network there is normally more than one path connecting two routers: not being able to exploit such multipath forwarding is thus likely to lead

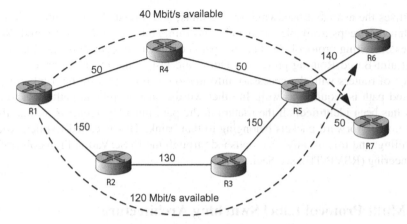

Fig. 3.1. "Fish" network

to unbalanced traffic scenarios, in which some links are overloaded while others are almost empty.

Consider for instance the simple example network, often nicknamed the "fish" network, shown in Fig. 3.1. The bandwidth of each link is also depicted. Assume that two traffic trunks flow from router R1 to R6 and from R1 to R7, respectively. In a plain IP scenario, *both* traffic trunks will follow the same path up to R5. Whether that path is the shortest one (i.e., R1–R4–R5) or the other one, i.e., R1–R2–R3–R5 (which, although longer, is capable of carrying a larger amount of traffic), is a matter of link cost configuration, and it is therefore under the control of the network administrator. However, suppose now that the two above-mentioned traffic trunks are expected to carry 120 and 40 Mbit/s of traffic. Clearly, they cannot both be routed through the selected path to R5 (whichever) without creating congestion. On the other hand, one can easily see that the network actually has enough bandwidth for accommodating both trunks: specifically, if the 40 Mbit/s trunk were routed through the R1–R4–R5–R6 path, and the other trunk through R1–R2–R3–R5–R7 path, no congestion would take place. Unfortunately, IGP routing and destination-based forwarding make such a solution impossible. Thus, the only possible choice is to over-provision one path, thus actually wasting bandwidth.

The above example is purposefully trivial. Simple as it is, it makes a reader wonder what may happen in a *complex* network consisting of several tens of nodes and links. In such a case, the amount of overprovisioning required in order to support a given traffic demand would surely be larger. Three requirements are therefore mandatory for traffic engineering: the first one is a more flexible forwarding scheme than standard, destination-based IP forwarding. Multi-Protocol Label Switching (MPLS), described in Sect. 3.3, allows the forwarding of IP packets to be performed based on arbitrary rules. With reference to the above example, it would allow the two traffic trunks to be routed along different paths, given proper configuration of the routers. As a second requirement, routers have to be provided with some means to *discover* paths of a given bandwidth to a destination. In other words, a dynamic routing protocol that advertises the available bandwidth on the links, and a related path computation algorithm that keeps available bandwidth constraints into account are required. Such classes of routing protocols (and related path computation algorithms) are known as Constraint-Based Routing protocols. Third, and last, some means to provide a sequence of routers with the necessary information to forward a traffic trunk along a selected path is required as well. In other words, once a suitable path for a traffic trunk has been identified, all the routers in the path must be *signalled*, so that they learn how to forward packets belonging to that trunk. This is called Explicit Route Signalling, and it is usually accomplished through the ReSerVation Protocol-Traffic Engineering (RSVP-TE), see Sect. 3.4.

3.3 Multi-Protocol Label Switching Architecture

All routing today in IP networks is destination-based; that is, the decision about where to forward a packet is made based only on its destination address. Suppose we want router R2 to implement the following policy: "packets arriving from R8 that are going to router R5 should go via router R3, while all other packets destined for R5 should go via router R6". A forwarding mechanism that only looks at destination addresses clearly cannot implement this policy. A standard label switching technique was successfully accepted in 1997 by IETF and was called Multi-Protocol Label Switching (MPLS) [68]. MPLS is a new forwarding mechanism in which packets are forwarded based on their *label*. An MPLS label is attached, or *pushed*, onto a packet at the ingress router of an *MPLS domain* (i.e., of a network employing MPLS under the control of a single administrative authority), and removed, or *popped*, before the packet leaves the MPLS domain (we will be more precise on where exactly labels actually get popped in Sect. 3.3.3.1). Within the MPLS domain, the routers do not forward packets based on their IP destination address: rather, they *only* examine the MPLS label. More specifically, the set of all possible packets is partitioned into a number of *Forwarding Equivalence Classes* (FECs). An FEC is assigned a label. This means that all packets belonging to the same FEC are indistinguishable within the MPLS domain, and therefore they will follow the same path. To one end of the spectrum, an FEC may correspond to an IP destination prefix, thus falling back into traditional IP forwarding. However, an FEC can be defined by much finer constraints than mere IP destination prefixes. More specifically, it can be any combination of the latter: IP source and destination prefixes, the Protocol field in the IP header, and it can also include layer-4 information such as the source and destination port. Thus, an FEC can be as fine-grained as to represent traffic from a specific application between two remote end-hosts. Such a great degree of freedom, however, has to be used wisely, sometimes trading forwarding accuracy for network manageability. Within an MPLS domain (Fig. 3.2), routers capable of handling labels are called *Label Switching Routers* (LSRs). They are further distinguished into *core* and *edge* LSRs, depending on whether they are or are not surrounded only by LSRs of the same MPLS domain.

MPLS has two major components that are described in the following sections:

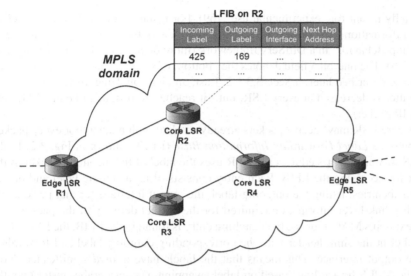

Fig. 3.2. An MPLS domain

- The Forwarding Component (or Forwarding Plane), which is responsible for forwarding packets (based on labels).
- The Control Component (or Control Plane), which is responsible for exchanging Layer-3 routing information and labels. For instance, it tells each LSR which label to use for which FEC.

3.3.1 The Forwarding Component

In MPLS, a 32-bit label, shown in Fig. 3.3, is prepended to a layer-3 (e.g., IP) packet. When the packet is forwarded on a link, the label usually sits between the layer-2 header and the layer-3 packet, in the so-called "shim" header. For some specific layer-2 technologies (like ATM or Frame-Relay) the MPLS label can be directly encoded in the layer-2 header, using some dedicated field (e.g., VPI/VCI or DLCI, respectively). However, in the remainder of this chapter, we will not make further reference to these particular cases.

The MPLS label consists of several fields: a 20-bit *Label* field encodes the label. This allows for a theoretical maximum of roughly 1 million different FECs (although some label values are reserved for particular purposes). A three-bit *exp* field was

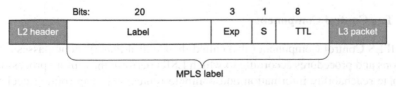

Fig. 3.3. MPLS label

originally meant for "experimental use" [69]. For instance, this field can be used to carry information regarding the forwarding treatment of the packet, e.g., to encode its "Per-hop Behavior" in a DiffServ framework (more details on this issue are given in Sect. 3.5). The one-bit S field denotes the "bottom of stack", which is related to *label stacking*, described later in Sect. 3.3.3.2. Last, an eight-bit Time-To-Live is defined. The latter is decreased at every LSR, until it reaches zero (much like the TTL field of an IP packet).

A core LSR may receive packets already marked with a label. For every packet, it browses a *Label Forwarding Information Base* (LFIB), shown in Fig. 3.2. In the MPLS forwarding procedure, each LSR uses the label of the incoming packet as the index for accessing the LFIB. Each entry consists of an incoming label and one or more subentries, listing the outgoing label, the output interface for that packet, and possibly link-layer information required for the correct delivery of the packet, e.g., the next hop's MAC address. If a matching entry is found in the LFIB, the LSR *swaps* the label in the shim header with the corresponding outgoing label and forwards it to the output interface. This means that the labels have a *local* significance. Note that the MPLS forwarding, based on label swapping, is considerably faster than the conventional IP forwarding: in fact, the former only requires just one memory access (using the label as an address), to take a forwarding decision, whereas the latter requires a much more time-consuming longest-prefix matching in the IP forwarding table.

Instead, an ingress edge LSR receives unlabelled IP packets, to which it imposes (or "pushes") a label based on a packet-to-FEC mapping. The rules according to which a packet is classified to a FEC can include any combination of layer-3 information, such as IP addresses, layer-4 information, UDP/TCP ports, or an incoming interface number.

Finally, an egress edge LSR receives labelled packets and removes (or "pops") the label from them. After that, it forwards the packet to a neighbour router outside the MPLS domain, using standard IP forwarding. The sequence of LSRs traversed by packets of a given FEC, from an ingress edge LSR to an egress edge LSR, is called a *Label Switched Path* (LSP). An LSP is *unidirectional*. If, as it often happens in practice, bidirectional connectivity between two edge LSRs is required, two separate LSPs in the opposite directions must be set up.

In order to achieve a consistent forwarding treatment (e.g., to avoid loops, to begin with), the content of the LFIBs in the LSRs have to be made mutually coherent within the whole MPLS domain. This requires LSRs to exchange routing information and to inform their neighbours regarding which label they are using for which FEC. These issues are dealt with within the MPLS Control Component.

3.3.2 The Control Component

The MPLS Control Component (also called the Control Plane) encompasses all the functions and procedures according to which LSRs perform the routing process (i.e., distribute reachability information and compute routes) and map routing decisions into a consistent forwarding treatment. As such, it includes the routing protocols (e.g., OSPF, BGP, etc.) used by the control component of the conventional IP routing architecture. Furthermore, it includes procedures for an LSR to:

- associate (or *"binding"*) a label to a FEC;
- advertise its bindings to its neighbours; and
- use its own bindings and the ones advertised by its neighbours to populate its LFIB.

Each LSR maintains a pool of free labels: labels are drawn from the pool when a new binding is created, and returned to the pool when the binding is no longer needed. In MPLS, labels are always assigned by the *downstream* LSR. This means that the downstream LSR tells its upstream neighbours which outgoing label to use for an FEC when forwarding a packet. The opposite choice, i.e. an upstream LSR telling its downstream neighbour "Packets for this FEC will be sent to you with this label", is instead not allowed.

MPLS does not require that label bindings to be distributed through a specific protocol. However, the Label Distribution Protocol (LDP) has been standardised for this specific purpose in RFC 3036 [70]. LDP runs on both UDP and TCP, using port 646. It uses UDP for discovering neighbours, and TCP to exchange label binding information. The use of TCP is motivated by the need of reliability and in order delivery: if a binding or request for a binding is not successfully delivered, traffic cannot be correctly forwarded along an LSP. Moreover, a binding advertisement followed by a withdrawal of that binding, for example, would have a very different effect if the messages were received in the reverse order. LSRs discover directly connected neighbours (a layer-2 connection exists between them) by sending LDP HELLO messages to the 224.0.0.2 multicast address (all routers on a subnet). Once a neighbour has been discovered, a TCP session is established. At session establishment, a number of parameters are negotiated (e.g., keep-alive timer values, version, label-binding distribution mode, etc.). As for label-binding distribution, two alternative modes are defined:

- Downstream-on-Demand: Label bindings are distributed (by the downstream LSR) only on request from the upstream LSR.
- Unsolicited Downstream: A downstream LSR distributes label bindings to LSRs that have not explicitly requested them. Label bindings will be distributed to all adjacent neighbours.

The LDP messages involved in label binding distribution are the following:

- A LABEL REQUEST is sent in a downstream-on-demand mode by the upstream LSR to request a label for a particular FEC.
- A LABEL REQUEST ABORT is used to abort an unfulfilled LABEL REQUEST.
- A LABEL MAPPING is sent by a downstream LSR to advertise the binding between FECs and labels.
- A LABEL WITHDRAW is sent by a downstream LSR to revoke a previously advertised binding.
- A LABEL RELEASE is sent by an upstream LSR to notify its downstream neighbour that a previously received label binding is no longer needed.

Neighbours that receive a label binding from an LSR that is not the next hop for that FEC may decide to keep track of such bindings (*Liberal* Label Retention Mode) or discard (i.e., release) such bindings (*Conservative* Label Retention Mode). The main advantage of the liberal retention mode is that an LSR can quickly react to a routing change. However, such a mode wastes labels unnecessarily. All received bindings are stored in the *Label Information Base* (LIB). The ones actually used are also installed in the LFIB, which was described in Sect. 3.3.

Besides deciding whether label bindings are advertised on demand or unsolicited, it remains to be decided *when* a known label binding can be advertised. Two options exist with respect to this issue:

- Independent Control: Each LSR assigns a label to an FEC independently. It then can advertise its label bindings to its neighbours, either on demand or unsolicited.
- Ordered Control: an LSR does not assign a label to a FEC unless it knows how to forward packets of that FEC to the next hop. As a consequence, label bindings proceeds in an orderly fashion from the egress edge LSR to the ingress edge LSR.

An ordered control paradigm guarantees better protection against routing loops, which might instead arise with independent control. Furthermore, it guarantees that a coherent label binding is performed in a network. On the downside, ordered control requires more time to setup an LSP than independent control.

Finally, note that commercial routers allow an administrator to define label bindings *statically*, much like they allow him/her to define static IP routes. In this case, LSPs are manually configured, and consistent label binding must be enforced by the administrator itself.

3.3.3 MPLS Optimisation

This section presents some optimisations on the MPLS forwarding and control procedures.

3.3.3.1 Penultimate Hop Popping

An egress edge LSR in an MPLS domain might have to perform two lookups on a packet received from a neighbour to be forwarded outside the MPLS domain. In fact, it must inspect the label so as to realise that the label has to be popped. Then, it must inspect the underlying IP packet and process it according to standard IP forwarding, in order to know which neighbour to send it to. This obviously reduces the performance of that node and increases the complexity of the hardware implementation. Penultimate Hop Popping addresses this issue by allowing the label to be removed from the packet *before* the latter reaches the egress edge LSR: the egress edge LSR can request its upstream neighbour to perform a label pop operation. This way, the egress edge LSR just performs IP address forwarding. Recall that labels are allocated by the downstream LSR. This implies that the egress edge LSR has to signal its upstream neighbour that it has to pop the label itself. This is achieved by advertising a special label, called the *implicit-null* label, as shown in Fig. 3.4.

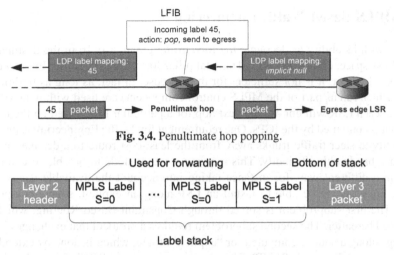

Fig. 3.4. Penultimate hop popping.

Fig. 3.5. Label stack example

3.3.3.2 Label Stacking

So far we have described MPLS assuming that each packet carries a *single* MPLS label. More generally, in MPLS a labelled packet may carry an arbitrary number of labels, organised as a last-in, first-out *Label Stack*, as shown in Fig. 3.5. The top of the stack appears right after the link layer header, and the bottom of the label stack appears right before the network layer header. As far as forwarding is concerned, the label at the top of the stack is the only one taken into consideration at an LSR. Note that the "bottom of stack" field in the MPLS label is always set to zero except for the inmost label, which in fact represents the bottom of the stack. When label stacking is used, core LSRs are allowed to push or pop labels (besides swapping them). However, the bottom-of-stack label is pushed and popped only at the ingress and egress edge LSRs, respectively. In order to allow for label stacking, each entry in the LFIB of a core LSR also specifies one among the following actions: push, pop, swap. Furthermore, an LFIB entry that specifies a pop action can list the address of the *same* LSR as the next hop. This allows the same packet to be processed more than once: for instance, a packet carrying a stack of two labels can first have its top label popped, then "be sent" to the router itself, i.e., be processed again, and be forwarded based on the *bottom* label. Label stacking allows LSPs to be tunnelled into one another, which is useful for Traffic Engineering purposes. For instance, a set of LSPs sharing a given path from R1 to R2 can be tunnelled into a single, higher level LSP by simply having R1 and R2 push and pop a label, respectively. This way, the number of labels exchanged on the path between R1 and R2 is reduced, which preserves scalability. Label stacking is also employed for Fast Rerouting, as will be explained in Sect. 3.4.3. Note that the Penultimate Hop Popping procedure can take place at any level of the label stack.

3.4 MPLS-Based Traffic Engineering

MPLS, with its ability to decouple the forwarding granularity from the destination IP address space, constitutes a fundamental pillar for setting up Traffic Engineering policies. However, it is not sufficient for this purpose. In fact, as long as traditional IGPs (which run as part of the MPLS control component) are used within an MPLS domain, each LSR will choose the next hop for a particular FEC based on the least-cost routes computed by the IGPs. One requirement for Traffic Engineering is instead the ability to steer traffic trunks away from the least-cost route to a destination, so as to use bandwidth efficiently. This requires a source node to be able to compute paths in a different way, for instance taking into account the available bandwidth on the links, and to be able to install an LSP along an explicit, source-computed route. The first subproblem is solved through Constraint-Based Routing, which is described hereafter. The second subproblem requires a protocol that exchanges label bindings along a source-computed (or "explicit") route, which is done by extending the Reservation Protocol (RSVP). This extension, known as RSVP-TE, is described in Sect. 3.4.2.

3.4.1 Constraint-Based Routing

Constraint-Based Routing (CBR) is the set of algorithms and protocols that enable a node to compute a path to a destination, which (i) is optimal with respect to a certain *scalar metric*, and (ii) does not violate a set of *constraints*. While the principle is fairly general, the current Traffic Engineering practices use the administrative cost as the scalar metric to be optimised (much like in conventional IGPs), whereas the constraints can be of the following types:

- Performance constraints: an administrator may want a minimum bandwidth to be available along the entire path.
- Administrative constraints: for instance, links can be classified into a number of administrative classes, and an administrator may want a link to traverse only (or exclude) links of a given class.

Three requirements are necessary to enable CBR. First of all, all links have to be characterised through a coherent set of attributes. For instance, it must be possible to configure an amount of *available bandwidth* on each link, beside the administrative cost. Second, the attributes of each link must be conveyed to each node through a suitable routing protocol. Third, a path computation algorithm that is able to compute the optimal path subject to a specific set of constraints is required on each node. As anticipated above, a routing protocol that conveys the link attributes to all nodes is required. Note that this mandates the routing protocol to be of the link-state class. In fact, in order to enable CBR, each node has to know the value of the attributes at each and every link, which would not be possible with a distance vector protocol. Rather than devising a completely new routing protocol, existing link-state routing protocols have been extended to support CBR. The extended versions of the two most popular link-state IGPs, namely, IS-IS and OSPF, have been standardised and are customarily referred to as IS-IS-TE [71], and OSPF-TE [72], respectively. For both protocols, the set of possible link attributes includes:

- Maximum Bandwidth, i.e., the link capacity.
- Maximum Reservable Bandwidth, i.e., the amount of bandwidth that can be *reserved* on a link. This is normally configured to be smaller than (or equal to) the Maximum Bandwidth, unless the administrator wants the link to be oversubscribed.
- Unreserved Bandwidth, i.e., the amount of bandwidth still available on the link (for Traffic Engineering purposes).
- Administrative Group (or *color*). A link can be a member of up to 32 groups.

In a domain using a TE-IGP, each router stores the link attributes in its Traffic Engineering Database (TED), which can be thought of as an extension of the Link State Database in use with a standard link-state IGP. Some of these attributes, e.g., the Maximum Bandwidth and the Administrative Group, are static and are configured manually by an administrator. Others instead, like the Unreserved Bandwidth, change as new LSPs are opened. Therefore, the TE IGP has to propagate those changes as they happen, and the TED has to be updated accordingly. Note that while a standard link-state IGP only floods information when the underlying *topology* changes, a TE-IGP might do that also when new LSPs are setup and torn down. However, during normal operation this happens seldom enough for TE-IGP traffic and does not cause a significant overhead. Furthermore, thresholds can be set on dynamic attributes: for instance, a router may be configured so that a change in the Unreserved Bandwidth of a link would trigger flooding of this information only if the attribute crosses a certain threshold. This further limits the amount of TE-IGP traffic. The alert reader will already have noticed that, at a given moment in time, the content of the TED of a router might not be up to date because of the latency involved in flooding the link state attributes. We will come back to this issue later on in this section, after introducing RSVP-TE.

When a router is required to compute the optimal path subject to some constraint to a given destination, it runs a modified version of the well-known Dijkstra's algorithm (or Shortest Path First, SPF), called *Constrained Shortest Path First* (CSPF), to compute the path. Note that the words "distance" and "cost" are used interchangeably, reflecting a long-established parallel between the two, and so are "shortest" and "least-cost". CSPF uses the information in the TED, flooded by the TE-IGP, *and* locally specified constraints on the link attributes. The most common constraint is that a minimum Unreserved Bandwidth be available at all links along the path. Moreover, excluding or mandating links of a certain colour is also common. A router has the complete picture of the underlying network graph stored in its TED. The CSPF algorithm just consists of: (i) applying the constraints to all the links in the TED, so as to obtain a "pruned" network graph, which only includes those links that meet the constraints, and (ii) using Dijkstra's algorithm on the pruned network graph so as to find the *Shortest Path Tree* that connects the source to any reachable destination.

As an example, we report the CSPF computation for a path from router R1 to router R8 in the network shown in Fig. 3.6. For simplicity, we assume that links

{Cost, Unreserved Bandwidth, [Groups] }

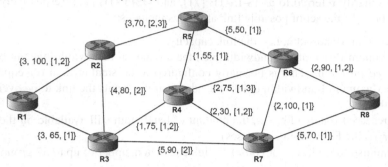

Fig. 3.6. Scenario for the CSPF example

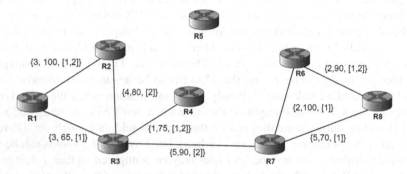

Fig. 3.7. How the network looks after applying the constraints

are characterised only by their administrative cost, an Unreserved Bandwidth and Administrative Group. Furthermore, although the attribute values may be different in the two directions of a single full duplex link, we assume that they are equal in both directions. The constraints specified at the source are that the minimum Unreserved Bandwidth along the path must be at least 60 Mbit/s, and that the path must exclude links belonging to Administrative Group 3.

As a first step, the network graph obtained from the TED is pruned, and all the links that do not meet the constraint are removed (see Fig. 3.7). Then, the shortest path tree rooted at R1 is computed on the pruned network graph, by applying Dijkstra's algorithm. The outcome is shown in Fig. 3.8. Such a tree obviously includes the constrained shortest path to the selected destination R8, i.e., R1–R3–R7–R6–R8, with a cost of 12. Note that the *unconstrained* shortest path to R8 would have been different, i.e. R1–R3–R4–R6–R8, whose cost is 8. Furthermore, note that R5 is not reachable from R1 under the specified constraints.

While Dijkstra's algorithm computes the shortest path tree rooted at the source node, i.e. a set of paths connecting the latter to *any* reachable destination, the goal of CSPF is to compute *one* path from the source to a target destination, which is fed as input to the algorithm. This allows an optimised version of the SPF to be run on the pruned network graph, which stops exploring the shortest path tree as soon as the

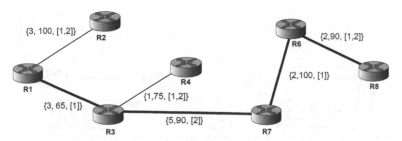

Fig. 3.8. The shortest path tree on the pruned network graph

target destination is reached. Finally, we observe that, when running CSPF, it may actually be possible that more than one feasible path with the *same* cost is found for the target destination. In a practical implementation of a TE-IGP, a tie-breaking rule between two equal cost paths is thus required. Some tie-breaking rules used in commercial routers are the following:

- largest minimum Unreserved Bandwidth first: the path with the largest minimum Unreserved Bandwidth is selected, so as to balance (up to some extent) the reservation on all links.
- smallest minimum Unreserved Bandwidth first: the path with the smallest minimum Unreserved Bandwidth is selected, so as to fully exploit the resources on links already traversed by LSPs before considering alternative links.
- whichever: one path, possibly the first in the list, is picked, without considering bandwidth attributes and no possibility of control by the administrator.

3.4.2 Explicit Route Signalling

Once we have computed—through Constraint-Based Routing—a suitable path for a given destination, traversing a sequence of MPLS-enabled routers, we need to actually set up an LSP along that path. This is called Explicit Route Signalling, where the term "explicit" reflects the fact that the sequence of hops is provided as an input, rather than being decided implicitly by the IGP. Explicit Route Signalling actually entails that label bindings are installed in the LFIBs of the routers along the computed path, which is done through a signalling protocol. Two existing protocols have been extended to support explicit route signalling, namely the Reservation Protocol (RSVP) [73], originally designed in 1994 as a component of the Integrated Services (IntServ) architecture, and the Label Distribution Protocol, described in Sect. 3.3.2. Their extensions are called RSVP-TE [74] and Constraint-based Routing LDP (CR-LDP) [75]. The functions and capabilities of RSVP-TE and CR-LDP are very similar. However, in 2003 it was decided within the IETF that maintaining two different protocols for performing the same job represented an unnecessary duplication of efforts, and CR-LDP was abandoned in favour of RSVP-TE, which was by far the most widely implemented of the two. For this reason, we only describe RSVP-TE in some detail. We first recall the basic RSVP functionalities, and after that we describe

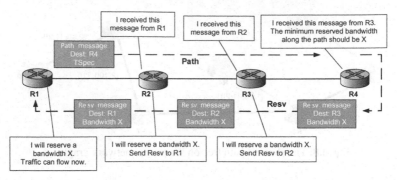

Fig. 3.9. An RSVP Path/Resv handshake

the TE extensions. As the name suggests, RSVP is used to reserve resources (i.e., a queue with a minimum guaranteed bandwidth and buffer space) along a path from a source to a destination. The usual RSVP communication is the exchange of a pair of messages called Path (going from the source to the destination) and Resv (going in the opposite direction), as shown in Fig. 3.9. The Path message includes the Traffic Specification of the flow, i.e. its traffic profile, including the sustainable rate of the flow. As the Path message travels from the source to the destination, each hop records the address of the previous hop. When the Path message arrives at the destination, the amount of resources to be reserved at each hop is computed, based on the TSPEC and on the accumulated latency along the forward route. Then, the Resv message is sent along the reverse route (which includes *exactly* the same routers as the Path message in the reverse order), and the amount of resources specified in the Resv message are actually reserved at each hop. Resource reservation along a path can be explicitly torn down through a similar message exchange pattern, which involves PathTear and ResvTear messages.

Three enhancements are required for making RSVP suitable for explicit route signalling in a Traffic Engineering context:

(i) the ability to request and install label bindings;
(ii) the ability to route a Path message through a precomputed sequence of hops; and
(iii) the ability to control the admission of a new LSP, i.e. to verify whether the Unreserved Bandwidth on each link is actually sufficient for the LSP *and*, if so, to decrease it of the amount of bandwidth required by the LSP.

The RSVP message format includes a common header, which also specifies the message type (i.e., Path, Resv and so on), and a list of *objects*, e.g. the above-mentioned TSPEC. This makes RSVP easy to extend: in fact, you only need to add new object types. As far as point (i) is concerned, two new objects, namely Label-Request and RSVPLabel, have been defined. The former is sent in the Path message to inform downstream routers that they are expected to provide a label. The latter is inserted in a Resv message to provide the label itself to the upstream router. When the Path message reaches the destination, the latter selects a label and inserts it in the

RSVPLabel object of the Resv message. As the Resv message travels back along the reverse route, each intermediate router selects a new incoming label, installs an entry in its LFIB specifying that the incoming label has to be swapped with the outgoing label and sent to its downstream neighbour, and propagates the incoming label to its upstream neighbour. In other words, RSVP-TE enforces an *ordered downstream* label binding. Note that the destination router can exploit Penultimate Hop Popping by inserting an implicit-null label in the RSVPLabel object of the Resv message. The procedures for handling the label bindings are in addition to—not instead of—the basic RSVP procedures. For instance, an RSVP-TE Resv message may also reserve resources along the route, besides binding labels. Whether and how this is actually done is largely implementation-dependent.

Regarding point (ii), we observe that, in RSVP Path, messages are sent to the IP address of the destination and are, therefore, forwarded according to conventional destination-based IP routing. The TE extension, instead, allows an Explicit Route Object (ERO) to be specified in the Path message. The latter is in fact the path computed at the source through Constraint-Based Routing. The ERO consists of a sequence of *abstract nodes*. An abstract node is often a single router. However, it can also be a *group* of routers (e.g., a whole area of an MPLS-TE domain) whose internal topology is, however, opaque to the router that computes the ERO.

As far as point (iii) is concerned, we first observe that the Path message carries a TSPEC object, which contains the bandwidth requested for the LSP. Recall that the ERO was computed through Constraint-Based Routing. This means that the source router has already checked, by comparing the Unreserved Bandwidth of the links in its TED to the LSP bandwidth, that there *is* enough bandwidth to support the LSP to the destination. Why, then, do we need an admission control procedure at all? The answer lies in the fact that, due to flooding latencies the TED of the source router may not be up to date. In other words, the fact that enough bandwidth was available at the time the ERO was computed does not guarantee that it will still be available when we setup the LSP. Thus, we do need to check the Unreserved Bandwidth at each hop, which is done when the Path message is processed, as routers along the path must have the final decision on the LSP setup. If the admission control test fails at a link (a likely cause being that some *other* LSP traversing that link was recently established), a PathErr message is returned to the source along the reverse route. A sample RSVP-TE Path/Resv message exchange is shown in Fig. 3.10. When an LSP is established (i.e., after the Resv message has reached the source), each router along the path has to flood the network with a new link-state advertisement, in which a suitably reduced Unreserved Bandwidth is advertised. This way, each router will update its TED, and—after a while—a steady state will be reached again, in which all TEDs are aligned. Once again, we remark that the decision to set up an LSP is taken (by the administrator) at time scales that are larger by orders of magnitude, than the flooding latency. Therefore, the latter is hardly going to be a problem in practical cases.

RSVP-TE inherits the "soft state" approach of RSVP. Soft state means that a reservation (and, for the TE extension, label binding) is no longer valid after a given timeout, unless it is periodically refreshed. To this purpose, Path and Resv messages

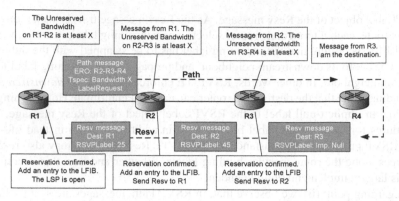

Fig. 3.10. The setup of an LSP through RSVP-TE

are exchanged between neighbours at regular intervals, also after the setup of the LSP. However, in RSVP-TE, after the LSP has been set up, Path and Resv messages are not sent in a "request/ack" fashion on the end-to-end path. Rather, each node sends them periodically and independently to its upstream and downstream neighbours. If the timeout expires, the LSP is removed. The timers are obviously set so that this happens only if a relatively large number of consecutive messages are lost. Note that the bandwidth waste of such a mechanism is limited, since messages are sent (roughly) at 30-second intervals. On the other hand, periodic refreshes also partially compensate for the lack of a reliable message delivery mechanism, since RSVP and RSVP-TE run either on UDP or directly on IP. Finally, note that, while RSVP was originally devised for signalling *single sessions* (e.g., one stream of an ongoing Voice over IP call between two remote hosts), RSVP-TE signals LSPs, which are *traffic trunks*, i.e. paths through which a large amount of such sessions will be routed. Therefore, they are assumed to be semipermanent and their number in a MPLS-TE domain is expected to be relatively small. Thus, the overhead of control and signalling traffic related to LSP setup and management hardly represents an issue.

3.4.3 Traffic Engineering Practices

Having presented the basic concepts and mechanisms of Traffic Engineering, we now present two applications of the above in practical contexts. More specifically, we describe how to optimise the placement of LSPs in an MPLS-TE domain, and how MPLS-TE mechanisms can be used to quickly recover from a link failure with minimal data loss.

3.4.3.1 LSP Optimisation

As already stated, LSPs act as semipermanent paths. While Constraint-Based Routing ensures that an LSP is placed on the optimal path, the network topology may change *after* the LSP has been created, either because new links appear, or because other existing LSPs are torn down. Therefore, the once-optimal path for a given LSP may no longer be so after a while. MPLS-TE implementations include tools that, either on a periodic basis (normally in the range of hours or days), or as a consequence of topology changes, recompute the Constraint-Based Routing paths for open LSPs. If a *new* path is found to be optimal for a given LSP, the latter can be rerouted on the new path. Rerouting an LSP on a new path can be done without losing traffic. In fact, the new path is signalled through RSVP-TE *before* the old one is torn down (which is often called "make-before-break"). Note that the new path may actually have some links in common with the old one. If this happens, a make-before-break approach would lead to temporarily reserving double the bandwidth on the common links, or cause the admission control test to fail for lack of bandwidth. However, when opening an LSP through RSVP-TE it is possible to specify that a reservation is of the *Shared Explicit* type. This allows the source router to state that the required bandwidth for the new LSP is to be *shared* with the one for the old LSP.

3.4.3.2 Fast Rerouting

The topology of a network can also change because of link failures. In this case, all the LSPs traversing a failed link would experience a considerably long service disruption. In fact, in a TE context, at least three things should happen before a failed LSP is reestablished: first, the link failure should be detected by the ingress LSR, which normally takes some time (on the order of seconds, due to the link-state flooding latencies). Second, after routing has reached convergence again, a new path for the LSP should be computed through Constraint-Based Routing. Third, the new computed path should be signalled through RSVP-TE, which again involves the forwarding of messages to the egress LSR and back. In order to alleviate this problem, a "proactive" approach, known as *Fast Rerouting* is taken in MPLS-TE. The basic idea is to preprovision a *backup LSP* that circumvents a critical link. Such backup LSPs are kept in standby (i.e., not used to carry traffic) until a failure occurs. This way, as soon as an LSR (not necessarily the ingress one) detects a failure, it can reroute the traffic through the backup LSP, without waiting for the failure to be advertised to the ingress LSP and so on. With reference to Fig. 3.11, we want the link R2–R3 to be protected against failures. That link is currently carrying an LSP from R1 to R6, for which labels are allocated in the LFIBs of all routers. During normal operation, R2 would swap an incoming label with the value of 124 to an outgoing label of 152 and send packets on the link to R3. Furthermore, assume that R2 and R3 have opened a backup LSP through R4 and R5, with respect to which R2 and R3 are edge LSR. The action that R2 would take to forward a packet along that LSP would be to push label 35 on an incoming packet and forward it on the link R2–R4. R4 would swap label 35 with 38, and R5 would pop label 38, being the penultimate hop. When router R2 detects a failure on the link R2–R3, it does the following: it still swaps 124 with 152, but it also *pushes* label 35 and forwards the packet along the link R2–R4. This way, the packet arrives untouched to router R3, and may further proceed on its journey. In other words, Fast Rerouting uses label stacking.

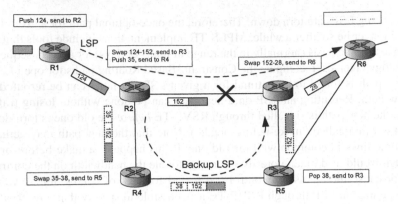

Fig. 3.11. Fast rerouting

Clearly, Fast Rerouting may result in suboptimal routing. However, backup LSPs are not expected to carry traffic for a long time. As soon as the IGP propagates the link failure to the ingress LSR, a new optimal LSP can be computed according to the make-before-break approach, and normal operation is resumed. Note that the backup LSP protects a *link*, rather than a single LSP. Therefore, if several LSPs share a common link and that link goes down, the same backup LSP circumventing that link can be used to quickly reroute all those LSPs. However, *links* are not the only components that happen to fail. In fact, *nodes* may go down as well. For instance, the backup LSP of Fig. 3.11 would be useless if R3 itself fails. In order to protect against node failures, a backup LSP circumventing a *node*, for instance traversing R2–R4–R6, can be created. Note that this LSP would also protect against failures of links R2–R3 and R5–R6. However, this requires the incoming label for the standard LSP at R6 to be made known at R2, which is something that would not happen normally. In fact, after a failure of node R3, R2 should swap label 124 with 28 (and not 152), push label 35 and route the traffic to R4. Finally, we observe that backup tunnels can be protected against congestion by reserving a suitable amount of bandwidth through RSVP-TE. How large is "suitable" actually depends on the number and bandwidth of LSPs that will be quickly rerouted through the backup LSP, and on how critical their traffic is.

3.5 Traffic Engineering and Quality of Service

MPLS-TE provides a powerful means to control the amount of congestion that traffic may experience in a network domain. However, conventional MPLS traffic engineering does not provide direct support for Quality of Service (QoS). As a matter of fact, MPLS and MPLS-TE are oblivious of service classes. MPLS allows each LSR to select the next hop based on the labels attached to incoming packets. However, once the forwarding decision has been made, it provides no means to differentiate the scheduling treatment and dropping precedence among packets sharing the same outgoing interface. On the other hand, with MPLS-TE, bandwidth accounting is performed during path establishment at each LSR along a given LSP across all classes of service and not on a per-class basis. However, bandwidth allocation on a per-class basis is a key requirement in order to provide QoS guarantees in a network domain.

A reference QoS architecture in today's IP-based networks is the DiffServ architecture defined in RFC 2475 [14], which provides a scalable solution based on traffic policing at the network ingress, and queueing, scheduling and dropping mechanisms implemented on a per-class basis at each hop of the DiffServ domain. In order to allow network operators to benefit from both traffic engineering techniques provided by MPLS-TE and QoS guarantees in terms of delay, jitter and packet loss provided by DiffServ, additional mechanisms are needed. These are the ability to specify how to map DiffServ onto LSPs, and to account for bandwidth on a per-class basis during LSP setup. These mechanisms have in fact been defined by IETF as extensions to MPLS and MPLS-TE, respectively, and will be described in the next sections.

3.5.1 QoS Support over MPLS

In a DiffServ domain, a *Behaviour Aggregate* (BA) is a set of IP packets traversing the domain and requiring the same scheduling and, in some cases, dropping treatment at each hop. At the ingress node of the domain, packets are classified into BAs and marked with a corresponding *DiffServ Code Point* (DSCP), which is used at each next hop to determine their *Per Hop Behaviour* (PHB). RFC 2475 [14] specifies the rules to carry the DSCP into the IP packet header. However, in an MPLS domain, once an IP packet at the ingress LSR is encapsulated into the shim header, forwarding decisions at each next LSR are based solely on the label contained in that header, i.e. the IP header is no longer inspected. Therefore, the basic issue in supporting DiffServ over MPLS is to let each LSR be able to map DiffServ BAs onto LSPs, i.e. to infer the appropriate PHB of each packet by looking at the MPLS shim header only.

However, there is a second, more subtle issue to be considered. In fact, as stated in RFC 3260 [76], specific BA groups, called *Ordered Aggregates* (OAs), may be defined in DiffServ so that packets of the same microflow cannot be reordered if they belong to different BAs of the same OA. The set of PHBs corresponding to BAs of the same OA is called a *PHB Scheduling Class* (PSC). An example of OA—presently, the only one—is the *Assured Forwarding* (AF) BA class defined in RFC 2597 [19]: packets belonging to the same AF class, e.g. $AF1$, are entitled to get the same scheduling treatment, i.e., they are buffered to the same queue, but possibly different dropping precedences, which are mapped onto different PHBs, i.e., $AF11$, $AF12$, or $AF13$. In order to not violate the ordering constraint, it is then necessary to prevent an LSR from forwarding packets of the same OA but different BAs over different LSPs, since this would eventually result in packet disordering.

RFC 3270 [77] describes the mechanisms that are needed in an MPLS domain to support DiffServ. In particular, depending on the adopted solution, two LSP types are envisaged:

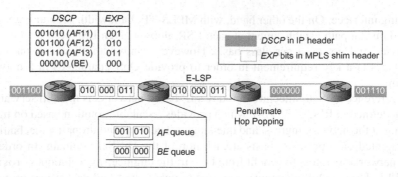

Fig. 3.12. An example of E-LSP

- EXP-Inferred-PSC LSPs (E-LSPs); and
- Label-Only-Inferred-PSC LSPs (L-LSPs).

With E-LSPs, the PHB to be applied to the packet is directly encoded into the three EXP bits of its MPLS shim header, which therefore determine both the PSC of the packet and its dropping precedence. The same E-LSP can then carry a traffic mix of a given FEC from any set of up to eight BAs—possibly spanning multiple Ordered Aggregates—versus a maximum number of 64 for DSCP. An example of a single E-LSP supporting four different PHBs is reported in Fig. 3.12. When an IP packet arrives at the ingress LSR, it is first classified (as usual) into its FEC, which determines the label to be included in the MPLS shim header. In addition, the PHB is identified by, e.g., looking at the DSCP value in the IP header, assuming that it has been already set at a prior hop. Based on the configured EXP-to-PHB mapping, the EXP bits are then set accordingly. In particular, in this example, it is assumed that the EXP-to-PHB mapping for the E-LSP has been configured so that $EXP = 001$, $EXP = 010$, and $EXP = 011$ are mapped onto the $AF11$ ($DSCP = 001010$), $AF12$ ($DSCP = 001100$) and $AF13$ ($DSCP = 001110$) PHBs, respectively, and $EXP = 000$ is mapped onto the Best Effort (BE) PHB ($DSCP = 000000$). When the packet arrives at a core LSR, the next hop is determined as usual by looking up the LFIB with its MPLS label. However, once the packet has been bound to its output interface, the queue to which it will be buffered, as well as its dropping precedence, are solely determined by the value of the EXP bits through the configured EXP-to-PHB mapping.

In general, the EXP-to-PHB mapping is specific to each FEC and corresponding E-LSP but, as a special case, it can also rely on a preconfigured mapping. In the former case, the mapping must be explicitly signalled at an E-LSP setup; to this aim, RSVP and LDP protocols have been extended to support such signalling (see [77] for details). In the latter case, instead, no signalling is needed, since it is assumed that a kind of "default" mapping is manually configured in a consistent manner across the whole MPLS domain. Preconfigured mapping is in fact the usual case when E-LSPs are used in production networks, since it reduces signalling overhead and label consumption, and simplifies network management.

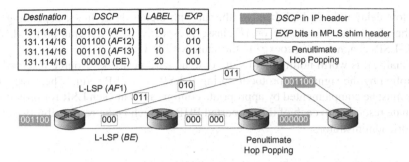

Destination	DSCP	LABEL	EXP
131.114/16	001010 (AF11)	10	001
131.114/16	001100 (AF12)	10	010
131.114/16	001110 (AF13)	10	011
131.114/16	000000 (BE)	20	000

Fig. 3.13. An example of L-LSP

With L-LSPs, instead, the scheduling treatment of a packet is bound to the label itself. Therefore, L-LSPs can carry only packets from a single BA or OA. In the latter case, however, the problem is to let each LSR be able to infer the specific BA, i.e., the dropping precedence of each forwarded packet. To this aim, with L-LSPs the MPLS label is in fact bound to the PSC of the packet, which determines the scheduling treatment, whereas the actual PHB *among those belonging to that PSC* that determines the dropping precedence is encoded into the EXP bits of the shim header. Note that since the per-hop behaviour with L-LSPs depends on the label value, its determination cannot in any case rely on a preconfigured mapping, and therefore must necessarily be signalled during LSP setup. Both RSVP and LDP protocols have been extended to support this kind of signalling [77].

An example of two L-LSPs carrying two different PHB scheduling classes is reported in Fig. 3.13. The basic difference with the previous example is that here, when the IP packet arrives at the ingress LSR, *both* its FEC *and* its PHB, identified as usual, are used to determine the label to be included in the shim header, which places the packet in the correct L-LSP to the destination. In this example, for the same destination network, the ingress LSR binds $LABEL = 10$ to the L-LSP carrying traffic of the AF1 class, and $LABEL = 20$ to the L-LSP carrying traffic of the BE class. Furthermore, the EXP bits are determined depending on the PHB scheduling class. In this example, for the $AF1$ L-LSP, $EXP = 001$, $EXP = 010$, and $EXP = 011$ are set in case of $AF11$ ($DSCP = 001010$), $AF12$ ($DSCP = 001100$) and $AF13$ ($DSCP = 001110$) PHBs, respectively, whereas $EXP = 000$ is always set for the BE L-LSP.

To summarise, a solution based on E-LSPs resembles quite strongly the DiffServ operation in a native IP network, since QoS treatment required by each packet is directly encoded in a specific field of its header. However, the number of different PHBs in the same network is limited to eight (in case of preconfigured mapping). On the other hand, with L-LSPs there is no such limitation, but additional signalling is required at LSP setup and network management gets complicated because of the increase of the overall number of LSPs that are required to be established. However, L-LSPs also give the advantage of allowing us to engineer different paths for different classes of service. For example, packets to the same destination could be routed over low-delay links or high-bandwidth, but with higher delay links, depending on whether they belong to the *EF* or *AF* classes, respectively. In general, both E-LSPs and L-LSPs can, however, coexist in the same MPLS domain.

Finally, it is worth noting that in any case no hard network resource reservation is implied by the signalling protocol during E-LSP or L-LSP setup. Therefore, the latter must be complemented by appropriate configuration at each LSR for providing adequate resources to each of the supported PHBs, which is the responsibility of the network administrator.

3.5.2 Traffic Engineering Extensions for DiffServ

By means of E-LSPs and L-LSPs, or a combination of both, MPLS is enabled to support DiffServ, thus combining QoS treatment of packets at each hop with label-switched forwarding in the same network domain. DiffServ alone, however, may not be sufficient to meet the expected QoS, if adequate resources are not provisioned along the forwarding paths, independently of the forwarding technique. To this aim, MPLS-TE could potentially provide great benefits, since it allows selecting forwarding paths—not necessarily the shortest ones—by explicitly taking bandwidth availability into account. However, as already mentioned at the beginning of this section, the issue is that MPLS-TE is oblivious to classes of service, since it accounts for available bandwidth without distinguishing among possible different classes of service.

As an example, consider an IP/MPLS network in which a considerable fraction of traffic is expected to be VoIP traffic, so that its amount could even approach—in face of failure scenarios—the capacity of some of its links. In order to provide the required QoS to such delay-sensitive traffic, the challenge for the service provider is to reserve adequate resources at all nodes of the network, combined with appropriate policing and admission control mechanisms at the network ingress. In particular, in order to keep delay and jitter sufficiently low, a possible approach would be that of enforcing the amount of VoIP traffic traversing a link to stay below a certain percentage of its overall capacity. This would ensure that the queueing component of the delay experienced by VoIP packets is kept low. In such a scenario, the service provider could not take advantage of MPLS-TE in order to benefit from constraint-based routing of traffic, since bandwidth constraints could only be expressed as a common constraint for both VoIP and Best Effort traffic. A real support for engineering traffic in such a scenario would instead require the ability to specify a *specific* bandwidth constraint as a "certain" percentage of the link capacity. This would only be for LSPs carrying VoIP traffic, while specifying a different constraint for the BE traffic—possibly allowing it to have access to all of the remaining link capacity.

In order to overcome the limitations of MPLS-TE, *DiffServ-aware Traffic Engineering* (DS-TE) was recently standardised by the IETF in RFC 3564 [78], which combines the advantages of both DiffServ and MPLS-TE. DS-TE makes MPLS-TE aware of service classes (Classes of Service, CoS), allowing resource reservation with CoS granularity and providing the fault-tolerance properties of MPLS at a per-CoS level. The result is the ability to give strict QoS guarantees while optimising use of network resources. DS-TE is thus the state of the art for combining QoS and traffic engineering, and is already supported by off-the-shelf network products (e.g., it is implemented by *Cisco IOS XR* v3.4 and *Juniper JUNOS* v8).

RFC 3564 [78] introduces two concepts in order to enforce separate bandwidth reservations for different classes of traffic. The first concept is that of a *Class-Type* (CT) defined as "the set of traffic trunks crossing a link that is governed by a specific set of bandwidth constraints". Each LSP can only carry traffic from one CT, and LSPs that are traffic-engineered to guarantee bandwidth from a particular CT are referred to as DS-TE LSPs. Link bandwidth allocation, constraint-based routing and admission control for each DS-TE LSP are performed depending on its CT. This implies, for example, that all routers throughout the network must keep track of reserved bandwidth, on each link and at any given time, *on a per-CT basis*. DS-TE requires support for up to eight CTs referred to as *CT0* through *CT7*.

The concept of Class-Type is complemented by the concept of *Bandwidth Constraint Model*, which is "the set of rules defining: (i) the maximum number of Bandwidth Constraints; and (ii) which CTs each Bandwidth Constraint applies to and how". In particular, a *Bandwidth Constraint* (BC) is an amount of available bandwidth expressed, for example, as a percentage of the link's capacity, which can be maximum reserved by one, or a set of CT(s). More than one BC—up to eight, referred to as *BC0* through *BC7*—can be configured on each link of the network. The specific bandwidth constraint model adopted will then establish how many of such BCs must actually be defined, and the relationship between them and the set of defined CTs.

Two models are currently standardised by IETF and implemented by routers: The Maximum Allocation Bandwidth Constraints Model (MAM), defined in RFC 4125 [79], and the Russian Doll Bandwidth Constraints Model (RDM), defined in RFC 4127 [80]. The MAM model basically sets a one-to-one correspondence between BCs and CTs, that is the link capacity is simply divided among the different CTs. As an example, on a link of 1 Mbit/s capacity where *CT0* and *CT1* class types are supported, the network administrator might configure two bandwidth constraints, say e.g. *BC0* = 600 kbit/s and *BC1* = 400 kbit/s, respectively, so that LSPs carrying traffic from *CT0* cannot reserve more than 600 kbit/s, whereas LSPs carrying traffic from *CT1* cannot use more than 400 kbit/s. Note that, in general, the sum over all the bandwidth constraints on a given link is allowed to be greater than the maximum reservable bandwidth on that link. In such a case, however, there is the additional constraint that the latter cannot be exceeded by the overall amount of bandwidth reserved by all CTs.

The MAM achieves complete isolation between different CTs, but at the price of possibly wasting bandwidth, or not making an optimal use of it. This may happen since it is possible that an LSP fails to setup or it has to follow a nonoptimal path, due to not enough bandwidth being available on a given link for its CT, even though the overall maximum reservable bandwidth on the same link is far from being consumed. The RDM model tries improving bandwidth efficiency over the MAM model by allowing CTs to share bandwidth. As with MAM, the RDM model requires that as many BCs are defined as the number of supported CTs. However, assuming that all

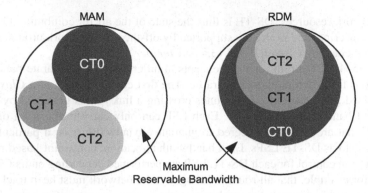

Fig. 3.14. The MAM and RDM bandwidth allocation models

eight CTs are defined, mapping between the two sets is as follows: each bandwidth constraint BCi, $0 \leq i \leq 7$, represents the maximum amount of bandwidth reservable altogether by CTj, $i \leq j \leq 7$. $BC0$ is in addition restricted to be equal to the maximum reservable bandwidth on the link. Considering the same example above, i.e. a 1 Mbit/s link with two class types $CT0$ and $CT1$ supported, configuring bandwidth constraints as $BC0 = 1$ Mbit/s and $BC1 = 400$ kbit/s, respectively, implies with the RDM model that LSPs carrying traffic from $CT1$ cannot reserve more than 400 kbit/s, whereas LSPs carrying traffic from *both* $CT1$ *and* $CT0$ cannot use more than 1 Mbit/s. It then follows that traffic from $CT0$ can consume up to all the maximum reservable bandwidth in case there is no traffic from $CT1$, differently from what would happen if the MAM model were applied. On the other hand, this also means that there is no perfect isolation between the two CTs, and therefore, when needed, preemption must be used to ensure that each CT is guaranteed its share of bandwidth. This can be achieved by making use of preemption priorities.[1] Figure 3.14 schematically represents the relationship between BCs and CTs in the MAM and RDM allocation models, respectively. A performance comparison between the two can be found in RFC 4128 [81].

Constraint-based path computation, regardless of the particular bandwidth constraint model applied, obviously also requires a number of extensions to conventional MPLS-TE protocol operations. First, CSPF needs to be extended to handle per-CT reservation requirements. Second, TE-IGPs, such as OSPF and IS-IS, must also be extended in order to convey per-CT reservable bandwidth information at different priority levels. Finally, for each LSP, the CT must be signalled during LSP setup in order to perform a correct computation of available resources and subsequent admission or rejection of the path request. All such protocol extensions are defined in RFC 4124 [82].

---

[1] For the sake of simplicity, we intentionally omitted mentioning setup and hold preemption priorities associated to DS-TE LSPs. We refer the reader to [78] for details on how preemption priorities are managed in DS-TE domains.

Recalling the scenario with VoIP traffic described at the beginning of this section, it is now clear how it could be easily supported by means of DS-TE, both with the MAM or the RDM bandwidth constraint models. On the other hand, it is also equally clear that, once DS-TE LSPs have been set up, carried traffic must receive the appropriate scheduling behaviour at each LSR, corresponding to its class type. To this aim, DiffServ can be used. However, recalling that a DS-TE LSP can carry traffic from just one CT, it follows that class types must consistently be mapped onto per-hop behaviours encoded into packets. One simple solution is to map each CT to a different OA supported by the network. In such a case both L-LSPs or E-LSPs can be used but, in the latter case, provided that they are enforced to carry traffic from just one OA. The class type of the LSP is then immediately determined by the transported OA. On the other hand, it might be possible in principle to make use of E-LSPs carrying traffic from multiple OAs. However, in this case, it is much more difficult to ensure that bandwidth reservation at setup time and scheduling treatment at forwarding time are always consistent (see RFC 3564 [78] for details).

To conclude, it is worth highlighting that even if resources are correctly reserved throughout the network on a per-class-of-service base by means of DS-TE, and traffic receives the appropriate treatment at each hop of the network conforming with its class of service, due to DiffServ, QoS guarantees still cannot be provided. They can be provided only if further mechanisms, such as policing and admission control, are configured at the ingress of the network so as to ensure that the traffic stays within the limits assumed when the resource reservation was made.

3.6 Conclusions

In this chapter, Traffic Engineering with Quality of Service support has been illustrated in the context of the MPLS forwarding network technology. The MPLS technology was first introduced, showing how it decouples the forwarding decision process from the destination IP address space. In particular, the forwarding and control procedures of MPLS have been described, including some of the optimisation options implemented within them. Extensions to MPLS in order to explicitly support Traffic Engineering were then illustrated. In particular, the fundamental ability to compute paths based on the available resources, implemented by Constraint-Based Routing, was discussed. Moreover, the RSVP-TE protocol, through which an LSP can be established along a source-computed path, was described. Finally, extensions to MPLS and MPLS-TE in order to support Quality of Service were introduced, along with the mechanisms needed in an MPLS domain to implement DiffServ, so as to combine the advantages of both DiffServ and MPLS-TE.

4

Signalling

Ilaria Marchetti, Antonio Pietrabissa, Massimiliano Rossi, Fernando Boavida,
Luís Cordeiro, Edmundo Monteiro, and Marilia Curado

Summary. Although the Internet does not rely on a connection-oriented paradigm
as the PSTN does—including connection establishment, data transfer and connection termination—several signalling protocols are nonetheless required. The need
for signalling protocols is manifold. Three such routing protocols with rather different purposes and goals are the Session Initiation Protocol (SIP), the Next Steps In
Signalling (NSIS) framework and the Common Open Policy Service (COPS) protocol. SIP supports application-level signalling to establish, maintain and terminate
Voice over IP calls, while NSIS and COPS instead operate at the network level.
NSIS is a signalling framework supporting network-level signalling of QoS parameters between network elements such as routers. COPS supports policy-based network
management and configuration of network elements.

4.1 Introduction

There are several approaches to signalling on the current Internet. All of them have
the common objective of providing some form of control over—and support of—user
traffic and services, thus contributing to the smooth operation of the network.

For many years in the past, Internet users have looked at signalling-based approaches as something to avoid. Ideally, signalling on the Internet should be reduced
to a minimum and performed by end-systems in order to keep the network as simple as possible. The current use of the Internet is showing that this is not possible
anymore and that, for several reasons, some forms of signalling must be used.

Although the current Internet is still data-driven—as opposed to the signalling-
driven nature of, for instance, the telephone network—signalling is present in virtually all its components for network operation support, quality of service support,
management and application/user support. Routing protocols, such as OSPF and
BGP, can be considered operation-oriented signalling protocols, as they are indis-
pensable to the operation of the current Internet. RSVP, MPLS and NSIS are examples of signalling protocols for the support of Quality of Service. SNMP and COPS

are examples of management protocols. On the other hand, SIP and H.323 are examples of application/user-support signalling protocols.

The purpose of this chapter is to address and explain three of the most-used and most-promising signalling protocols/frameworks employed in the current Internet: the Session Initiation Protocol (SIP), the Next Steps In Signalling (NSIS) framework and the Common Open Policy Service (COPS) architecture and protocol.

We start off with a description of the Session Initiation Protocol. The description addresses the protocol components, SIP messages, session description, session establishment and SIP extensions. The next section is dedicated to the NSIS framework, providing some background and main characteristics, presenting the overall architecture and an overview of the protocol structure, as well as describing the main aspects of the NSIS Layer Transport Protocol and of the two main NSIS Signalling Layer Protocols. COPS is described in the last section of the chapter. The description includes architectural and protocol overviews, message formats, common operation and some examples.

4.2 Session Initiation Protocol (SIP)

4.2.1 SIP and Its Value Propositions

The SIP protocol was developed with the main purpose of establishing a session with two or more clients wishing to communicate with each other. It is similar to the two major Internet protocols—HTTP (World Wide Web) and SMTP (e-mail)—in that it uses symbolic addresses to represent persons in a session. Like both of them, SIP is a textual client–server protocol, in which the client issues requests and the server returns responses. SIP uses much of the syntax and semantics of HTTP: its response code architecture, many message headers and its overall operations. Also like HTTP, each SIP request is an attempt to invoke some method at the server. There are six SIP methods to establish a session: INVITE, ACK, CANCEL, REGISTER, OPTION and BYE. The most basic is the INVITE method used to initiate a call between the client and the server. Unlike HTTP and SMTP, SIP can run on top of either the Transmission Control Protocol (TCP) or the User Datagram Protocol (UDP). To assure the Quality of Service during the transmission of the messages, the SIP protocol uses the time-out and request-response mechanisms. When the server sends a request, if the answer does not return in a preestablished time (time-out), it assumes that the request was lost and it reissues the request. In the same way, the caller must receive an ACK message when the response is received. But, if the request is unsuccessful for several times, the client can decide to open the connection with TCP. However, the preferred transport protocol for the SIP is UDP, in order to avoid the time spent in TCP connection set-up and tear-down. When used with TCP, SIP allows many requests and responses to be sent over the same TCP connection, as in HTTP. The SIP protocol allows a perfect integration with other protocols developed for the IP network (e.g., SAP, RTPRTCP, RTSP, RSVP, SDP, MEGACO), but it does not depend on these, so it can be used with other signalling protocols. In the following the most important capabilities of SIP protocol will be analysed, such as:

- Identification of the locations of the target endpoint: SIP supports address resolution, name mapping and call redirection.
- Identification of the media capabilities of the target endpoint: conferences can be established knowing only the media capabilities supported by all endpoints.
- Identification of the target endpoint availability: if the called party is already connected to a call or did not answer in the allotted number of rings, the SIP protocol sends a message indicating why the target point was unavailable.
- Establishment of a session with two or more parties.
- Handling of transfer and termination of calls: during a call transfer, SIP can establish a session between the transferee (a proxy server in-between) and a new endpoint and terminates a session between transferee and the transferring party.
- Supporting of the advanced personal mobility service: if an endpoint has two addresses (for instance, one for the office and one for home), the user can set up his/her computer to automatically forward the calls to the address where he/she is.

4.2.2 Protocol Components

The SIP protocol is able to create, modify and terminate voice, video and multimedia sessions thanks to messages sent between two or more parties (clients and servers). SIP is a client–server protocol that involves the following four basic entities: User Agents (that contains both a client protocol, called User Agent Client (UAC) and a server protocol called User Agent Server (UAS)), Registrar, Proxy Server and Redirect Server.

4.2.2.1 User Agent Client (UAC)

The User Agent Client is an entity that allows a session to be initiated by sending a request. When a client has to forward a call by the UAC SIP component, the UAC determines the essential parameters to establish a conversation, which is the protocol, the port and the IP address of the UAS to which the request is being sent. The UAC is also capable of using the information in the request URI to establish the path of the SIP request to its destination, as the request URI always specifies the host, which is essential.

4.2.2.2 User Agent Server (UAS)

The UAS is the server that hosts the application responsible for receiving the SIP requests from a UAC, and on reception it returns a response to the request back to the UAC. The UAS can answer more requests from the UAC. The communication between the UAC and the UAS is client–server and peer-to-peer.

4.2.2.3 Proxy Server

Proxy Servers are SIP routers. They receive a message and forward it to a user agent or another proxy along the path. The Proxy Server is the most important entity to understand how the SIP protocol routing works. A typical SIP session is initiated by the user agent client thanks to the services provided by the proxies. Users have their UA configured to be directed to their respective proxy servers. The proxy servers then communicate with each other to convey the message. If the proxy server is used, the caller UA sends an INVITE message to the proxy server. When the proxy server determines a path to send the call and then forwards it Fig. 4.1(a), the callee responds to the proxy server, which forwards the response to the caller Fig. 4.1(b). Once the proxy server forwards the acknowledgements of both parties, a session is then established between the two clients Fig. 4.1(c).

A proxy server can also be used for name mapping. A proxy server can ask a location service and map an external SIP identity to an internal SIP identity. These proxy servers are not firewalls, they are independent servers on the Internet that proxy the request on behalf of the user for various possible reasons. The Proxy Server can use an interorganisational configuration through which SIP communications are

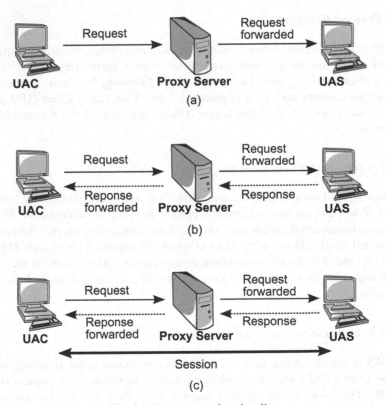

Fig. 4.1. Proxy server functionality

routed. This configuration is used when the messages are routed through the proxy servers before the messages are relayed to the destination SIP client. This can be useful for internal communications where security over an Internet link can be a problem.

4.2.2.4 Registrar

The Registrar server allows a call to be redirected to where the client is usually reachable. This is possible by sending a request to change the address to the registrar server. When the server receives these messages, it forwards the requests to the registered address. For instance, a client (who we will call Alice) can be reachable by two addresses:

- at home, where she has a computer—sip: `alice@pc1.home.com`
- and on her computer at the university laboratory—sip: `alice@pc2.lab.uni.edu`

Alice registered both addresses with the registrar message at domain.com. She wants to receive the calls at the university between 9:00 and 13:30 and at home from 16:00 to 20:00. When the registrar server receives a message addressed to the Alice's public URI (sip:`Alice.Bianchi@domain.com`) it decides where to forward the request by checking when the message will be sent. In this example, we saw that the registrar server routed the messages to Alice's user agent. However, the entity responsible for routing the message is the proxy. Proxies and registrars play only logical roles. In the previous example, the registrar and proxy servers are within the same box: when Alice registered her current location it acts as a registrar, when the server routes the SIP messages it acts as the proxy. However, we can find a box for each server to separate the roles.

4.2.2.5 Forking Proxies

An important feature of SIP is the possibility of forwarding single request calls to multiple destination addresses during session establishment. This function supports the provision of several advanced telephony services, such as automatic call forwarding to voice mail or simply user location. The SIP proxy servers that route messages to more than one destination are called forking proxies. For instance, if all the telephones ring at the same time in a house, the client has the time to pick up the call in any rooms of the house. This is called parallel forking. A forking proxy can also route a message sequentially. For instance, if a client has two addresses, the server can let a user agent ring for a certain time at the first location. If the client does not pick up the call, the forking proxy forwards the call to the second address.

4.2.2.6 Redirect Server

The Redirect Server helps the UAC to find a new location of the receiver of the message. When it receives a message, it contacts the location server to determine the path to the callee and then sends a reply, which provides the client with information about the next hop (or hops) that the message should take. The caller then sends a message directly to the device indicated in the redirection information. Note that the redirect server does not forward the message to its destination as proxies do.

4.2.3 SIP Messages

As previously mentioned, SIP is based on HTTP, thus it is a textual request-response protocol. In order to establish a session, the clients send the requests and the servers answer with responses. The format of SIP messages is composed by *Start Line*, a number of *header fields*, an *Empty Line* and an *Optional message body*.

4.2.3.1 Start Line

The *Start Line* differs dependent on a *request* or a *response*. Indeed, the *Request Line* consists of a method name (indicating the purpose of the request), the *Request*-URI (containing the address of the callee), and the protocol version (e.g., SIP2.0). For instance, if the client wants to send an INVITE message to Alice Bianchi, it must compile the *Status Line* as shown in Table 4.1.

The *response* to the *Start Line* is named *Status Line* and it contains the protocol version (SIP2.0) and the status of the transaction, which is in numerical (status code) and in human-readable (reason phrase) format. For instance, Bob can answer the previous invite request as follows:

In responses, the status code is described with an integer of three ciphers that indicate the meaning of the response. The first cipher defines the class of the response and the others have no particular meaning. Some possible response classes are shown in Table 4.3.

4.2.3.2 Header Field

All messages have the mandatory header fields. In the SIP messages there are different header fields. The most used are:

* *To*: contains the URI of the destination of the request. However, this address cannot be definitive; in fact, as previously said, a client can change its location. In the presence of forking proxies, this field includes a tag value to distinguish among the different user agents that are identified with the same URI.

Table 4.1. Start line

Method name	Request-URI	Protocol version
INVITE	sip:Alice.Bianchi@domain.com	SIP/ 2.0

Table 4.2. Invite request

Protocol version	Status code	Reason phrase
SIP/ 2.0	200	OK

Table 4.3. Possible responses for the example

Status code	Meaning
1XX (100−199)	Provisional: the request has been received but at the server there is not definitive response so it is continuing to process the request
2XX (200−299)	Success: the request has been successful
3XX (300−399)	Redirection: the callee has a new location
4XX (400−499)	Request Failure: the request has a syntax error so the server does not understand the message
5XX (500−599)	Server Failure: the server does not implement the request that appears to be good
6XX (600−699)	Global Failure: the request is not identified from any server

- *From*: contains the URI of the caller. Like the *To* header field it can specify a tag value.
- *Call-ID*: provides a unique identifier for a SIP message exchange.
- *Cseq*: contains a number and a method name. They are used to match requests and responses.
- *Contact*: contains a list of addresses where the callee can find the caller.
- *Via*: indicates the request's path among proxies. The response uses this header field to keep the same proxies traversed by the request. So it returns more quickly.
- *Max-Forwards*: is used to avoid routing loops. Every proxy that handles a request decrements its value by one, and if it reaches zero, the request is discarded.

Some header fields contain information on call services, addresses and protocol features to establish a session, and a set of header fields provides information about the message body, such as:

- *Content-Type* indicates which is the protocol used in the message body (in general it uses the SDP protocol).
- *Content-Length* contains the length of the body expressed in bytes.

4.2.3.3 Message Body

The message body is separated from the header field by an empty line. SIP messages can carry any type of body, also multipart bodies using Multipurpose Internet Mail Extensions (MIME) encoding. The MIME is a format that allows sending a message with multiple attachments of different formats. For example, an e-mail message can carry a JPEG picture and an MPEG video. The most important aspect of the message bodies is that they are transmitted end-to-end. In fact, the proxy server does not need the message body to route the message. Note that the body can be empty.

4.2.3.4 SIP Methods

SIP defines some several methods that are summarised in Table 4.4.

Table 4.4. SIP methods

Method name	Meaning
INVITE	Establishes a session inviting a user to a call
ACK	Confirms reliable message exchanges
CANCEL	Terminates a pending request
INFO	Transports PSTN telephony signalling
OPTIONS	Solicits information about the capabilities of the callee, but does not set up a call
REGISTER	Conveys location information to a SIP server Allows a user to tell a SIP server how to map an incoming address into an outgoing address that will reach that user
BYE	Terminates a session
NOTIFY	Notifies the user agent about a particular event
PRACK	Acknowledges the reception of a provisional response
PUBLISH	Uploads information to a server
SUBSCRIBE	Requests to be notified about a particular event
UPDATE	Modifies some characteristic of a session
MESSAGE	Carries an instant message
REFER	Instructs a server to send a request

4.2.4 Session Description

So far, we have seen the SIP body message where the information about the client and the server are contained. The details of the session are not described using SIP. Rather, the body of a SIP message contains a description of the session, encoded in some other protocol format, called Session Description. SIP can use different formats to describe the multimedia session. It is independent of the format of the objects it transports.

An example of session description is:

- *Subject*: Conference about Internet Communication
- *Time*: 12 April from 9:00 to 12:00
- *Location*: La Sapienza

The most common format used by SIP, however, is the Session Description Protocol (SDP), a textual format for describing unicast and multicast multimedia sessions. It contains information about codec, ports and protocol to be used for transmitting media to the caller. A caller can use this information to invite a callee to participate in an existing multicast session. For example, the information found in SDP is sufficient to allow a caller to send and receive audio immediately. SDP enables a user to indicate the ability to send and receive with multiple audio and video codecs, and SDP can also rank those codecs in preference of usage. The SDP lines consist of *type = value*, where *type* is always one character long. Table 4.5 shows all the types defined by SDP.

For example, Alice's client wants to send an INVITE message to Bob to talk about the holidays. Alice's IP address is 123.4.5.6 and she wants to receive audio via

Table 4.5. SDP types

Type	Meaning
v	Protocol version
b	Bandwidth information
o	Owner of the session and session identifier
z	Time zone adjustments
s	Name of the session
k	Encryption key
i	Information about the session or the media line
a	Attribute lines
u	URL containing a description of the session
t	Times when the session is active and will be repeated
e	E-mail address to obtain the information about the session
p	Phone number to obtain information about the session
m	Media line
c	Connection information

the port number 4561. The codec audio that Alice supports is G.711, which corresponds to the number 0 in the example:

v = 0
o = Alice 2649376915 734564836585 IN IP4 123.4.5.6
s = Talk about the next holidays
c = IN IP4 123.4.5.6
t = 0 0
m = audio 4561 RTP/AVP 0
a = sendrecv

As we can see in this example, an SDP description consists of two parts: session-level information and media-level information. The first part (before the m-line) provides version and user identifiers (v-line and o-line), the subject of the session (s-line), Alice's IP address (c-line) and the time of the session (t-line). Note that in this case the session is supposed to take place at the moment this session is received, which is why the t-line is t = 0 0. The second part is stream-specific and consists of an m-line and a number of optional a-lines that provide further information about the media stream. The a-lines in the example indicate that the stream is bidirectional (user and server receive media).

4.2.5 Establishment of an SIP Session

SIP supports five ways of establishing and terminating multimedia sessions:

- *User location*: determination of the end system to be used for communication.
- *User availability*: determination of the willingness of the called party to engage in communications.
- *User capabilities*: determination of the media and media parameters to be used.

- *Session setup*: "ringing", establishment of session parameters at both called and calling party.
- *Session management*: including transfer and termination of sessions, modifying session parameters, and invoking services.

To establish a session the caller sends an INVITE message addressed to the callee's SIP URI, which he/she wants to contact. The INVITE message contains a number of header fields that provide additional information about the message (the destination address, the caller's address, session information etc.) and the session description. The session is established when the caller receives the OK response by the callee. The 200 (OK) message contains a message body with the SDP media description of the type of the session that the callee is willing to establish with the caller. As a result, there is a two-phase exchange of SDP messages—the first in the request and the second in the response. This two-phase exchange provides basic negotiation capabilities and is based on a simple request/response model of SDP exchange. Now that we have introduced the generic information about the session establishment, let us give some examples of how SIP works.

4.2.5.1 Message Flow for Session Establishment

First of all, to establish a multimedia session, Alice must register her current location with the REGISTER message at the domain.com by sending a REGISTER request, indicating that all messages addressed to the URI specified in the *To* header field

sip:Alice.Bianchi@domain.com

must be forwarded to the URI specified in the CONTACT header field

sip:Alice@pc1.home.com

The OK response by the domain.com confirms that the request has been registered. If Bob wants to contact Alice to talk about a meeting, he sends an INVITE message to Alice's public URI. The proxy at the domain.com routes the INVITE request to Alice's current location. Alice accepts the invitation by sending a *200 OK* response. The proxy at the domain.com routes the *200 OK* message to the Bob's URI.

Note that in the *200 OK* response Alice specifies her current location in the Contact header field. This header field is used by Bob to send subsequent messages directly to Alice, bypassing the proxy server. As soon as the session has been established, Bob and Alice can talk about whatever they want. If, in the middle of the session, they want to make any changes to the session (e.g., add video), they should issue another INVITE request with an updated session description.

When Bob and Alice finish their conversation, Bob sends a BYE request directly to Alice without interaction with the proxy. Alice confirms the request with an OK response. Session description is summarised in Fig. 4.2.

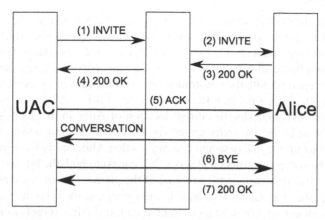

Fig. 4.2. Session description

4.2.5.2 Home Phone

One of the most interesting technical challenges for IP telephony is to mimic standard residential phone services. In particular, IP telephony requires the following features:

- All phones in a home must ring if someone calls its number.
- When one of the lines is picked up, all other phones in the home must stop ringing.
- A user can join an existing call by picking up any other telephone in the home.
- A home can have multiple lines, enabling a user on another handset to initiate a new call while one or more are in progress.
- All users involved in a single call are essentially involved in a multiparty conference call, and are thus able to hear each other.

A simple example further explains these features: Alice sends an invite message to Bob's parents. When the network server receives the message, it consults the database to find the list of contact addresses, each of which constitutes a single extension of the line. The server thus forks and sends out the INVITE messages to all members of the family and the lines ring at each address. When a user picks up the call (Member 3), an acceptance message is sent back to the server. When a forking proxy receives a call acceptance, it should send a cancel request on all unanswered members of the family (Member 1 and Member 2). Then, the server forwards the call acceptance. After that, if another callee picks up the call, an acceptance message is acknowledged by the server and the new participants join the call. To terminate the session, the caller sends a BYE message that is forwarded by the proxy to the two currently active lines.

4.2.5.3 Personal Mobility

Alice is a university researcher. So, in addition to having a computer at home (sip: Alice.Bianchi@domain.com), she also has two location addresses at the university, at the laboratory (sip: `Alice@lab.uni.com`) and at the office (sip: `Alice@office.uni.com`). When Alice is at the university, she sends a REGIS-TER message to the `domain.com` server listing the university address (sip: `Alice@uni.com`) as a forwarding address. Once at the university, Alice registers both her lab and office machine with the registration server of the university. Now, if someone sends a request to Alice's public URL (sip: `Alice.Bianchi@domain.com`), the `domain.com` server checks the current location of Alice in the database and forwards the request to the university server. As soon as the request arrives, the university server looks up the database and determines that Alice has two potential means of contact. The server then forks and sends the request to both the lab and office machines at the same time, causing the ringing of the phones. When Alice picks up the call, an acceptance message is sent back to the server and the session is established, as we have seen earlier. We have a different situation if Alice forgets to register the lab machine, for instance, and restarts her user agent in the lab to forward the call to her `domain.com` server. When the lab phone receives the request, according to its outdated configuration, it forwards it to the `domain.com` server. Using the loop detection capabilities in SIP, this server determines that an error has occurred and returns an error response to the lab machine. In turn, it returns an error code to the university server. If, in the meantime, Alice responds to the call from the office, the university server also receives an acceptance message. Having now received both responses, the server forwards the acceptance answer establishing a session.

4.2.6 SIP's Extension

SIP's extension negotiation mechanism uses three header fields: Supported, Required, and Unsupported. When a SIP session is being established, the user agent client lists in the Required header field all the names of the extensions it wants to use for that session, and all the names of the extensions it supports are not listed previously in a Supported header field. When the user agent server receives the Required header field, it checks the list and, if it does not support any of the extensions listed, it sends back an error message specifying that the session could not be established. This error response contains an Unsupported header field listing the extensions the user agent server did not support. If the user agent server supports all the required extensions, it should decide whether or not it wants to use any extra extensions and, if so, it includes the option tag for the extension in the Required header of its response. If this option was included in the Supported header field of the request, the session will be established. Otherwise, the user agent server includes the extension that is required by the server in a Required header field in the error response.

4.3 The Next Steps In Signalling (NSIS)

4.3.1 Background and Main Characteristics

The IETF's Next Steps in Signalling Working Group is responsible for standardising an IP signalling protocol with QoS signalling as the first-use case. This working group will concentrate on a two-layer signalling paradigm. The intention is to reuse, where appropriate, the protocol mechanisms of RSVP, while at the same time simplifying it and applying a more general signalling model. The existing work on the requirements, the framework and analysis of existing protocols will be completed and used as input for the protocol work. The NSIS WG is developing a transport layer signalling protocol for the transport of upper layer signalling. In order to support a toolbox or building-block approach, the two-layer model will be used to separate the transport of the signalling from the application signalling. This allows a more general signalling protocol to be developed to support signalling for different services or resources, such as NAT, firewall traversal and QoS resources. The initial NSIS application will be an optimised RSVP QoS signalling protocol. The second application will be a middle box traversal protocol. Security is a very important point for NSIS and the working group will study and analyse the threats and security requirements for signalling. Compatibility with authentication and authorisation mechanisms such as Diameter, COPS for RSVP (RFC 2749) and RSVP Sessions will be addressed. NSIS is a signalling protocol framework for conveying information about data flows along their path in the network, and interacting with nodes along the data path. Moreover, the NSIS messages pass directly through the same nodes as the data and only unicast data flows are considered. The intention is that the components of the NSIS protocol suite will be usable in different parts of the Internet, for different needs, without requiring a complete end-to-end deployment (signalling is intended not only for QoS). This flexibility is achieved by dividing the signalling protocol stack in two layers: a generic (lower) layer and an upper layer specific for each signalling application.

In the signalling architecture, the messages are only received, processed and sent by Signalling Entities (SE) that can be placed on all devices on the data path (to support signalling purposes) or on some devices not included on the data path. Two different signalling architectures can be realised (distributed and centralised) and will be analysed in the following sections. In the distributed signalling architecture, SEs are placed on all devices (e.g., routers) on the data path. Thus, all devices are signalling-aware and take part in signalling. In the centralised signalling architecture, signalling is managed by a centralised SE in a domain. This architecture reduces the signalling charge on the interior devices in the domain.

4.3.1.1 Signalling Entities (SE)

A Signalling Entity (SE) is the function that implements the signalling protocol. It can be placed in a network device (e.g., router, policy server) or in end systems. SE can support many signalling applications (for instance resource reservation). A Signalling Initiator (SI) is the SE that initiates the signalling, while a Signalling Responder (SR) is the SE at the end of the signalling path and terminates the signalling. Signalling Forwarder (SF) is an SE that is on the signalling path between SI and SR. SF receives, processes and forwards signalling messages from SI to SR. Finally, Signalling Controller (SC) is the centralised SE in a domain. A SC is responsible for receiving, processing and sending signalling messages in a domain and it is used in the centralised signalling architecture to reduce the charge on the edge routers and interior routers.

4.3.1.2 Distributed Signalling Architecture

In the distributed signalling architecture, SEs are placed in the network devices on the data path and the signalling messages pass through the same network devices as the data packets. Figure 4.3 shows a simple example of the architecture. After a trigger from an application, the SE in user A initiates the signalling for a data flow from A to B via nodes R1, R2, R3 and R4. Signalling entities are installed on all routers between two end points to support the signalling. In the case where the request of the user must be done by multidomains, signalling will be done between the devices at the edge of the domain and the interior devices. The advantage of this architecture is that nodes on the data path can receive, process and send signalling messages. When there is a change on the network (e.g., overload, errors), the nodes can notify other entities in the network and rapidly adapt themselves to the change.

Every router uses the same routing mechanism for data packets to route signalling messages. As a result, signalling message propagation does not require global information for routing signalling messages. When a routing change happens (e.g., handover in the case of a mobile user), the network devices can detect this change and rapidly establish a new signalling path that follows the data path. The disadvantage of the distributed architecture is that an SE must be installed on all network devices on the data path with consequently increased load of signalling on the intermediate nodes between two end points. Moreover, when the number of user flows increases, the information of state per flow contained in intermediate nodes can also increase. This could cause serious scalability problems.

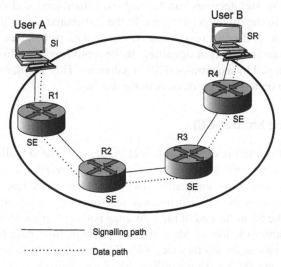

Fig. 4.3. Distributed signalling architecture

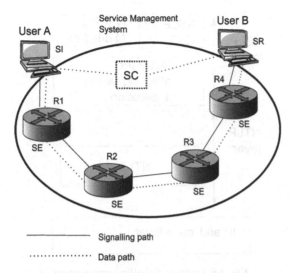

Fig. 4.4. Centralised signalling architecture

4.3.1.3 Centralised Signalling Architecture

In the centralised signalling architecture, a particular SE, called SC (Signalling Controller) is in charge of managing the signalling in the domain. An SC can be installed on a centralised service management system (SMS), which manages services in a domain. It can also be installed in a resource management server, on a policy server or in any server in a domain. Figure 4.4 shows the centralised signalling architecture.

   User A can make direct contact with the SC to ask the network to support a signalling application. When the SC receives signalling messages from user A, it transfers them to the SMS that knows the key information on the domain (e.g., topology of domain, routing table, resource availability of devices in the network) and is able to answer the request from the user. Finally, the SMS can invoke signalling entities or other entities implementing the request of user by configuring devices in the network.

4.3.2 Overview of Signalling Scenarios and Protocol Structure

4.3.2.1 Layer Model for the Protocol Suite

In order to achieve a modular solution for the NSIS requirements, the NSIS WG proposed a split-layer protocol suite structured in two layers: (1) The NSIS Transport Layer Protocol, named General Internet Signalling Transport (GIST) [83], is responsible for moving signalling messages among network entities. This process should be independent of the signalling applications. (2) The NSIS Signalling Layer Protocol (NSLP) contains the specific functionalities of the signalling applications. As described in the following section, this two-layer protocol model allows the support of

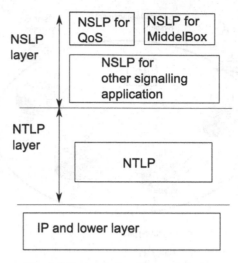

Fig. 4.5. Protocol signalling architecture

various signalling applications, such as QoS [84] and Network Address Translation (NAT) & Firewall (FW) [85] (see Fig. 4.5).

4.3.2.2 Signalling Application Properties

For some signalling applications and scenarios, signalling may only be considered for a unidirectional data flow. However, in other cases, there may be interesting relationships between the signalling for the two flows of a bidirectional session. An example is QoS for a voice call. Note that the path may be different for two directions, due to asymmetric routing. In the basic case, bidirectional signalling can simply use a separate instance of the same signalling mechanism in each direction. In constrained topologies, where parts of the route are symmetric, it may be possible to use a more unified approach to bidirectional signalling, e.g. carrying the two signalling directions in common messages. This optimisation might be used for example to make mobile QoS signalling more efficient. In either case, the correlation of the signalling for the two flow directions is carried out in the NSLP. The NTLP would simply be enabled to bundle the messages together. Moreover, to provide additional flexibility in defining the objects carried by the NSLP such that only the objects applicable in a particular setting are used. One approach for reflecting the distinction is that local objects could be put into separate local messages that are initiated and terminated within one single domain; an alternative is that they could be "stacked" within the NSLP messages that are used anyway for interdomain signalling. We are assuming that the NTLP provides a simple message transfer service, and any acknowledgements or notifications it generates are handled purely internally (and applied within the scope of a single NTLP peer relationship). However, we expect that some signalling applications will require acknowledgements regarding the failure/success of state installation along the data path, and this will be an NSLP function. Acknowledgements can be sent along the sequence of NTLP peer relationships toward the signalling initiator, which relieves the requirements on the security associations that need to be maintained by NEs and can allow NAT traversal in both directions (if this direction is toward the sender, it implies maintaining reverse routing state in the NTLP). In certain circumstances, e.g. trusted domains, an optimisation could be to send acknowledgements directly to the signalling initiator outside the NTLP, although any such approach would have to take into account the necessity of handling denial-of-service attacks launched from outside the network. The semantics of the acknowledgement messages are of particular importance. An NE sending a message could assume responsibility for the entire downstream chain of NEs, indicating for instance the availability of reserved resources for the entire downstream path. Alternatively, the message could have a more local meaning, indicating for instance that a certain failure or degradation occurred at a particular point in the network. Notifications differ from acknowledgements, because they are not (necessarily) generated in response to other signalling messages. This means that it may not be obvious to determine where the notification should be sent.

4.3.3 The NSIS Layer Transport Protocol

4.3.3.1 GIST Description

The GIST layer is responsible for the transport of signalling messages. When a signalling message is ready to be sent, it is given to the GIST layer along with information about the flow it is for; it is then up to the GIST layer to get the message to the next network element (NE) along the path (downstream, in the flow direction from the source to the destination; or upstream, in the opposite direction of the flow from the destination to the source), where it is received and the local GIST responsibility ends.

In the receiving NE, the GIST either forwards the message directly to the next hop or, if there is an appropriate signalling application, passes it upward for further processing; the signalling application can then generate another message to be sent via GIST.

Figure 4.6 is an example of the NSIS two-layer architecture, showing two different signalling applications and how NEs handle the signalling messages accordingly.

In this example, the first NE in the path has the NTLP and NSLP 1. NSLP 1 generates a signalling message and sends it to the local NTLP so that it can be forwarded to the flow destination. In the next NE, there are no NSLPs, so the message is forwarded without being processed by the NTLP. In the next hop the NTLP and NSLP 2 are present. Since the message NSLP ID does not correspond to the connected NSLP 2, the message is forwarded to the flow destination again. In the next hop there is again NTLP and NSLP 1. Since the correct NSLP is available, NTLP sends the message to NSLP 1. When NSLP receives the message from NTLP, it processes it accordingly.

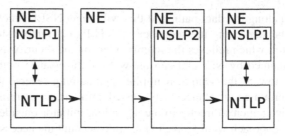

Fig. 4.6. Signalling with heterogeneous NSLPs

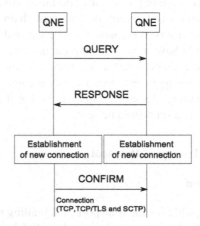

Fig. 4.7. GIST three-way handshake

GIST allows two modes of operation, the Datagram mode (D-mode) and the Connection mode (C-mode). D-mode uses UDP to encapsulate the messages and is used for small and infrequent messages. All Query messages must be sent in D-mode. The C-mode uses TCP or any other stream- or message-oriented transport protocol (currently only Stream Control Transmission Protocol, SCTP [86], is being researched in addition to TCP) which allows GIST to support reliability and security (e.g., using Transport Layer Security, TLS, [87] over TCP) in the message transport.

To meet the routing requirement, GIST defines a three-way handshake to set up the necessary connection with the adjacent peers. This three-way handshake contains a QUERY, a RESPONSE and an optional CONFIRM message. Figure 4.7 describes the three-way handshake process between two entities that support GIST. In this handshake, the QUERY message is the first message to be sent. This message is always sent in D-mode and with the IP Router Alert Option (RAO) [88] flag active. With this flag, the message sent by GIST travels along the network and every router that checks this flag analyses the packet content. GIST entities in the network analyse all packets flagged with the IP RAO and process all QUERY messages.

When a QUERY message is intercepted, the NSLP ID is checked and if the corresponding NSLP is present, the message is processed by GIST. Otherwise, the message is forwarded to the flow destination so that other GIST entities can intercept the message, or the destination is reached.

The purpose of the QUERY message is the discovery of the next NSIS hop in the path and the transport of a proposal for the establishment of a connection between the two entities. These messages contain a QUERY Cookie object and when a connection is requested, the association characteristics (for instance the protocol and port to use in the association) are also present. The QUERY Cookie is a security payload that is carried by the QUERY message, which allows the detection and prevention of several security problems in the handshake.

GIST entities that receive a QUERY message need to reply with a RESPONSE message. This message is sent to the previous GIST entity by getting its identity from the QUERY message. This message contains a RESPONSE Cookie, which is a cryptographic key based on the received QUERY Cookie. This RESPONSE Cookie increases the security of the protocol, allowing the upstream hop to check if the Response message is not sent by a fake NSIS entity. If the received QUERY message requested an association, the RESPONSE message also includes the association response.

If the association between the two GIST entities is requested (by the NSLP or by a local GIST decision/configuration) when the RESPONSE message is received in the upstream GIST, the association is created and a CONFIRM message is sent to the downstream GIST using the association. This association can be supported through TCP, secure TCP with Transport Layer Security (TCP/TLS) or the Stream Control Transmission Protocol (SCTP). Only after the CONFIRM message is sent, the NSLPs payloads can start flowing between the two GISTs.

The associations created via the three-way handshake can be reused for different sessions and NSLPs when the downstream peer and the association characteristics are the same. Even though the three-way handshake is needed for each new session, the RESPONSE and CONFIRM messages are sent using the already established association.

GIST was designed as a soft-state protocol to manage all the messages and associations. GIST uses states for each action occurred in the system and associates a timer to each state. Each time the state is updated, the timer is restarted. If the state is not updated, the timer expires and the state is removed. GIST has two main state tables: Message Routing State (MRS) and Message Association State (MAS). The MRS is responsible for managing individual flows and the MAS is responsible for managing the associations between individual peers. When a timer expires (if no message is received for the corresponding flow or association), the state automatically is removed from the state tables. If a state is required again, a new handshake is needed and a new association must be created.

After the handshake is completed, data messages can be sent with the NSLP payload. GIST does not check the NSLP payload, the only processing done to the message is the decrement of the message hop-count, the corresponding states are refreshed (MRS and MAS) and finally the payload is sent to the corresponding NSLP.

QoS NSLP is described in the following section. This NSLP is one example of an NSLP that uses GIST as its transport protocol.

4.3.3.2 Signalling for Quality of Service

In the case of signalling for QoS, we can apply all the basic NSIS concepts. In addition, there is an assumed directionality of the signalling process in that one end of the signalling flow takes responsibility for actually requesting the resources. This leads to the following definitions:

- The protocol employs a client/server model where the PEP requests, updates and deletes to the remote PDP and the PDP returns decisions back to the PEP.
- QoS NSIS Responder (QNR): the signalling entity that acts as the endpoint for the signalling and can optionally interact with applications as well.
- QoS NSIS Forwarder (QNF): a signalling entity between a QNI and QNR, which propagates NSIS signalling further through the network.
- COPS provides message-level security for authentication, replay protection and message integrity. COPS can also reuse existing protocol for security (IPSEC) or to authenticate and secure the channel between the PEP and the PDP.

Each of these entities will interact with a resource management function (RMF), which actually allocates network resources (router buffers, interface bandwidth etc.). Note that there is no constraint on which end of the signalling flow should take the QNI role: with respect to the data flow direction it could be at the sending or receiving end.

4.3.3.3 Protocol Message Semantics

The QoS NSLP will include a set of messages to reserve resources along the signalling path. A possible set of message semantics for the QoS NSLP is shown later. Note that the "direction" column in Table 4.6 only indicates the "orientation" of the message. Messages can be originated and absorbed at QNF nodes as well as the QNI or QNR. An example might be QNFs at the edge of a domain exchanging messages to set up resources for a flow across it. Note that it is left open whether the responder can release or modify a reservation, during or after setup. This seems mainly a matter of assumptions about authorisation, and the possibilities might depend on resource

Table 4.6. NSIS protocol messages

Operation	Direction	Description
Request	I to R	Create a new reservation for a flow
Modify	I to R	Modify an existing reservation
	(R to I)	
Release	I to R	Delete (tear down) an existing reservation
	(R to I)	
Accept/Reject	R to I	Confirm or reject a reservation request
Notify	I to R	Report an event detected within the network
	(R to I)	
Refresh	I to R	State Management

type specifics. The table also explicitly includes a refresh operation. This does nothing to a reservation except extend its lifetime, and is one possible state-management mechanism.

4.3.3.4 Route Changes and QoS Reservations

The normal operation of the NSIS protocol will lead to the situation depicted in Fig. 4.8, where the reserved resources match the data path.

A route change can occur while such a reservation is in place. The route change will be installed immediately and any data will be forwarded on the new path. This situation is depicted in Fig. 4.9.

Resource reservation on the new path will only be started when the next control message is routed along the new path. This means that there is a certain time interval during which resources are not reserved on (part of) the data path, and certain delay or drop-sensitive applications will require this time interval to be minimised. Several techniques to achieve this could be considered. As an example, RSVP has the concept of local repair, where the router may be triggered by a route change. In that case the RSVP node can start sending PATH messages directly after the route has been changed. Another approach would be to preinstall back-up state, and it would be the responsibility of the QoS-NSLP to do this, but mechanisms for identifying back-up paths and routing the necessary signalling messages along them are not currently considered in the NSIS requirements and framework. It is not guaranteed that the new path will be able to provide the same guarantees that were available on the old

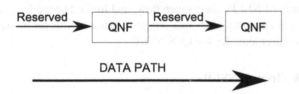

Fig. 4.8. Normal NSIS protocol operation

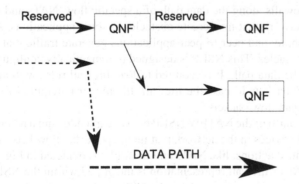

Fig. 4.9. Route change

path. Therefore, it might be desirable for the QNF to wait until resources have been reserved on the new path before allowing the route change to be installed (unless of course the old path no longer exists). However, delaying the route change installation while waiting for reservation setup needs careful analysis of the interaction with the routing protocol being used, in order to avoid routing loops. This solution adapts to a route change when a route change creates congestion on the new routed path.

4.3.3.5 Resource Management Interactions

The QoS NSLP itself is not involved in any specific resource allocation or management techniques. The definition of an NSLP for resource reservation with Quality of Service, however, implies the notion of admission control. For a QoS NSLP, the measure of signalling success will be the ability to reserve resources from the total resource pool that is provisioned in the network. Resource Management Function (RMF) is responsible for all resource provisioning, monitoring and assurance functions in the network. A QoS NSLP will rely on the RMF to do resource management and to provide input for admission control. In this model, the RMF acts as a server toward the client NSLP(s). It should be noted, however, that the RMF may in turn use another NSLP instance to do the actual resource provisioning in the network. In this case, the RMF acts as the initiator (client) of an NSLP. This essentially corresponds to a multilevel signalling paradigm with an "upper" level handling Internet working QoS signalling, possibly running end-to-end, and a "lower" level handling the more specialised intradomain QoS signalling, running between just the edges of the network. Given that NSIS signalling is already supposed to be able to support multiple instances of NSLPs for a given flow, and limited scope (e.g., edge-to-edge) operation, it is not currently clear that supporting the multilevel model leads to any new protocol requirements for the QoS NSLP.

4.3.3.6 NAT & Firewall NSLP

The NAT and Firewall (NATFW) NSIS Signalling Layer Protocol (NSLP) [89] is being defined in the NSIS IETF Working Group to provide dynamic configuration of NATs and firewalls along the data path of a specific flow. NATs and firewalls are devices in the network that may create obstacles to some applications. Applications such as IP telephony and peer-to-peer applications generate traffic that is unable to traverse these obstacles. This NSLP is designed to dynamically configure NATs and firewalls along the data path. It is required to load firewall rules with an action that allows data flow packets to pass the firewall. In NAT, it is required to create NAT bindings to the data flow packets.

A simple scenario of the NATFW NSLP between a sender and a receiver with two middle-boxes (a devices in the network that intercept packet flow between end hosts and perform control actions, like NATs and firewalls) is depicted in Fig. 4.10. In this example, the NAT or firewall representation is integrated within the NSIS entity, but they can be two separate entities where the NSIS entity requests the middle-box to change configuration.

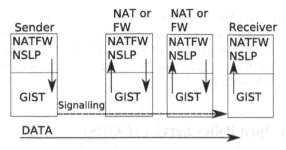

Fig. 4.10. Simple NATFW NSLP overview

This example describes a source host (sender) that generates a NATFW NSLP signalling message and sends it to the destination host (receiver). This message follows the data path and every NSIS entity along the data path with the NATFW NSLP application processes the message. Based on the processing of the message, the NATFW NSLP changes the middle-boxes accordingly and forwards the message to the receiver. After all the middle-boxes are configured for the specific flow, the data can start to flow with no obstacles.

If the sender or the receiver is not NATFW NSLP aware, the NSLP specification allows the usage of a NATFW NSLP proxy. This is referred to as proxy mode operation.

The described scenario does not work if the receiver is behind NATs. The sender cannot address the receiver directly. To solve this issue, a mode of operation was defined as the RESERVE-EXTERNAL-ADDRESS (REA) mode. This mode allows a receiver to locate upstream NATs and preallocate a public address.

NATFW NSLP signalling messages contain general information (like IP address, ports, protocol) and policy rules. The policy rules are abstractions of the network equipment policy rules that need to be installed. The request initiator generates the abstract policy rules and in each NATFW NSLP in the path these rules must be mapped to the particular NAT or firewall rules. This mapping is vendor- and model-dependent.

To provide the described functionalities, five message types have been defined: CREATE, RESERVE-EXTERNAL-ADDRESS, TRACE, NOTIFY and RESPONSE. The CREATE message creates, changes, refreshes and deletes NATFW NSLP sessions on the data path from the sender to the destination. The REA message is forwarded from the receiver to the edge NAT to allow inbound CREATE messages to be forwarded to the receiver. This message reserves an external address (and a port number if needed) in the edge router and requests the configuration of all intermediate middle-boxes (between the receiver and the edge NAT). The TRACE message gathers information from all NATFW NSLP in the data path. The NOTIFY message is an asynchronous message used by the NSLP to notify upstream peers about specific events. The RESPONSE message is a response to CREATE, REA and TRACE messages.

All messages received by a NATFW NSLP before being processed are checked as to whether the requested actions are authenticated and authorised. For this purpose all the NATFW NSLP messages carry the NATFW CREDENTIAL object. The information and structure of this object depends on the authentication and authorisation model used in each domain.

4.4 Common Open Policy Service (COPS)

4.4.1 COPS Overview

Common Open Policy Service (COPS) specified in the RFC 2748 [90] is a simple query-and-response protocol that can be used to exchange policy information between a policy server (Policy Decision Point or PDP) and its clients (Policy Enforcement Points or PEPs). COPS supports two models of policy control: outsourcing and configuration (also known as provisioning). In the outsourcing model the PEP contacts the PDP every time a policy decision has to be made. The PDP makes the decision and communicates it back to the PEP, which enforces it. In the configuration model the PDP configures the PEP with the policy to be used. The PEP stores the policy received from the PDP locally and uses it to make decisions instead of contacting the PDP every time a new event occurs. The main characteristics of COPS protocol include:

- The protocol employs a client/server model where the PEP requests, updates and deletes to the remote PDP and the PDP returns decisions back to the PEP.
- The protocol uses Transfer Control Protocol (TCP) as its transport protocol for reliable exchange of messages between policy clients and a server.
- The protocol is extensible in that it is designed to leverage off self-identifying objects and can support diverse client-specific information without requiring modifications to the COPS protocol itself.
- COPS provides message-level security for authentication, replay protection and message integrity. COPS can also reuse existing protocol for security (IPSEC) or to authenticate and secure the channel between the PEP and the PDP.
- The protocol allows the server to push configuration information to the client, and then allows the server to remove such state from the client when it is no longer applicable.
- The protocol is stateful in two main aspects:
  - The *Request/Decision* state is shared between client and server. The requests from the client PEP are installed or remembered by the remote PDP until they are explicitly deleted by the PEP. At the same time, decisions from the remote PDP can be generated asynchronously at any time for a currently installed request state.
  - In the *Interassociated* state, the server may respond to new queries differently because of previously installed *Request/Decision* state(s) that are related.

4.4.2 Basic Model

The basic model of COPS and the framework of policy-based admission control are shown in Fig. 4.11. The network nodes can be routers, switches or hubs. The resources are allocated or released inside a node by Policy Enforcement Point (PEP). A node can be a policy-ignorant node, which does not support the COPS protocol. The network nodes are grouped into administrative domains. There is always at least one policy server in each administrative domain. Inside the policy server there is the Policy Decision Point (PDP), which makes the final decision about the handling of the resources. There can also be a local PDP in the network node (see Fig. 4.11).

The PEP may communicate with a policy server to obtain policy decisions or directives. It is responsible for initiating a persistent TCP connection to a PDP, for notifying the PDP when a request state has changed on the PEP and, finally, for the deletion of any state that is no longer applicable. When the PEP sends a configuration request, it expects the PDP to continuously send the named units of configuration data until it is successfully installed, and then the PEP should send a report message to the PDP confirming the installation. The policy protocol is designed to communicate self-identifying objects that contain the data necessary for identifying request states, establishing the context for a request, identifying the type of the request, referencing previously installed request, relaying policy decisions, reporting errors and providing message integrity. When a failure is detected, the PEP must try to reconnect to the remote PDP or attempt to connect to an alternative backup PDP. While disconnected, the PEP should revert to making local decision with LPDP; once the connection is reestablished, the PEP is expected to notify the PDP of any deleted state or new event that passed local admission control after the connection was lost. The PDP can also send unsolicited decisions to the PEP, e.g., the PDP can force the PEP to change previous decisions. Respectively, the PDP can send information for accounting or monitoring purposes to the PDP. The PEP outsources the decision making to the PDP. Although the PEP can make local decisions with the

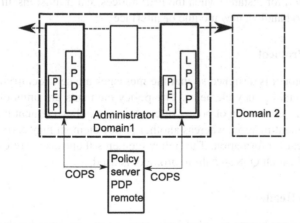

Fig. 4.11. COPS in the framework of policy-based admission

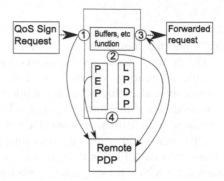

Fig. 4.12. COPS processing of QoS requests

LPDP, the final decision is made by the remote PDP. There are three different types of outsourcing events that need the decision from the PDP and one nonoutsourcing type (Fig. 4.12). These define the context of each request and decision. The incoming message (e.g., RSVP message) causes the PEP to ask the PDP how to handle the incoming signal (1), e.g. to accept or reject it. The next step is to allocate local resources (2) in order to process the message and finally the PEP enforces the forwarding decision made by PDP (3).

Thus, COPS processes QoS requests as follows:

1. arrival of an incoming message
2. allocation of local resources
3. forwarding of an outgoing message
4. configuration information

The fourth type of event, which is not counted as an outsourcing event, is the request for configuration information from the remote PDP. The PEP can make the request, for example when it is booting up. The PEP can also ask for configuration information later, for instance when the PEP notices that it must install new instructions in order to handle a new module or interface.

4.4.3 COPS Protocol

The COPS protocol is designed so that the messages are self-identifying policy objects which contain policy elements. The policy elements are units of information necessary for the evaluation of policy rules. A single policy element may carry user or application identification, whereas another policy element may carry user credentials or credit card information. The policy elements themselves are expected to be independent of which QoS signalling protocol is used.

4.4.3.1 COPS Header

COPS messages are binary-encoded and consist of the common header followed by a number of typed objects.

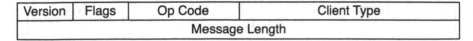

Version	Flags	Op Code	Client Type
Message Length			

Fig. 4.13. The COPS common header

The fields in the header are as follows:

- *Version*: 4 bits. COPS version number. Current version is 1.
- *Flags*: 4 bits. Defined the flag values (all other flags must be set to 0): 0x1 So-licited Message Flag.
- *Bit*: This flag is set when the message is solicited by another COPS message.
- *Op Code*: 8 bits. Contains a message type indicating the COPS operations, which are:
  1 = Request   (REQ)
  2 = Decision   (DEC)
  3 = Report State   (RPT)
  4 = Delete Request State   (DRQ)
  5 = Synchronise State Req (SSQ)
  6 = Client-Open   (OPN)
  7 = Client-Accept   (CAT)
  8 = Client-Close   (CC)
  9 = Keep-Alive   (KA)
  10 = Synchronise Complete (SSC)
- *Client-type*: 16 bits. It indicates the type of policy client. Interpretation of all encapsulated objects is relative to the client-type. Client-types that set the most significant bit in the client-type field are enterprise-specific (these are client-types 0x8000 - 0xFFFF). For KA Messages, the client-type in the header must always be set to 0 as the KA is used for connection verification (not per client session verification).
- *Message Length*: 32 bits. Size of message in octets including the standard COPS header and all encapsulated objects. Messages must be aligned on four octet in-tervals.

4.4.3.2 COPS-Specific Object Formats

The COPS header defines the message type. A number of policy elements follow af-ter the header. These elements are used for transferring the information for decision-making and the actual decisions. The contents of the policy elements depend on the QoS signaling protocol, but the main structure of the COPS protocol remains in-tact. The policy elements, which are defined in the COPS protocol, conform to the structure as shown in Fig. 4.14.

The length is a two-octet value that describes the number of octets (including the header) composing the object. If the length in octets does not fall on a 32-bit word boundary, padding must be added to the end of the object so that it is aligned to the next 32-bit boundary before the object can be sent on the wire. On the receiving

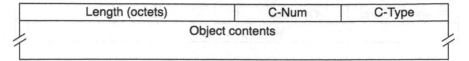

Length (octets)	C-Num	C-Type
Object contents		

Fig. 4.14. The COPS-specific object format

side, a subsequent object boundary can be found by simply rounding up the previous stated object length to the next 32-bit boundary. Typically, C-Num (8 bits) identifies the class of information contained in the object, and the C-Type (8 bits) identifies the subtype or version of the information contained in the object. For instance, with In Interface (C-Num = 3) and Out Interface (C-Num = 4) objects C-Type = 1 means that interface is IPv4 and C-Type = 2 means that the interface is IPv6.

The possible values of the C-Num fields and their meanings are presented in Table 4.7. Every COPS-specific object has respective contents of the object. This content is of variable length depending of the C-Num and C-Type. The messages between the PEP and the PDP are constructed from these objects. In the next section some examples of the messages are shown.

4.4.4 COPS Messages

A PEP and a PDP exchange COPS traffic over a TCP connection that is always initiated by the PEP. One PDP implementation per server must listen on a well-known TCP port number (COPS = 3288 by IANA). The location of the remote PDP can either be configured or obtained via a service location mechanism. If a single PEP can support multiple client-types, it may send multiple Client-Open messages, each specifying a particular client-type to a PDP over one or more TCP connections.

Request (REQ) [PEP → PDP]: The PEP establishes a request state client handle for which the remote PDP may maintain state. The handle is the identification with which the PDP communicates. If there are local changes in the PEP, the PEP is responsible for informing the PDP about the changes. The Context object tells the context where all the other objects must be interpreted. ClientSI is the client-specific information; it can be the contents of a message of some QoS signalling protocol. Also, the incoming and outgoing interfaces are depicted in the message. LPDPDecision contains the decisions that the local PDP has done and they must be verified, completed or overwritten by the remote PDP. There are five different kinds of remote and local PDP decisions. Flags indicate the normal request/decision, stateless data means local decision, which does not affect the state of the request, replacement data replaces the existing data in a signalled message, client-specific decision data is to used to introduce additional decision types and, finally, named data contains configuration information. The instructions on the usage of the four last-mentioned types should be specified in several documents on COPS extension for the given client-type.

Decision (DEC) [PDP → PEP]: The PDP responds to the REQ with a DEC message that includes the associated client handle and one or more decision objects grouped relative to a Context object and Decision Flags object-type pair. It is required

Table 4.7. COPS-specific objects

C Num	Name	Explanation
1	Handle	The Handle Object encapsulates a unique value that identifies an installed state. This identification is used by most COPS operations.
2	Context	Specifies the type of event(s) that triggered the query. Required for request messages.
3	In-Interface	This object is used to identify the incoming interface on which a particular request applies and the address where the received message originated.
4	Out-Interface	This object is used to identify the outgoing interface to which a specific request applies and the address for where the forwarded message is to be sent.
5	Reason Code	This object specifies the reason why a request state was deleted. It appears in the delete request (DRQ) message.
6	Decision	Appears in the reply as the decision taken by the PDP.
7	LPDP Decision	May appear in the request as local point decision.
8	Error	Identifies a particular COPS protocol error.
9	Client-Specific Info (SI)	This contains client-type specific information, e.g. the contents of RSVP Path-message, if the client is RSVP.
10	Keep-alive timer	Maximum time interval over which a COPS message has to be sent or received.
11	PEP Identification	Allows client identification to the PDP, required for Client-Open messages.
12	Report Type	Type of report in request state associated with handle.
13	PDP Redirect Address	A PDP when closing a PEP session for a particular client-type may optionally use this object to redirect the PEP to the specified PDP server address and TCP port number.
14	Last PDP Address	Used from PEP to specify the PDP the last PDP that has accepted to open session since he last rebooted, when PDP sends Open message.
15	Accounting timer	Optional timer value used to determine the minimum interval between accounting type reports.
16	Message Integrity	Sequence of number used for authentication and validating COPS messages.

that the first decision message for a new/updated request will have the Solicited Message flag set (value = 1) in the COPS header. This avoids the issue of keeping track of which updated request (that is, a request reissued for the same handle) a particular decision corresponds to. It is important that for a given handle there will be at most one outstanding solicited decision per request. This essentially means that the PEP should not issue more than one REQ (for a given handle) before it receives a corresponding DEC with the solicited message flag set. The PDP must always issue decisions for requests on a particular handle in the order they arrive, and all requests must have a corresponding decision. To avoid deadlocks, the PEP can always timeout after issuing a request that does not receive a decision. It must then delete the expired handle, and may try again using a new handle. The Decision message may include either an Error object or one or more context-plus associated decision objects. COPS protocol problems are reported in the Error object (e.g., an error with the format of the original request including malformed request messages, unknown COPS objects in the Request, etc.). The applicable Decision objects depend on the context and the type of client. The only ordering requirement for decision objects is that the required Decision Flags object type must precede the other Decision object types per context binding.

Report State (RPT) [PEP → PDP]: The RPT message is used by the PEP to communicate to the PDP its success or failure in carrying out the PDP's decision, or to report an accounting related change in state. The Report-Type specifies the kind of report and the optional ClientSI can carry additional information per Client-Type. For every DEC message containing a configuration context that is received by a PEP, the PEP must generate a corresponding Report State message with the Solicited Message flag set, describing its success or failure in applying the configuration decision. In addition, outsourcing decisions from the PDP may result in a corresponding solicited Report State from the PEP depending on the context and the type of client. RPT messages solicited by decisions for a given Client Handle must set the Solicited Message flag and must be sent in the same order as their corresponding Decision messages were received. There must never be more than one Report State message generated with the Solicited Message flag set per Decision. The Report State may also be used to provide periodic updates of client-specific information for accounting and state monitoring purposes depending on the type of the client. In such cases, the accounting report type should be specified, using the appropriate client specific information object.

Delete Request State (DRQ) [PEP → PDP]: This message indicates to the remote PDP that the state identified by the client handle is no longer available or relevant. This information will then be used by the remote PDP to initiate the appropriate housekeeping actions. The reason code object is interpreted with respect to the client-type and signifies the reason for the removal. The format of the Delete Request State message is as follows: It is important that when a request state is finally removed from the PEP, a DRQ message for this request state is sent to the PDP so the corresponding state may likewise be removed on the PDP. Request states not explicitly deleted by the PEP will be maintained by the PDP until either the client session is closed or the connection is terminated.

Synchronise State Query (SSQ): This message indicates that the remote PDP requests the client (which appears in the common header) to resend its state. If the optional Client Handle is present, only the state associated with this handle is synchronised. If the PEP does not recognise the requested handle, it must immediately send a DRQ message to the PDP for the handle that was specified in the SSQ message. If no handle is specified in the SSQ message, all of the active client state must be synchronised with the PDP. The client performs state synchronisation by reissuing request queries of the specified client-type for the existing state in the PEP. When the synchronisation is complete, the PEP must issue a synchronise state complete message to the PDP.

Client-Open (OPN) [PEP → PDP]: The PEP uses the Client-Open message to tell the PDP what kind of client-types the PEP support. The PEP can also specify the last PDP to which the PEP connected. The PEPID is a symbolic name of the PEP, which identifies it inside the administrative domain. The identifier is an ASCII string that can be an IP address or DNS name of the PEP. The PEP can forward some additional client-specific information to the PDP. The last PDP address describes the last PDP for which the PEP is still caching decisions. The integrity object is used if security is in use or when the security is wanted in the usage.

Client-Accept (CAT) [PDP → PEP]: The Client-Accept message is used to positively respond to the Client-Open message. This message will return to the PEP a timer object, indicating the maximum time interval between keep-alive messages. Optionally, a timer specifying the minimum allowed interval between accounting report messages may be included when applicable. If the PDP refuses the client, it will instead issue a Client-Close message. The Keep-Alive (KA) timer corresponds to maximum acceptable intermediate time between the generation of messages by the PDP and PEP. The timer value is determined by the PDP and is specified in seconds. A timer value of 0 implies no secondary connection verification is necessary. The optional Accounting (ACCT) timer allows the PDP to indicate to the PEP that periodic accounting reports should not exceed the specified timer interval per client handle. This allows the PDP to control the rate at which accounting reports are sent by the PEP (when applicable). In general, accounting-type Report messages are sent to the PDP when deemed appropriate by the PEP. The accounting timer is merely used by the PDP to keep the rate of such updates in check (i.e., preventing the PEP from blasting the PDP with accounting reports). Not including this object implies that there are no PDP restrictions on the rate at which accounting updates are generated. If the PEP receives a malformed Client-Accept message, it must generate a Client-Close message specifying the appropriate error code.

Client-Close (CC) [PEP → PDP, PDP → PEP]: The Client-Close message can be issued by either the PDP or PEP to notify each other that a particular type of client is no longer being supported. The Error object is included to describe the reason for the closing (e.g., the requested client-type is not supported by the remote PDP or client failure).

Keep-Alive (KA) [PEP → PDP, PDP → PEP]: The keep-alive message must be transmitted by the PEP within the period defined by the minimum of all KA Timer values specified in all received CAT messages for the connection. A KA message must be generated randomly between $\frac{1}{4}$ and $\frac{3}{4}$ of this minimum KA timer interval. When the PDP receives a keep-alive message from a PEP, it must echo a keep-alive back to the PEP. This message provides validation for each side that the connection is still functioning even when there is no other message exchange. Note: The client-type in the header must always be set to 0, as the KA is used for connection verification (not per client session verification). Both client and server may assume the TCP connection is insufficient for the client-type with the minimum time value (specified in the CAT message), if no communication activity is detected for a period exceeding the timer period. For the PEP, such detection implies the remote PDP or connection is down and the PEP should now attempt to use an alternative backup PDP.

Synchronise State Complete (SSC) [PEP → PDP]: The Synchronise State Complete is sent by the PEP to the PDP after the PDP sends a synchronise state request to the PEP and the PEP has finished synchronisation. It is useful, since the PDP will know when all of the old client state has been successfully rerequested and, thus, the PEP and PDP are completely synchronised. The Client Handle object only needs to be included if the corresponding Synchronise State Message originally referenced a specific handle.

4.4.5 Common Operation

COPS supports two models of policy control: outsourcing and configuration (also known as provisioning). In the outsourcing model the PEP contacts the PDP every time a policy decision has to be made. The PDP makes the decision and communicates it back to the PEP, which enforces it. In the configuration model the PDP configures the PEP with the policy to be used. The PEP stores the policy received from the PDP locally and uses it to make decisions instead of contacting the PDP every time a new event occurs.

4.4.5.1 Outsourcing Operation

In the outsourcing scenario the PEP contacts the PDP every time a policy decision needs to be made. Since the request is stateful, the request will be remembered, or installed, on the remote PDP. The unique handle (unique per TCP connection and client-type), specified in both the request and its corresponding decision identifies this request state. The PEP is responsible for deleting this request state once the request is no longer applicable. The PEP can update a previously installed request state by reissuing a request for the previously installed handle. The remote PDP is then expected to make new decisions and send a decision message back to the PEP. Likewise, the server may change a previously issued decision on any currently installed request state at any time by issuing an unsolicited decision message. At all times the PEP module is expected to enforce the PDP's decisions and notify the PDP of any state changes. An example of this model is COPS usage for RSVP. RSVP-enabled routers, which act as PEPs and use COPS client-type 1, query the PDP when an RSVP message is received. The client specifies which RSVP message was received (e.g., PATH or RESV) and the expected behaviour of the router. The PDP decides whether or not the requested reservation is acceptable, according to the policy of the domain and communicates its decision back to the PEP (e.g., remove the resources assigned to a particular flow).

4.4.5.2 Configuration Operations

In the configuration scenario (known as COPS-PR), the PDP provides PEPs with policies and the PEP applies these policies. The PDP will then potentially send several decisions containing named units of configuration data to the PEP. The PEP is expected to install and use the configuration locally. When the PDP no longer wishes that the PEP uses a piece of configuration information, it will send a decision message specifying the named configuration and a decision flags object with the remove configuration command. The PEP should then proceed to remove the corresponding configuration and send a report message to the PDP that specifies it has been deleted. When the client downloads this policy, it does not need to contact the server to make individual decisions. This makes COPS-PR a highly scalable protocol; moreover, the COPS-PR could potentially be used to transfer configuration parameters beyond policy information.

4.4.5.3 Security

In the typical exchanges between remote PDP servers and PEP clients there are also the COPS security messages. If COPS-level security is required, it must be negotiated during the initial Client-Open/Client-Accept message exchange specifying a Client-Type of zero (which is reserved for connection-level security negotiation and connection verification). Security can be initiated by the PEP, if the PDP accepts the PEP's security key and algorithm by validating the message digest using the identified key, the PDP must send a Client-Accept message with a Client-Type of zero to the PEP carrying an Integrity object. This Integrity object will contain the initial sequence number that the PDP requires the PEP to increment during all subsequent communication with the PDP and the Key ID, identifying the key and algorithm used to compute the digest. The COPS protocol provides the Integrity object that can achieve authentication, message integrity and replay prevention. Furthermore, it is good practice to use localised keys specific to a particular PEP such that a stolen PEP will not compromise the security of an entire administrative domain. The COPS Integrity object also provides sequence numbers to avoid replay attacks. The PDP chooses the initial sequence number for the PEP and the PEP chooses the initial sequence number for the PDP. These initial numbers are then incremented with each successive message sent over the connection in the corresponding direction. The initial sequence numbers should be chosen such that they are monotonically increasing and never repeat for a particular key. Security between the client (PEP) and server (PDP) may be provided by IP Security [IPSEC]. In this case, the IPSEC Authentication Header (AH) should be used for the validation of the connection. Additionally, IPSEC Encapsulation Security Payload (ESP) may be used to provide both validation and secrecy.

4.4.6 Using Examples: COPS for RSVP

4.4.6.1 Unicast Flow Example

This section details the steps in using COPS for controlling a Unicast RSVP flow. It details the contents of the COPS messages with respect to Fig. 4.15.

The PEP router has two interfaces (if1, if2). Sender S1 sends to receiver R1. A Path message arrives from S1:

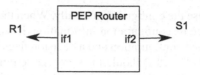

Fig. 4.15. Unicast example: a single PEP view

```
PEP --> PDP  REQ := <Handle A>
                    <Context: in & out, Path>
                    <In-Interface if2> <Out-Interface if1>
                    <ClientSI: all objects in Path message>

PDP --> PEP  DEC := <Handle A> <Context: in & out, Path>
                    <Decision: Command, Install>
```

A Resv message arrives from R1:

```
PEP --> PDP  REQ := <Handle B>
                    <Context: in & allocation & out, Resv>
                    <In-Interface if1> <Out-Interface if2>
                    <ClientSI: all objects in Resv message>

PDP --> PEP  DEC := <Handle B>
                    <Context: in, Resv>
                    <Decision: command, Install>
                    <Context: allocation, Resv>
                    <Decision: command, Install>
                    <Decision: Stateless, Priority=7>
                    <Context: out, Resv>
                    <Decision: command, Install>
                    <Decision: replacement, POLICY-DATA1>

PEP --> PDP  RPT := <Handle B>
                    <Report type: commit>
```

Notice that the Decision was split because of the need to specify different decision objects for different context flags. Time passes, the PDP changes its decision:

```
PDP --> PEP  DEC := <Handle B>
                    <Context: allocation, Resv>
                    <Decision: command, Install>
                    <Decision: Stateless, Priority=3>
```

Because the priority is too low, the PEP preempts the flow:

```
PEP --> PDP  DRQ := <Handle B>
                    <Reason Code: Preempted>
```

Time passes, the sender S1 ceases to send Path messages:

```
PEP --> PDP  DRQ := <Handle A>
                    <Reason: Timeout>
```

4.5 Conclusions

This chapter provided an overview on the signalling protocols and analysed in detail three of the most popular and promising signalling protocols/frameworks that are used in the current Internet: the Session Initiation Protocol (SIP), the Next Steps In Signalling (NSIS) framework, and the Common Open Policy Service (COPS) architecture and protocol.

For each signalling protocol/framework, background information was given and the main characteristics were described, presenting the overall architecture and overview of the protocol structure. The descriptions included architectural and protocol overviews, message formats, common operation and some examples.

5

Enhanced Transport Protocols

Nicolas Van Wambeke, Ernesto Exposito, Guillaume Jourjon, and
Emmanuel Lochin

Summary. The deployment of QoS network services and the entitled set of services
offered by existing transport protocols have motivated the design of new transport
protocols. In this chapter, we present a set of standardised transport protocols and
advanced transport protocol mechanisms to support Quality of Service and satisfy
new application requirements.

5.1 Introduction

At the network layer, despite several studies on the end-to-end QoS guarantees provisioning, the high complexity of these mechanisms results in the domination of
Best-Effort service as the only Internet network service available. The aim of the
enhanced transport protocols is to provide an end-to-end QoS-oriented service and
QoS optimisations or guarantees for current and future multimedia applications by
using available resources and network services (i.e., new network services).

In Sect. 5.2, we introduce the basic transport mechanisms provided by standard
transport protocols (i.e., TCP, UDP, SCTP and DCCP) and, in particular, congestion
and error-control mechanisms. Then, Sect. 5.3 details transport mechanisms used to
implement common transport services. We will see that traditional and more recent
transport protocols are not designed to offer QoS-oriented services. Indeed, these
protocols have mainly focused on the implementation of congestion-control mechanisms to protect and save network resources (i.e., TCP, SCTP and DCCP) while satisfying application requirements only partially. Finally, Sect. 5.4 presents enhanced
transport protocol mechanisms based on QoS-aware error- and congestion-control
mechanisms. Both error-control and congestion-control mechanisms take into account intrinsic media flow characteristics, network QoS and application time constraints. The QoS-aware error-control mechanisms are intended to provide partially
ordered and partially reliable (PO/PR) services. A differentiated and partially reliably service (D-PR) is proposed to satisfy specific reliability requirements of scalable multimedia streams. In order to satisfy specific time requirements, the service

is enhanced to provide a time-constrained and differentiated, partially reliable (TD-PR) service. The TFRC congestion-control mechanism allows enhanced transport protocols QoS awareness provided by the network, while at the application level the TD-TFRC congestion-control mechanism takes into account the time and reliability constraints. The composition of error- and congestion-control mechanisms aimed at supporting a large set of transport services is finally presented.

5.2 State of the Art of Transport Protocols

The different services available at the transport layer include the conceptual OSI transport layer model.

The Open System Interconnection (OSI) reference model describes how information from an application in one computer moves through a communication medium to an application in another computer. The OSI reference model is a conceptual model composed of seven layers, which details specific communication functions. The model was developed by the International Standardisation Organisation (ISO) in 1984, and it is now considered the base model for interconnected computers. Indeed, while layers 5 to 7 of this model have been considered as too complex for the service they provide, layers 1 to 4 represent the very basic parts of communication systems.

The transport layer in the OSI model is the lowest layer that operates on an end-to-end basis between two or more communicating hosts [91]. This layer is located at the boundary between the host applications and the network layer. A "service" is defined as the abstraction capability offered by an OSI model layer to a higher one. Transport services enable applications to abstract from the details of the available network services. A transport user generally performs three phases of operation: connection establishment, data transfer and connection termination. A connection-oriented transport service provides primitives for the three operations and a connectionless service supports only the data transfer phase. Moreover, a connection-oriented service maintains state information about the connection (i.e., messages sequence number, buffer sizes, etc.). Transport services and protocols can differ in several characteristics:

- Message and byte-stream services: In the case of a message service, users send messages or service data units (SDUs) having a specified maximum size and message boundaries are preserved. In the byte-stream service the data sent by the user are transported as a flow of bytes and message boundaries are not preserved.
- Reliability: comprising no-loss, no-duplicates, ordered and data integrity transport service.
- Blocking and nonblocking: A nonblocking service allows the sender to submit data and continue operating without taking into account the transport layer buffering capabilities or the rate at which the user receiver consumes data. A blocking service avoids overloading the transport layer with incoming data.

- Multicast and unicast: A multicast service enables a sender to deliver data to one or more receivers. A unicast service limits the data delivery to exactly one user receiver.
- Priority: A priority service enables a sending user to indicate the relative importance of various messages.
- Security: authentication of transport users, access control to resources, confidentiality and integrity of data, etc.
- Feedback or status-reporting service: allows a transport user to obtain specific information about the transport entities (i.e., performance, addresses, current timer values, statistics, etc.).
- Quality of service: A transport layer that explicitly provides QoS allows the quality specification of the required transmission service by a sender (i.e., delay, jitter, order, reliability, throughput, security, priority, etc.).

5.2.1 TCP and UDP

Transmission Control Protocol (TCP) offers a reliable and in-sequence end-to-end data transfer service between two interconnected systems [92]. TCP is a connection-oriented and byte-stream-oriented service. The User Datagram Protocol (UDP) has been proposed to offer a light transport service for messages or datagrams [93]. This UDP light transport service is implemented without the (time-consuming) connection phase and without the (resource-consuming) errors, congestion- and rate-control mechanisms. Therefore, UDP offers a connectionless and message-oriented service with no order and no reliability guarantees. Both TCP and UDP implement a multiplexing mechanism to support different applications transmitting several data flows using the same IP address. Both protocols implement mechanisms for the detection of corrupted data (i.e., checksum), where if a given set of bit errors is detected at the receiving side, the data packet is discarded. TCP implements error reporting and recovery mechanisms in order to provide a fully reliable service. Moreover, TCP implements flow and congestion-control mechanisms in order to avoid exceeding receiver buffers capacities and network congestion. Error, flow and congestion-control mechanisms implemented by TCP may induce transmission delay and variable throughput. Sometimes these effects are not compatible with application requirements such as multimedia applications, which demand throughput and delay guarantees. As a result, these applications have been implemented using UDP in combination with other protocols, i.e. Real-Time Transport Protocol (RTP)/Real-Time-Control Protocol (RTCP) [94], in order to obtain a more suited transport service.

5.2.2 TCP Evolution

TCP is at present the most widely used transport protocol in the Internet. Nevertheless, while the generic name has remained the same, the current TCP version used is different from the first TCP version in the early 1980s by Postel [92]. In this section, we describe four main TCP variants and the reasons that have led to the definition of these different versions: TCP Tahoe [95], TCP Reno [96], TCP Vegas [97] and TCP New Reno [98] with SACK [99]. Finally, we present the latest version of TCP algorithms that has better performance over high-throughput networks and wireless networks.

5.2.2.1 TCP Tahoe

In the first TCP version described by Van Jacobson in [95], the congestion control mechanism is based on the estimation of losses by the sender, and a congestion window regulates the number of packets that can be sent over the network (i.e., emitted rate). The increase of this congestion window follows two different stages: the slow-start and the congestion-avoidance phase. In the slow-start phase, the congestion window grows exponentially until a certain threshold has been reached. Once the protocol has reached this value, it follows a congestion-avoidance phase where it only increases the congestion window by a value of one more segment.

This version of TCP suffered from numerous drawbacks. The first concerns the Go-back-N error-recovery mechanism. This mechanism is not efficient, mainly because it can only retransmit packets that have already been received. The second drawback of this TCP version concerns the method for the detection and recovery of losses. Loss detection in this version is done using a timer that is triggered for every packet and staying active, either until the reception of the corresponding acknowledgement packet or until a fast-retransmit occurs. Furthermore, when the loss is finally detected, the protocol goes back to the slow-start phase with a threshold value of the half of the actual congestion window.

In order to solve these problems, new mechanisms are required: the selective repeat mechanism for the problem of the error-recovery mechanism, and fast-recovery added to the fast-retransmit mechanism for the problem of the loss detection.

5.2.2.2 TCP Reno

TCP Reno took into account the drawbacks of TCP Tahoe in order to improve the protocol. It modifies the fast-retransmit algorithm that could have been implemented in the Tahoe version to integrate the fast-recovery algorithm. The fast-recovery algorithm halves the congestion window instead of going back to the slow-start algorithm. This congestion window is increased during this period by the number of duplicate ACKs. Furthermore, this version applies the selective repeat mechanism for the recovery of packets lost. Nevertheless, these mechanisms also contain some minor drawbacks: the successive fast-retransmit problem or the false fast-retransmit followed by a false-recovery problem. This version also suffers from performance problems when multiple packets are dropped in the same sending window.

5.2.2.3 TCP Vegas

TCP Vegas [97] proposes new algorithms for the slow-start phase, the estimation of the available bandwidth in the congestion-avoidance phase and loss detection.

In order to detect congestion in the network, TCP Vegas defines a *BaseRTT* as the minimum measured *RTT* and the *ExpectedRate* as the ratio of the congestion window to the *BaseRTT*. Furthermore, the sender measures the *ActualRate* based on the sample *RTT*. Then, if the difference between the *ExpectedRate* and the *ActualRate* is superior to an upper bound, the sender linearly decreases the congestion window during the next *RTT*. Otherwise, if this difference is lower than a lower bound, the sender linearly increases the congestion window. According to [97], this TCP version achieves a better rate than the Tahoe and Reno TCP versions. Nevertheless, this version was never deployed due to scalability and stability concerns identified later in [100, 101]. One of the main drawbacks of TCP Vegas concerns its poor performance when mixed with other TCP versions.

5.2.2.4 TCP New Reno

In order to improve the behaviour of TCP Reno when multiple packets are lost in the same window, TCP New Reno has been proposed. In this version, a modified version of the fast recovery algorithm has been integrated, where partial ACKs are used to indicate multiple losses in the same window. This new fast-recovery algorithm has been described in [98]. This version of TCP appears to be adequate for wired networks where the bandwidth-delay product is not too high, but performs poorly over high bandwidth-delay product and wireless networks. For instance, the problems over wireless networks are due to the interpretation of a lost packet, because the TCP loss-detection mechanism supposes that packets are lost because of congestion in the network. However, in a wireless network, these losses can be due to channel errors or bad transmission.

These facts have motivated new TCP enhancements that are presented in the following section.

5.2.2.5 TCP Variants for High-Throughput and Wireless Networks

Nowadays, networks offer increasing bandwidth capacities to the end user. Nevertheless, TCP alone cannot take advantage of these new services, because of the additive increase/multiplicative decrease (AIMD) algorithm, which makes TCP too slow to adapt its sending rate to the network's bottleneck. In order to solve this problem, two kinds of transport protocols, based on a variation of the TCP AIMD congestion avoidance phase algorithm, have been proposed. The first proposals remain close to TCP as they do not require routers to modify their internal algorithms and marking, such as in BIC, HSTCP or STCP protocols [86, 102, 103]. The second set of proposals, such as XCP [104] and VCP [105], performs better than both TCP New Reno, but requires the network to provide information about the actual network congestion level using an ECN-like mechanism [106].

Nowadays, another TCP problem concerns its poor performance over wireless networks. TCP has been designed to perform over wired networks where a packet lost means network congestion. As a result, the congestion-control mechanism—as described above with the fast-recovery and fast-retransmit mechanism—decreases

the congestion window, in order to reduce the congestion in the network. Nevertheless, in the case of wireless communications, losses can also be due to urban obstacles, mobility of devices or channel interferences. In this context, new versions of
TCP congestion control have been proposed such as WTCP [107] or TCP Westwood
[108]. Another solution, TCP Veno (Vegas + Reno), proposed to let TCP Vegas estimate the available bandwidth and to act as TCP Reno when a loss is detected due
to congestion [109]. Nowadays, the current TCP used in the Internet are TCP New
Reno (*BSD), TCP Westwood (Microsoft Windows Vista), and a TCP BIC variant
(GNU/Linux) all with selective acknowledgement (SACK) enabled by default.

5.2.3 SCTP

The Stream Control Transmission Protocol (SCTP) is a reliable transport protocol,
which operates on top of a connectionless packet network protocol, such as IP, and
offers a reliable transport service [86]. SCTP is unicast and session oriented. An
SCTP session is an association established between two end systems. When end systems present several network addresses, the address list is exchanged during the association establishment phase. Supporting several IP addresses within the same SCTP
session is known as multihoming. The SCTP error control detects lost, disordered,
duplicated or corrupted packets and uses retransmission schemes to implement the
error-recovery mechanism. SCTP uses selective acknowledgements (SACK) in order to confirm data reception. Retransmission is done after a time-out or when the
SACKs indicate that some SCTP packets have not been received. In contrast to TCP,
SCTP is a message-oriented transport protocol. SCTP packets are composed of a
common header and data chunks. Multiple chunks may be multiplexed into one
packet up to the path-MTU size. A chunk may contain either control information
or user data. SCTP offers a multistream service, which means that application data
can be partitioned in multiple flows that can be delivered using several independent-
ordered streams. SCTP does not enforce any ordering constraints between the different streams. It provides a full-ordered intrastream service and a full-unordered inter-
stream service. This service guarantees that data delivery over the rest of streams is
not affected if some loss or disordering is detected in a stream. In contrast, flow and
congestion control are implemented on the association basis and not independently
for every stream. These mechanisms are based on the TCP algorithms: the receiver
informs the sender about the reception buffer capacity and a congestion window
is maintained for the SCTP association. The slow-start, congestion-avoidance, fast-
recovery and fast-retransmission mechanisms are implemented following the TCP
algorithms, but using the SCTP packets as the acknowledgement unit. Applications
accepting a partially ordered transport service can take advantage of the multistream
service provided by SCTP. However, the effects of the fully reliable service of SCTP
can be incompatible with multimedia applications presenting bandwidth, delay, jitter and synchronisation constraints. Currently, a partial reliability extension to SCTP
has been proposed [110]. In this proposal only a timed reliability service has been
specified. Timed reliability means that the user can specify the lifetime of a message.
However, this mechanism could be insufficient for time-constrained applications pre-

senting specific ADU reliability requirements and interdependency constraints (e.g., I, P and B frames of MPEG video).

5.2.4 DCCP

The Datagram Congestion Control Protocol (DCCP) offers a nonreliable transport service for datagram flows [111]. DCCP provides a congestion-control mechanism in order to behave fairly with other TCP flows. DCCP uses a Congestion Control Identifier or CCID to identify the congestion control to be used for each direction of the DCCP connection. This congestion control can be configured according to two profiles numbered Congestion Control ID (CCID) 2 or 3. In CCID 2 [112], a congestion control similar to the window-based congestion control is provided. In CCID 3 [113], a rate-based congestion control is provided. This congestion control is based on the TCP-Friendly Rate Control (TFRC) [114].

DCCP is suited to applications currently using UDP. In order to avoid network congestion, applications that use UDP should implement their own congestion-control mechanism. DCCP aims to deliver a transport service that combines both the efficiency of UDP and the congestion control and network friendliness of TCP. DCCP allows the negotiation of some connection properties to be used such as the congestion-control mechanism.

DCCP can be used by applications presenting time constraints and which are able to adapt their transmission rate to the limitations imposed by the congestion-control mechanism. If a certain reliability is needed, DCCP designers propose to implement error-recovery mechanisms (i.e., data retransmission or redundancy) at the application level. Nevertheless, the implementation of these mechanisms at the user space increases development efforts and can be less efficient than transport mechanisms operating in the kernel space.

5.2.5 Discussion

In this section a survey of the main transport protocols has been presented. This study demonstrates that traditional and new generation transport protocols have been designed taking into account only a subset of the QoS requirements of multimedia applications. These protocols have mainly focused on the implementation of congestion-control mechanisms to save network resources (i.e., TCP, SCTP and DCCP) while providing either full order and full reliability or nonorder and non-reliability. Moreover, mechanisms intended to satisfy time constraints are not supported at the transport layer. A QoS-oriented transport service based on the delay, jitter, throughput and synchronisation constraints of the multimedia applications and taking into account the partial order and partial reliability tolerance, as well as the scalable characteristics of multimedia flows, has not yet been provided. This is the reason that led us to propose the design of a new generation transport protocol aimed at providing end-to-end QoS guarantees. These protocols have to be designed to be easily configured from the requirements of current and future multimedia applications. This means that, first, the services provided by enhanced transport protocols should be transparently deployed for existing applications, minimising the adaptation efforts (i.e., preservation of standard transport API, transparent adaptation to legacy RTP streaming applications, etc.). Second, these specialised services should be accessible to new multimedia applications that are able to explicitly specify their QoS requirements (i.e., providing a QoS-enhanced transport API). Moreover, transport mechanisms taking into account underlying communication services (i.e., network services) could be implemented to provide soft or hard end-to-end QoS guarantees. A survey of common transport mechanisms implemented at the transport layer is presented in the next section.

5.3 Transport Mechanisms

The previous section presented services provided by common transport protocols. In this section, the basic mechanisms generally used to implement these common transport services are introduced. In particular, the congestion-control and error-control mechanisms are described.

5.3.1 Overview

In [115], the authors gave the following definitions of the basic transport layer mechanisms. They focused particularly on error and congestion, which are the two pillar mechanisms of a transport protocol.

- Error-control techniques protect against loss or damage of user data and control information. Error control is performed in two phases: error detection, and error reporting and recovery. Error detection identifies lost, disordered, duplicated and corrupted Transport Protocol Data Units (TPDUs). Error reporting is a mechanism where the transport receiver informs the sender about errors detected. Error reporting may be implemented by positive acknowledgement of data received (ACK) or negative acknowledgement of errors detected (NACK). Error recovery mechanisms are used by the sender or receiver in order to recover from errors. They can be implemented by retransmission strategies (i.e., Automatic Repeat request or ARQ) or redundancy mechanisms (i.e., Forward Error Correction or FEC).
- Flow and congestion control: Flow control is a mechanism implemented by the transport layer to limit the rate at which data are sent over the network in order to avoid exceeding the capacity of the transport receiver entity. Congestion-control mechanisms are intended to preserve network resources in order to avoid network congestion.
- Multiplexing and demultiplexing are mechanisms implemented by a transport protocol in order to associate several Transport Service Access Points (TSAPs) to a single Network Service Access Point (NSAP). In other words, this mechanism enables supporting several transport layer connections using the same network

layer connection. The use of protocol port numbers to perform the multiplexing/demultiplexing operations allows multiple transport users to use the same network address.

• Segmentation and reassembly: When the size of the Transport Service Data Units (TSDUs) is bigger than the allowed size of the Network Service Data Units (NSDUs), the TSDUs have to be segmented into smaller TPDUs by the transport sender. The transport receiver reassembles the TPDUs in order to rebuild the TSDUs to be delivered to the user receiver.

• Other mechanisms: Some transport protocols implement other specialised mechanisms, such as concatenation/separation and splitting/recombining. Concatenation combines several TPDUs into one NSDU in order to reduce the number of NSDUs submitted to the network layer. Separation of concatenated TPDUs will be performed by the transport receiver entity. The splitting operation is opposite to the multiplexing functions. Several NSAPs can support a single TSAP, thus providing additional resilience against network failures and increasing the throughput capabilities.

The next paragraphs will present a detailed study related to congestion-control and error-control mechanisms intended to evaluate the most adequate mechanisms for enhanced transport protocols.

5.3.2 Congestion-Control Mechanisms

The Internet protocol architecture is based on a connectionless end-to-end packet service using the IP protocol. These characteristics offer advantages in terms of flexibility and robustness, but a careful design is also required to provide good service under a heavy load. In fact, lack of attention to the dynamics of packet forwarding can result in severe service degradation. This phenomenon is technically called "congestion collapse" [116]. Network congestion is characterised by excessive delay and losses in delivering data packets. Congestion-control mechanisms are intended to avoid network congestion and its consequences. In [117] congestion-control mechanisms are classified into rate-control, rate-shaping and rate-adaptive encoding. Rate-control and rate-shaping mechanisms can be implemented as transport layer functions. In contrast, rate-adaptive encoding is based on compression techniques, being suitable for implementation as an application layer function. In this work, only rate-control and rate-shaping mechanisms able to be implemented at the transport layer will be studied.

5.3.2.1 Window-Based Congestion Control

Window-based congestion control was originally proposed for the TCP transport protocol [118]. This mechanism probes the available network bandwidth by slowly increasing a congestion window limiting the data being inserted into the network by the source. Detection of packet loss is considered as an indication of network congestion and the congestion window is reduced in order to avoid network collapse.

TCP-like congestion-control mechanisms are typically coupled with error-correction mechanisms (i.e., retransmissions), which can increase data delivery delay. For this reason, these mechanisms are considered as being noncompliant with the time constraints of multimedia flows.

5.3.2.2 Rate-Based Congestion Control

The rate-based congestion control mechanisms are characterised by the use of an estimation of the available network bandwidth as the allowed transmission rate. Rate-based mechanisms may use information about losses in order to calculate the transmission rate. This characteristic makes the rate-based mechanisms more suitable for controlling network congestion when full reliability is not required. Rate control can be performed by the source, the receiver or a combination of both [117]. The available network bandwidth can be estimated following a probe-based or a model-based approach.

5.3.3 Reliability Mechanisms

Packet loss is one of the consequences of network congestion in traditional IP networks. During data transmission, packets are temporarily stored in intermediate nodes before being forwarded to their final destination. When storage capacities are exceeded, some packets are dropped. As explained in previous sections, the degree of tolerance of packet loss depends on the type of application. Some applications are able to tolerate a certain degree of packet losses (i.e., audio, video, images, etc.), while for other applications packet loss is unacceptable (i.e., data files, text, etc.). Two main error-control mechanisms have been proposed for implementation at the transport layer. The first mechanism is known as Forward Error Correction or FEC [117]. FEC is performed by the data source and it is based on adding redundant information to the data packets to be transmitted. Redundant information will be used by the receiver to recover lost packets. The second error-control mechanism, called Automatic Repeat Request or ARQ, is based on the retransmissions of lost packets. Retransmissions can be demanded by the receiver when losses are detected or be performed by the source if the packets are not acknowledged after some time. Other mechanisms, such as error resilience and concealment, have been proposed at the application layer. Error-resilience mechanisms are intended to prevent error propagation or to limit the consequences of packet losses in the compressed data flow (i.e., synchronisation marks, data partitioning, etc.) [119]. Error-concealment mechanisms are performed by the receivers in order to hide the consequences of losses to the final user (i.e., spatial or temporal interpolation, replacement of lost frames by the previous ones, etc.) [120]. Hereafter, only the error-control mechanisms capable of implementation at the transport level will be studied.

5.3.3.1 Automatic Repeat Request

Automatic Repeat Request (ARQ) is an error-control mechanism based on the retransmission of packets considered as lost or damaged. This mechanism has been used to provide reliability in a number of communication protocols. Loss detection and recovery signalling techniques are specific to each communication protocol. The next paragraphs introduce some of these protocols and show how the ARQ mechanism has been implemented.

Stop-and-Wait ARQ offers the simplest reliability service at the transport level. A sender using the Stop-and-Wait protocol transmits a TPDU and then waits for a response. The receiver waits for a TPDU and sends an Acknowledgement (ACK) if the TPDU has been correctly received or a Negative Acknowledgement (NACK) otherwise. In practice, the receiver may not be able to detect lost TPDUs, and the sender needs to implement a timer to retransmit the TPDU when no response has been received from the receiver. If an ACK has been received, the transmitter can start sending the next TPDU. In order to detect duplicated TPDU or ACKs, each message has to be uniquely identified using, for instance, a sequence number.

In contrast to the Stop-and-Wait mechanism, Go-Back-N ARQ allows the simultaneous transmission of multiple TPDUs, as allowed by the transmission window size. Each TPDU must be identified uniquely by a sequence number. The source must keep in memory all the TPDUs that have been sent, but have not been yet acknowledged. The receiver must keep in memory the highest TPDU sequence number correctly received. When a packet loss is detected, the receiver sends a negative acknowledgement packet and all the received packets with a sequence number higher than the lost packet are discarded. The source restarts the Go-Back-N retransmission, since the TPDU corresponding to the sequence number indicated in the NACK packet.

Selective Repeat is a more complex, but more efficient error-control mechanism. This scheme is employed by the TCP transport protocol. Similar to the Go-Back-N mechanism, the retransmission is performed in response to the selective repeat feedback sent by the receiver. However, the sender retransmits only the TPDU for which the selective repeat has been indicated. This feature reduces the number of retransmissions, but increases the complexity at the sender and receiver. Indeed, each TPDU must be acknowledged individually, and the receiver must keep in memory packets received out of sequence.

In [95] a TCP extension was proposed, implementing the concept of Selective Acknowledgement (SACK). By sending selective acknowledgements, the receiver of data can inform the sender about all segments that have arrived successfully, so the sender needs to retransmit only the segments that have actually been lost. In [121] an implementation of this Selective Acknowledgement mechanism combined with a selective repeat retransmission policy was proposed.

5.3.3.2 Flow Control

In order to prevent the receiver from dropping packets because its receiving buffer is full, the receiver needs to inform the sender about the available space in its buffer. Usually this mechanism is performed based on the exchange of information concerning the available buffer space at the receiver and the update of a variable representing this information at the receiver each time a packet is sent. As a result, the sender will stop sending data when it supposes that the buffer is full—even if this is not correct.

5.3.4 Discussion

In this section, a survey of different congestion and error control mechanisms has been presented. Congestion-control mechanisms including transport- and application-based approaches have been presented. Within these mechanisms, a rate-based congestion control seems to be more suitable. Indeed, rate-based mechanisms have been designed for implementation at the transport level and independently of error-control mechanisms. Furthermore, these mechanisms could be enhanced in order to be more compliant with time-constrained applications. This enhancement can be done using the scalable characteristics of media flows (i.e., using a rate-shaping approach) in order to take into account not only the available network resources, but also intrinsic time constraints as well as partial ordering and partial reliable tolerance of applications. Regarding error-control mechanisms, FEC and ARQ have been introduced. These mechanisms could be enhanced in order to be more compliant with time-constrained applications.

5.4 Enhanced Transport Protocol Mechanisms

5.4.1 TFRC and gTFRC, a QoS-Aware Congestion Control

TCP-Friendly Rate Congestion Control (TFRC) is an equation-based rate-control mechanism, which aims at reproducing the behaviour of TCP congestion control. The TCP equation presented in [122] and used in TFRC is

$$X = \frac{s}{\left(RTT \cdot \sqrt{\frac{p \cdot 2}{3}} + RTO \cdot \sqrt{\frac{p \cdot 27}{8}} \cdot p \cdot (1 + 32 \cdot p^2)\right)}. \tag{5.1}$$

The use of an equation instead of the AIMD algorithm (used by window-based congestion-control mechanisms) in order to estimate the sending rate produces smoother throughput variations. Furthermore, the TFRC congestion control is based on a datagram-based communication instead of the stream-based TCP connection.

Even if the knowledge of the guaranteed bandwidth could be provided to the transport level, the AIMD principle integrated into TCP does not use the instantaneous throughput as an input value for its congestion control. Only acknowledgements and time-out analysis allow TCP to act on the rate control. On the contrary, the TFRC mechanism makes use of the instantaneous throughput in conjunction with the flow RTT and loss events. These parameters are used in order to compute the controlled rate. In the following, we assume a network that is well-provisioned and that the whole in-profile traffic does not exceed the resource allocated to the considered class of service; for instance, the AF class. In case of excess bandwidth in the network, the application can send more than its given target rate, say g, so the network should mark its excess traffic out-of-profile. If the network becomes congested, this out-of-profile traffic is predisposed to be lost first. In such a case, the optimal rate estimated by TFRC still can be below the target rate g needed by the application and provided by an underlying CoS; for instance, a DiffServ network. In such a case, TCP would react in the same manner by halving its congestion window. As for TCP in the AF class, the TFRC flow is not aware that the loss is corresponding to an out-of-profile packet and that it should not decrease its emitted throughput below the target rate.

In contrast to TCP, the usage of the TCP equation allows the direct usage of the actual sending rate in conjunction with the flow RTT and loss event values. A new resulting congestion control mechanism, called gTFRC, can be thus made aware of the target rate negotiated by the application with the DiffServ-like network. Thanks to this knowledge, the application flow is sent in conformance with the negotiated QoS while staying TCP-friendly in its out-of-profile traffic part. This is achieved by computing the sending rate as the maximum between the TFRC rate estimation and the CoS target rate as given in (5.2):

$$G = \max(g, X). \tag{5.2}$$

G is the transmission rate in bytes/s; g is the target rate in bytes/s and X is the transmission rate in bytes/s computed by the TCP throughput algorithm. The rest of the gTFRC mechanism follow entirely the TFRC specification in [114].

gTFRC requires the knowledge of the underlying bandwidth guarantee provided by the DiffServ/AF network service to the session. This information is available to the mechanism at socket-creation time, directly by the application. This parameter is given to the application, after it has been previously negotiated in an end-to-end basis by the signalling mechanism provided by the QoS architecture (as an example see the EuQoS architecture in Chap. 6).

5.4.2 Application-Aware Transport Mechanisms

In this section, the enhancement of specific transport mechanisms in order to make them more compliant with the application's QoS requirements while taking into account constrained network services (i.e., Best-Effort service) is proposed. This enhancement is done by a cross-layer communication between the transport protocol and the application layers.

5.4.2.1 Application Profile-Aware Congestion Control

Currently, most commercial multimedia applications (i.e., streaming and conferencing applications) do not implement congestion-control mechanisms. The implementation of a congestion-control mechanism for these kinds of applications is required in order to reduce the risks of future congestion collapse of the Internet, due to flows that do not use end-to-end congestion control [116]. These applications are usually implemented using RTP/UDP protocols to transmit media flows. Real-time flows are either transmitted using a near-constant rate or an adjustable rate based on the feedback obtained from the receiving application (i.e., RTCP messages). But even when applications are able to adapt their sending rate, it is usually done in long time scales. Some studies have been conducted in order to propose congestion control mechanisms adapted to the characteristics of these applications [123]. As we have seen, one of these mechanisms is the TCP-Friendly Rate Control (TFRC).

The rate-control mechanism of TFRC is based on a delaying policy aimed at adapting the flow to the allowed sending rate. This mechanism can penalise applications with strict delay constraints. For these applications, received packets could be discarded if they arrive too late to be presented. An alternative to the delaying policy implemented by TFRC may be a quality adaptation policy. Quality adaptation mechanisms can be performed by applications (i.e., adaptive encoding, switching between multiple preencoded version, etc.). But usually these mechanisms are executed in long time scales. We propose performing quality adaptation at the transport level. This requires that QoS information describing the multimedia flows must be available at the transport layer. This information must include at least the time constraints associated to every ADU as well as specific QoS information aimed at performing the quality adaptation (i.e., ADU priorities, dependency, order, etc.). The delaying strategy of TFRC is based in a computation of the interpacket interval time (IPIT) for every data packet to be transmitted. TFRC calculates this IPIT value as follows:

$$IPIT = \frac{s}{r}, \tag{5.3}$$

where s is the packet size and r is the allowed sending rate. The IPIT value represents the time to delay the current data packet in order to respect the allowed sending rate. If the QoS information associated to data packets include the delivery time stamp of every packet to the receiving application, then the feasibility of this delaying strategy could be checked, taking into account the end-to-end delay of the applications. The one-way delay must be known in order to perform this temporal validation. The one-way delay can be estimated using the RTT estimated in TFRC:

$$oneWayDelay = \frac{RTT}{2}. \tag{5.4}$$

Using the one-way delay, the delivery time stamp of the current data packet can be calculated as follows:

$$eDeliveryTimestamp = now + IPIT + oneWayDelay, \tag{5.5}$$

where now is the current time. Data packets can be considered as obsolete by the receiving application if the following equation is valid:

$$eDeliveryTimestamp - timestamp > MAXDELAY. \tag{5.6}$$

The time stamp is the scheduled delivery date. MAXDELAY expresses the delay tolerance of the application (i.e., 400 ms for interactive application). These obsolete packets will be generally discarded by receiving applications. However, if the temporal validation is performed by the source, discarding could be anticipated in order to avoid wasted bandwidth. Nevertheless, this basic discarding policy could seriously affect the QoS perceived by the final user if important Application Data Units (ADUs) are discarded. Selective frame-discarding methods based on ADU-related QoS information can be used to optimise the QoS provided to the user, while preserving network resources and respecting the application delay constraints. This selective frame-discarding method can be applied if the medium has been encoded using specific compression and ADU segmentation techniques, which facilitate the implementation of this method at the transport layer (i.e., Application Level Framing/ALF approach for the segmentation of flows such as MPEG, H.263, MJPEG, etc.). This method could also be implemented at the multimedia transport level, where the TFRC sending rate can be shared between the flows comprising the multimedia session. In this case, scalable flows could grant part of the allowed rate to other flows presenting poor adaptive capabilities (i.e., audio flows). Similarly to the multilayered multicast flows, for transport-level quality adaptation strategy, several quality layers could be defined using the QoS description of the ADUs composing the multimedia flows. For instance, for an MPEG flow composed by I, P and B images, three quality layers could be defined:

- Layer 2: I, P and B images
- Layer 1: only I and P images
- Layer 0: only I images

If the TFRC sending rate is lower than the rate demanded for the layer 0, other layers composed by subsets of I images and presenting lower rates could be defined. For a multimedia session, the same scheme can be used. For instance, for a session composed by a H.263 video with I and P pictures and a GSM audio flow, the following quality layers could be defined:

- Layer 2: Video (I+P) + Audio
- Layer 1: Video(I) + Audio
- Layer 0: Only Audio

Likewise, new layers could be defined for this multimedia session using intermediate quality levels placed between the specified layers. The definition of these differentiated layers allow us to propose an enhancement to the TFRC algorithm (TD-TFRC) intended to provide a rate control compatible with the time constraints and the intrinsic characteristics of multimedia flows. The next algorithm describes this specialisation of the TFRC mechanism:

```
currentLayer=0 join layer(currentLayer) while (sessionIsActive)
{
/* When feedback received or noFeedBack timeout : estimation of
TFRC parameters and compute r */

    /* filtering */
    if (currentPacket.layer > currentLayer)
        currentPacket.discard = true
    else {
```

```
// inter-packets interval
IPIT = currentPacket.size / r;
// estimation of time of data delivery
eDeliveryTimestamp = (now + t_ipi + RTT/2 + delta)
// estimation of presentation delay eDelay =
eDeliveryTimestamp - currentPacket.timestamp

// quality adaptation action in response to the
// estimated delay
if (eDelay <= MinDelayThreshold) // i.e. 50 ms
    action=increase
else {
        //i.e. 400 ms action = decrease
        if (eDelay >= MaxDelayThreshold)
        // quality adaption decrease action
        if (action == decrease)
            if (currentLayer == MIN_LAYER && eDelay \
                                     < MinDELAY)
                drop layer(currentLayer) STOP
            else
                if (currentLayer > MIN_LAYER)
                currentLayer = currentLayer - 1;
                currentPacket.discard = true
        // quality adaption increase action
        if (action == increase && currentLayer < \
                                     MAX_LAYER)
            currentLayer = currentLayer + 1;
} //scheduling of current packet
transmission if not currentPacket.discard
scheduleTransmission
currentPacket,t_ipi
}
```

Now is the current time, RTT is the round-trip time and delta is a tolerance constant including error in time estimations. In order to avoid abrupt changes in the QoS provided to the final user, quality layer increase and decrease actions have been proposed to be tailored by the `MinDelayThreshold` and `MaxDelayThreshold` obtained from the QoS requirements.

5.4.2.2 QoS-Aware Error Control Mechanism

As previously explained, some multimedia applications present some preference for timeliness over order and reliability. Actually, many of these applications do not require a fully ordered and fully reliable transport service when the delay incurred by this service is not compatible with their time constraints. For this reason, most multimedia applications have been designed to use the UDP protocol without any guarantees of order and reliability. In some cases, these applications have to implement ad-hoc error control mechanisms to satisfy their requirements. In this section we present an error control mechanism based on the partial ordering and partial reliability constraints of multimedia flows aimed at improving the QoS delivered to the multimedia applications.

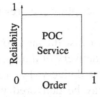

Fig. 5.1. Space of solution of the POC service

Transport protocols offering a partially ordered and/or a partially reliable (PO/PR) service have been proposed in several research works. The Partial Order Connection protocol (POC) was one of the first works proposing a partially ordered transport service for multimedia applications [124]. Unlike classic transport protocols that deliver objects either in the exact order transmitted or according to no particular order, POC provides a partial order service where some, but not all, objects have to be received in the order transmitted. This protocol has been designed to provide a partially reliable service, which accepts a subset of transmitted objects to be lost. A POC service specification can be defined by a subspace inside the whole space of partial ordered and reliable services, which can be realised for the delivery of a given set of Application Data Units (see Fig. 5.1).

In [125] the use of this family of protocols in the transport of video streams was studied. It was demonstrated that POC connections do not only fill the conceptual gap between TCP and UDP, but also provide real performance improvements for the transport of multimedia streams such as MPEG video. Other approaches, based on the POC concept and proposing the use of QoS requirements in order to offer a PO/PR services, have been presented. For instance, the partial reliability extension to SCTP (PR-SCTP) introduces the concept of timed reliability to implicitly regulate the error-control mechanism. However, a solution integrating the time, order, reliability and synchronisation constraints has not yet been proposed.

This section presents some error-control mechanisms aimed at providing PO/PR services. These mechanisms could be explicitly configured by specific order and reliability QoS requirements or implicitly deduced from the application requirements (i.e., delay, jitter, synchronisation, etc.). In both cases, specific QoS information describing the ADU characteristics has to be provided by applications in order to ensure that adequate order and reliability policies are applied by the error control mechanism.

5.4.2.2.1 Partially Ordered Service (PO)

A partially ordered service can be provided by the error-control mechanism at two levels:

- Medium or intraflow level: specific QoS information could be used by the transport protocol delivery mechanism in order to offer a partially ordered delivery service for the ADUs composing a flow. For instance, packets comprising the JPEG2000 or MJPEG2000 flows could be delivered by a partially ordered service deduced from the ADU description (i.e., resolution layers, region of interest, etc.).

- Multimedia or interflow: ETP can use the interflow synchronisation constraints to schedule the transmission and delivery of data packets for every flow, permitting a certain degree of out-of-order delivery. For instance, a session composed of two audio and video flows may be delivered with a partially ordered service between the audio and video ADUs, but respecting the interflow synchronisation constraints (e.g., 80 ms for lip synchronisation).

Transport mechanisms oriented to provide a PO service could be controlled by the source or receiver transport entities. Source control could be implemented following sending rate constraints imposed by congestion-control mechanisms in order to optimise the ADU transmission (i.e., sending first ADU with higher priorities). A partially ordered service could be scheduled taking into account intrinsic characteristics of ADUs (i.e., time stamp, dependency, etc.). A receiver controlled mechanism could optimise the delivery of data packets to the receivers when a partial order is permitted (i.e., ADUs corresponding to independent segments or tiles of JPEG2000 images). Furthermore, both PO source-based and receiver-based mechanisms could be implemented for unicast or multicast protocols.

5.4.2.2.2 Partially Reliable Service (PR)

A partially reliable service can be implemented based on the explicit reliability requirements of the application, or implicitly from intrinsic time constraints. FEC and ARQ mechanisms may be enhanced in order to provide this specialised error control mechanism. FEC mechanisms have been described as being very dependent on the traffic-loss characteristics. Furthermore, these schemes are usually designed to offer a full ordered and full reliable service when implemented at the transport layer. Partial order and partial reliability services using FEC have not been widely studied.

5.4.2.2.3 Partially Reliable, Differentiated and Time-Constrained ARQ (D-PR & TD-PR)

ARQ error-control mechanisms work as follows: when a loss is detected, the receiver sends a feedback message to ask the source to retransmit the message. This means that a retransmitted packet arrives at least three one-way delays after the transmission of the original packet. Sometimes, this delay could exceed the delay constraints of the application. However, if the one-way delay is short, this mechanism could be efficiently used to recover the losses. Time-constrained ARQ mechanisms could be implemented for unicast connections by receiver or source-based methods:

- Receiver-based: The objective of this mechanism is to avoid the request of retransmission demands, which would not arrive on time for their presentation. When a loss is detected before demanding its retransmission, the following condition has to be checked:

```
if (now + RTT < presentationTime)
    ask for retransmission
```

Now is the current time and RTT is the round-trip time. The problem with this method is that the receiver has to know the scheduled presentation time of lost packets.

• Source-based: This error-control method is intended to avoid retransmissions of packets that will arrive too late to be presented. The retransmissions can be demanded by the receiver when losses are detected. The source will check the following condition before performing the retransmission:

```
if (now + RTT/2 < presentationTime)
     retransmission of packet
```

This mechanism can be easily implemented by the source if QoS information related to the time presentation is available at the transport layer. Indeed this method can be used to provide a differentiated and partially reliable service, taking into account the notion of differentiated layers previously introduced.

5.5 Conclusions

The mechanisms discussed in this chapter include congestion-control mechanisms that are intended to preserve the resources of networks by providing a Best-Effort service. An error-control mechanism was presented that is intended to provide a partially ordered (PO) and partially reliable (PR) service, explicitly or implicitly configured from the application requirements. This error-control mechanism has also been enhanced in order to provide a differentiated and partially reliable service (D-PR). Both error- and congestion-control mechanisms have been enhanced in order to take into account intrinsic application time constraints (TD-PR & TD-TFRC). The composition of error- and congestion-control mechanisms to provide a large set of transport services has been discussed.

As it will be seen in the next chapter, the full design and implementation of the corresponding multi-QoS transport architecture and protocols was done within the framework of the EuQoS project.

6

The EuQoS System

Michel Diaz, José Enríquez-Gabeiras, Laurent Baresse, Andrzej Beben,
Wojciech Burakowski, María Ángeles Callejo-Rodríguez, Jorge Carapinha,
Olivier Dugeon, Ernesto Exposito, Mathieu Gineste, Enzo Mingozzi,
Edmundo Monteiro, Antonio Pietrabissa, Florin Racaru, Jarosław Śliwiński,
Giovanni Stea, Halina Tarasiuk, Nicolas Van Wambeke, and Markus Wulff

Summary. The European research project "End-to-End Quality-of-Service support over heterogeneous networks" (EuQoS) defined a novel architecture that builds, uses and manages the end-to-end (e2e) application exchanges and network paths with Quality-of-Service (QoS) guarantees across different administrative domains and heterogeneous networks. This chapter presents the architecture of the EuQoS system as a case study of the concepts introduced in previous chapters. The EuQoS architecture provides a clear interface that allows the end user to request a specific QoS level, without changing its application signalling protocol and using the basic connectivity of the local service provider. A complete set of supporting functions was implemented: (i) Security, Authentication, Authorisation and Accounting (SAAA); (ii) Admission Control; (iii) Charging; (iv) Signalling and Service Negotiation; (v) Monitoring and Measurements Functions and System (MMF/MMS); (vi) QoS Routing (QoSR); (vii) Failure Management; and (viii) Traffic Engineering and Resource Optimisation (TERO). The EuQoS system was deployed as a prototype including all the above features, encompassing the most common access networks, i.e., xDSL, UMTS, WiFi and Ethernet, connected through a core network composed by the National Research and Education Networks (NRENs) of the project partners and GÉANT (the European research network). This section describes the main features of the EuQoS system and presents the mechanisms, algorithms and protocols that were developed in the project. The results achieved validate the design choices of the EuQoS system, and confirm the potential impact that this project is likely to have in the near future.[1]

[1] This work was partially funded by the European Commission through the EuQoS Integrated Project (contract FP6-004503).

6.1 Introduction

Due to the increasing demand for new multimedia applications over the Internet (such as VoIP, video streaming or telemedicine), the provision of QoS to these novel services is becoming a key driver for ISPs in the future Internet. In this context, the main challenge is to guarantee the users' QoS requirements between the end points involved in the communication. Thus, a new architecture is needed in order to address this goal. Its main feature is the integration and synchronisation of the tasks performed in the different planes of the networks along the end-to-end path. In order to address this issue, the EuQoS system was designed to provide guaranteed e2e QoS over different underlying network technologies. The EuQoS system builds, uses and monitors e2e QoS paths across different administrative domains in heterogeneous networks.

This chapter presents the final architecture of the EuQoS system as a case study of the concepts introduced in previous chapters, providing a view on how QoS delivery can be supported in real environments using state-of-the-art technologies. The different aspects of the architecture and the implementation of the EuQoS system are introduced in the next sections:

- In Sect. 6.2 *a top-level description* of the architecture and the main characteristics of the EuQoS system are introduced. This high-level view presents the key actions and protocols used to coordinate the different technologies and domains in the e2e path. The behaviour of the network and the application levels, together with the way the main system components work, are described.
- Section 6.3 contains *the functional description* of the system based on the three main network design processes, i.e., Provisioning, Invocation and Operation, Administration and Management (OAM).
- Section 6.4 presents *the framework for QoS provision*, which specifies the EuQoS Classes of Service (CoS) and presents how they can be supported in different underlying network technologies.
- Section 6.5 shows, after the signalling and control phases, how the data will be transferred using an adequate transport layer. The six different transport layer services now needed for handling the e2e application-to-application QoS for the different underlying network CoSs are presented.
- Section 6.6 introduces the novel approach selected in the system to implement QoS multicast services. The EuQoS Multicast Middleware uses Scribe & Pastry for defining the Peer-to-Peer (P2P) network and for building the multicast trees. Pastry is a P2P routing substrate and Scribe builds an overlay structure on top of Pastry for multicast tree construction.
- Section 6.7 provides *a real-world example* of how commercial applications can be integrated into the EuQoS system. A telemedicine application (Medigraf) is introduced, and the key aspects needed to integrate it in the EuQoS environment are shown.

6.2 Architecture

6.2.1 Goals and Requirements

Following the *divide et impera* premise, the system is founded on a division of the e2e QoS paradigm along the vertical axis (Service, Control and Transport Planes) and the horizontal axis (the various network technologies, i.e., the access and the core networks). This is illustrated in Fig. 6.1.

Application signalling allows the caller to contact the callee, obtaining its IP address, and to agree on the codecs to be used. It works exactly the same as in the standard Internet nowadays.

The Service Plane, offers access to the EuQoS "QoS on demand" service to provide QoS connections using specific signalling, requesting the necessary resources to the network. Finally, this level is also responsible for authorising, authenticating and accounting of the user activity, and of filtering the QoS requests according to the user profile.

The Control Plane implements the mechanisms to translate the application requests to the network layer, and coordinates the e2e path management. The easy deployment of the EuQoS system was a key design principle, so as to facilitate different domain providers to adopt the EuQoS solution. This was met by the specification of a Network Technology Independent level (NTI), responsible for managing the domain at IP level, and a Network Technology Dependent level (NTD), for example performing the algorithms specific for each underlying network technology. The clear

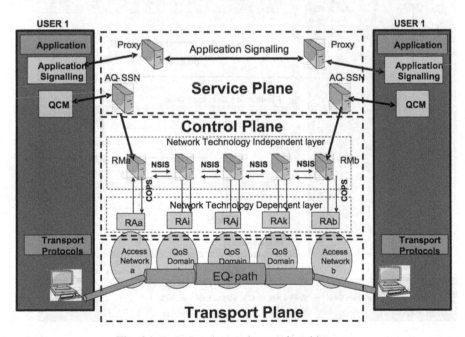

Fig. 6.1. EuQoS end-to-end network architecture

interface between them allows any provider to be integrated in the e2e QoS solution by just implementing its own components for the NTD.

The Transport Plane builds the actual e2e paths for the specified Network Classes of Service. It also includes in the hosts a new transport layer protocol, which can be optionally used to provide to the applications with different Transport Classes of Service, thus optimising the data transfer depending on the QoS requested by the applications and the selected Network Class of Service.

6.2.2 Functional Blocks and their Main Functions

Figure 6.2 gives a more detailed view of all these interfaces and of all functional entities that make up the EuQoS system, located at both the client and server sides. As shown in this figure, two sides are well differentiated in the EuQoS system: the EuQoS client and the EuQoS server. At the EuQoS client side, the main functions, located at the user equipment/host, are:

- The Application that the customer wants to use.
- The Application Signalling: it allows the caller to contact the callee side and to agree on their session parameters, e.g., codecs. This function can be performed by any legacy signalling protocol (as SIP).

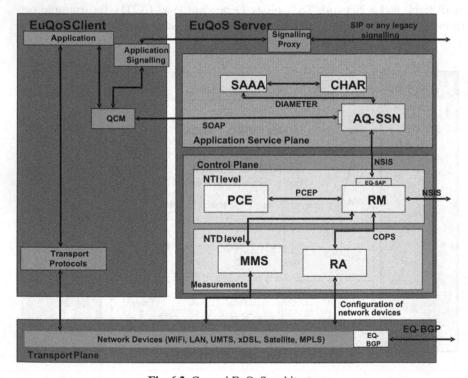

Fig. 6.2. General EuQoS architecture

- The Quality Control Module (QCM) is responsible for managing the data structures as required by the EuQoS server, and of asking the EuQoS server associated to its access domain to establish a QoS session, using the EuQoS "QoS on demand" service.
- The Transport Protocols that allow the application to send data to the Transport Plane in the network with an optimising protocol.

At the EuQoS server side, the structure of the different planes are as follows:

- The Service Plane: This plane must allow the EuQoS clients to request the establishment/release/modification of an EuQoS session with e2e QoS guarantees. In this plane, the key function is the Application Quality Service Signalling Negotiation (AQ-SSN) module, which provides the "QoS on Demand" Service to the end user. This plane also supports authorisation, authentication, accounting and billing for each user session. The SAAA is the module responsible for managing user access to network resources (Authentication), to grant services and QoS levels to the requesting users (Authorisation) and to collect accounting data (Accounting), while the CHAR module is responsible for charging the EuQoS customers and managing the bills.
- The Control Plane manages the Transport Plane in order to provide the e2e EQ paths (e2e QoS paths), according to the requests received from the Service Plane. So, the Control Plane has to enforce the QoS in its domain underlying technology of its domains, and to synchronise this process with the other domains involved in the provisioning of the EQ path. It is split into two different levels:
    - The Network Technology Independent level (NTI) is responsible for managing the domains at IP level. This level considers an abstraction of each domain including its topology. The main blocks at this level are the Resource Manager (RM) and the Path Computation Element (PCE).
    - The Network Technology Dependent level (NTD) is responsible for performing the resource reservation/release, provisioning of resources, configuring the network elements and algorithms, and using the Resource Allocator (RA) element. The Measurement and Monitoring Functions and System (MMF/MMS) is located at this level.
- The Transport Plane is composed of the network devices that should be managed by the Control Plane. The main goal of the EuQoS system Transport Plane is to build, use and manage the EQ paths across all different underlying network technologies.

It is important to note that the interaction with the EuQoS system does not imply the usage of a specific Application Signalling Protocol (such as SIP, H.323, etc.). This allows the easy integration of any application with the EuQoS system: the user must only use the QCM to invoke the "QoS on demand" service in order to request e2e QoS guarantees.

One of the major strengths of the EuQoS system is the clear specification of the interactions between the involved entities such as clients and QoS provider, Service,

Control and Transport planes, and EuQoS systems located at different ASs. The main interactions in the EuQoS system are:

- Application interaction: It allows the users to contact each other and to agree on the codecs that can be used to start the EuQoS session. Standard SIP is mostly used, but any other legacy signalling application could be used.
- EuQoS Client to server interaction: In order to set up QoS connections from the client side, several approaches can be followed:
  - EuQoS aware applications: This approach considers the application as part of the EuQoS system. In this way the Application invokes the QCM module to provide the QoS connection and, when an application signalling event is detected, the QCM contacts the AQ-SSN through a Simple Object Access Protocol (SOAP) interface to forward the request.
  - EuQoS nonaware applications: It allows any legacy application to use QoS connections, even when it is not integrated in the EuQoS system. To do this, an external program (like a Web application) can use the QCM at the client side to ask the AQ-SSN to establish/release/modify EuQoS sessions.
  - Home Gateway integration: When the operator-managed equipment (Home Gateway (HG)) represents the boundary between the operator network and the home network, the interaction can be considered an interdomain type. In this context, the Home Gateway can be considered as an extension of the EuQoS Control Plane, that interacts with its associated Operators Control Plane by means of the EQ-SAP interface to request e2e QoS guarantees in the segment that cannot be managed by the HG. These two interactions between the client and server sides are shown in Fig. 6.3.
- Interaction between the Service Plane and the Control Plane: The AQ-SSN module requests the services of the Control Plane using the EuQoS Service Access Point (EQ-SAP) interface that is implemented using the NSIS protocol.

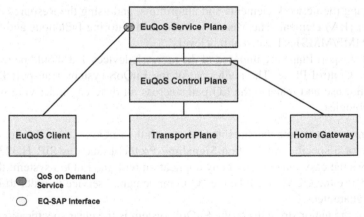

Fig. 6.3. Interaction between the EuQoS Client and the EuQoS server

- Interaction between NTI levels located in different domains: The NSIS protocol is used in order to exchange QoS invocation between different ASs (required to provide e2e QoS).
- Interaction between NTI and NTD levels: COPS primitives are used to ask for the resource reservation and commitment.

In addition to the mentioned functions, the following signalling protocols have been also implemented as part of the EuQoS system:

- Diameter allows the authentication, authorisation and accounting information exchange between the SAAA server and the AQ-SSN module.
- The EQ-BGP routing protocol conveys QoS information between each AS in the global system.
- The Path Computation Element (PCE) Protocol (PCEP) allows the communication between different PCEs of the hard model subsets of the EQ path.

6.2.3 Control Plane Elements: RM and RA

As explained earlier, the management and signalling at the Control Plane is mainly implemented by two components/entities, the Resource Manager (RM) at the Network Technology Independent level and the Resource Allocator (RA) at the Network Technology Dependent level.

6.2.3.1 Resource Manager Architecture

The RM is the Network Technology Independent entity responsible for managing the invocation and provisioning processes (see Sect. 6.3). RM entities can be deployed in each domain according to the size of the domain.

The RM provides the interface to the Service Plane and to trusted terminals— called EQ-SAP (EQ-Service Access Point)—in order to allow these entities to request QoS guarantees for specific flows. It also provides the interface to the RMs belonging to other network domains involved in provisioning e2e QoS guarantees. The main functions performed by the Resource Manager are:

- RM supports resource and admission control within a single administrative domain and between administrative domains: The RM is the core element of the EuQoS system that contacts the technology-specific Resource Allocators (RAs) to enforce the admission control decisions. It further contacts the RMs located in the other domains involved in the EQ path and configures the resources for guaranteeing the QoS requests.
- Verification of resource availability on an e2e basis: The RM applies an e2e Connection Admission Control (CAC) that checks whether there is a provisioned e2e path that meets the QoS requests.
- The final decision point is located at the RM, since it should decide the admission/rejection of a new session according the reservation results in its domain and in other domains.

- Network selection: The RM locates the core networks (via NSIS protocol) and the RAs that enforce the final admission decisions.
- The RM checks whether the connection requests meet the operator policies for this domain. These policies are a simple set of conditions formulated as the maximum bandwidth and QoS parameter limits supported by this domain for each e2e CoS.
- Network topology maintenance: The RM maintains the interdomain topology used during invocation process.
- Network resource maintenance: The RM maintains information about the expected usage of resources and collects information from different measurement MMF/MMS tools to infer the current usage of the network resources.

There is a complementary element in the NTI level, called the Path Computation Element (PCE), which is used during the provisioning process in case that MPLS-TE technologies are used (see Sect. 6.3.1.1). The rationale behind the PCE is to delegate the computation of the best MPLS path to a dedicated server, offloading the RM from this specialised task.

6.2.3.2 Resource Allocator Architecture

The Resource Allocator (RA)is a technology-dependent module responsible for providing and managing QoS in the underlying networks. The RA enforces the traffic-handling rules to implement the Classes of Service (CoS) in each network, as specified in Sect. 6.4. In general, the RA performs the tasks that come from the provisioning and invocation processes and from the monitoring functions (see Sect. 6.3).

The EuQoS architecture now assumes that a single RA (see Fig. 6.4) is deployed in a given domain and that it manages all the resources that are critical from the point of view of QoS assurance. A pool of RAs could be used instead. The main functionalities covered by this element are the following:

- QoS and priority mapping technology dependent: The CAC makes the final mapping from e2e CoSs (network CoSs) to technology dependent CoSs.
- Gate control: This function is limited and exists only if particular technology operates in a gateway (UMTS, possible for xDSL).
- IP packet marking and rate-limiting control: If a given technology is able to perform this function, the RA triggers this feature. Otherwise, one must provide a traffic conditioning module that marks packets generated by end users when they enter the network.
- Technology-dependent decision point: The RA will be responsible for accepting/rejecting one connection request to the specific technology policies.
- Network topology maintenance: The topology information managed by the RA is reduced and covers only access networks operating below IP level. Particularly, when the dynamic IP address allocation is used, the RA must be able to find out the exact location of the user.
- Network resource maintenance: The RA controls resources, taking into account provisioning and invocation point of view.

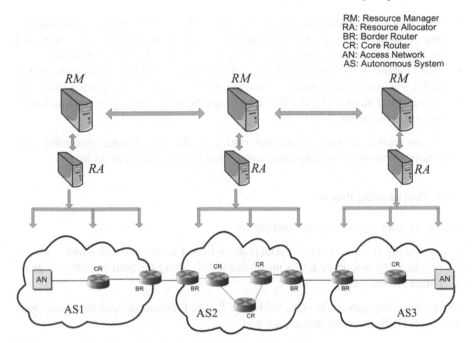

Fig. 6.4. Reference locations of RAs in EuQoS

- Element resource control: The RA provides configuration and management of transport elements not only at aggregate level, but also per-flow if access technology allows for it.

6.3 Provisioning, Invocation, and Operation, Administration and Management

EuQoS QoS guaranteed paths (EQ paths) are the EuQoS defined QoS paths providing a given end-to-end QoS. They are implemented in the Transport Plane over a wide variety of technologies and networks, and are built, used and monitored by the Control Plane in order to provide the QoS needed by the Service Plane. The purpose of these EQ paths is to provide quality guarantees to applications on an e2e basis. Each EQ path corresponds to a given set of QoS parameters, i.e., those corresponding to the selected Class of Service (CoS). The EuQoS system acts at three different levels:

- The provisioning process is responsible for building the EQ paths across network domains at both independent and dependent network levels. The time scale is on the order of hours or days and it is triggered according to interoperator agreements.

- The invocation process uses the EQ paths by selecting the most appropriate one, and performs CAC to protect EQ paths from congestion. This process is triggered by the end users when a new session request is sent to the EuQoS system.
- The Operation, Administration And Maintenance (OAM) process protects EQ paths from failure and interacts with the provisioning and invocation processes to repair EQ paths if needed. It also provides the necessary supervision and measurement functions.

In this section, a more detailed description of the provisioning, invocation, and operation, administration and management (OAM) processes is provided.

6.3.1 Provisioning Process

The provisioning process is responsible for:

- computing and setting up e2e data paths between access networks, and
- provisioning resources across the different ASs along the path so that QoS guarantees are enforced.

The provisioning process is managed by the Traffic Engineering and Resource Optimisation (TERO) module inside each RM.

6.3.1.1 Resource Provisioning

The EuQoS provisioning process defines two provisioning models, namely the *Loose Model* and the *Hard Model*, whose integration allows providers to control the balance between manageability and scalability of the system.

6.3.1.1.1 Loose Model

The loose model designs the transport path (between the sending and receiving entities) by starting from the data path. The data path is first selected by a routing protocol, and then the signalling protocol has to reserve the resources for this data path. In the loose model, resources are independently provisioned in every AS. Although resources are provisioned per CoS, there is no specific binding of reserved resources to e2e paths (EQ paths). Therefore, the resources required for establishing a single user connection along an EQ path are dynamically composed and associated to that path by the Call Admission Control (CAC) function at connection setup time, i.e., during the invocation process.

EQ paths are established by means of an EuQoS handling (EQ-BGP) of the Q-BGP protocol, an interdomain QoS routing protocol, whose objective is to establish e2e paths that offer the most suitable QoS guarantees, taking into account the QoS capabilities of each domain (see Sect. 6.3.1.2). EQ-BGP advertises the reachability of given destinations for each CoS, together with an estimate of the e2e QoS along the selected EQ path.

The main advantage of the loose model is that it requires minimum coupling among the Autonomous Systems (AS) along the EQ path. In fact, it only requires peering agreements between neighbouring Autonomous Systems, without any e2e concept (and related management requirements). As such, it can be considered as the basic Internet-wide model, which is suitable for any policies implemented by a provider with the single constraint of supporting EQ-BGP. For technologies that do not support EQ-BGP, or for domains where EQ-BGP is not suitable, the solution is to use EQ-BGP in the RM instead of in the border routers. In this case, the multihop classical BGP option is used to link the peering entities.

The main disadvantage of the loose model is the amount of signalling involved in the call setup/teardown process, due to the dynamic binding of resources to the EQ path.

6.3.1.1.2 Hard Model

The hard model is based on the concept of an EuQoS defined link, called the EQ link. An EQ link is a configured transport path, having known QoS characteristics between any two nodes in different (nonneighbouring) ASs, and behaving like a virtual interdomain link interconnecting a pair of neighbouring border routers. As such, it is associated to a specific CoS, not to a session (i.e., it carries traffic aggregates). Resources (bandwidth and buffers) are explicitly reserved for its exclusive use as part of the provisioning process. In practice, an EQ link is established as a DiffServ MPLS-TE tunnel, which may span over multiple domains or ASs (see Chap. 3). Thus, it is semistatic with resources associated to it, and it can be protected against failures. Based on this concept an EQ path may be simply built, at provisioning time, by establishing a corresponding EQ link on demand across the Internet between two networks.

EQ link establishment needs specific means for the computation of the AS path along which the EQ link is set up. In fact, today routers' online path computation is done at the head-end Label Switch Router (LSR), but this has some limitations. In particular, in an interarea and inter-AS context, the head-end routers only have a partial visibility of the topology and cannot compute an e2e path. To solve this issue, a two-step approach is implemented in the EuQoS system as shown in Fig. 6.5.

- First, the best AS path between the two ASs is computed through direct interaction of the TERO modules in neighbouring domains. The computation takes into account QoS objectives, resource availability and administrative constraints that may limit the reachability of the destination with the CoS of the EQ link.
- Then, the actual node-by-node path computation relies on a Path Computation Element (PCE) chain along the computed AS path (see [126]). The rationale behind the PCE is to delegate the computation of the best path to a dedicated server, i.e., the PCE itself. The PCE serves path computation requests sent by a client. Although the original Internet Engineering Task Force (IETF) charter for PCE was meant to take into account only intradomain path computations, the multiarea was in the scope of the PCE Working Group. In fact, since PCEs can communicate with each other, they can cooperate to compute a path that spans

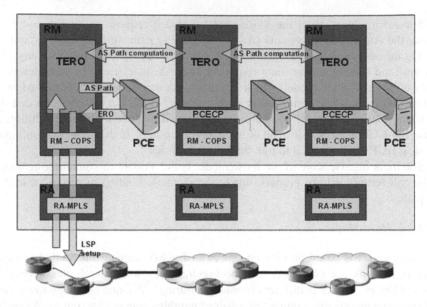

Fig. 6.5. PCE integration in EuQoS

across several ASs. The Path Computation Element Communication Protocol (PCECP) is used for the communication between the PCEs. The result of the computation is delivered as an Explicit Route Object (ERO) to the TERO module.

The EuQoS system relies on the PCE concept to implement multidomain EQ link setup. A detailed description of the functional requirements and specifications needed to setup EQ links is given in [127].

The advantages and disadvantages of the hard model are opposite to the loose model. First of all, it reduces the signalling required to set up connections. Signalling is required only in the access domains and at the entrance of an EQ link, and resources are already bound at the provisioning time. Furthermore, it can optimise resource provisioning by exploiting interdomain, multipath capabilities on a per-CoS basis. On the other hand, such a model entails complex path set up procedures, requiring a strong degree of cooperation between remote ASs. Furthermore, it requires support of DiffServ MPLS-TE in the whole core, and as such its applicability is limited to the domains where this mechanism is present.

In summary, regarding the EQ path building there are two possible approaches at the two ends of the spectrum:

- At one end, an EQ path is the result of a sequence (as determined by EQ-BGP) of a number of ingress-egress boarder router paths, each belonging to a single AS. Resources are provisioned e2e per session and per domain as part of the invocation process (loose model).
- At the other end, an EQ path is implemented by a dedicated complete e2e access network-to-access network EQ link, and resources are provisioned e2e per EQ

path as part of the provisioning process (hard model). Note that the latter would obviously imply that a full mesh of EQ links connecting access domains could be set up—at least theoretically.

As a consequence, network provisioning in EuQoS becomes quite flexible, as selecting any combination of loose/BGP-based and hard/MPLS-based paths is possible, depending on different type of constraints, as contexts, agreements, policies, etc.

6.3.1.2 EQ-BGP: Enhanced QoS Border Gateway Protocol

The Enhanced QoS Border Gateway Protocol (EQ-BGP) [128, 129] is the interdomain QoS routing protocol developed within the EuQoS project. Its objective is to advertise and select the interdomain routing paths taking into account QoS objectives of e2e CoSs (as defined in Table 6.2). EQ-BGP extends the currently used BGP (BGP-4) [130] interdomain routing protocol in several ways. First, it defines the QoS Network Layer Reachability Information (QoS NLRI) path attribute that conveys information about e2e CoSs offered on advertised paths. Second, it uses the QoS assembling function for computing aggregated values of QoS parameters guaranteed by each segment of a path. Third, EQ-BGP defines the QoS-aware decision algorithms for selecting routing paths. Fourth, EQ-BGP keeps separate routing table for each e2e CoS.

EQ-BGP performs QoS routing, taking into account the QoS guarantees provided by particular domains in multidomain networks. For that purpose, EQ-BGP routers advertise information about the reachable destinations jointly with aggregated values of the QoS parameters guaranteed by e2e CoSs on currently used paths. Those aggregated values are calculated, taking into account the impact of all domains and interdomain links on the path toward a given destination. Then, the neighbouring EQ-BGP routers update received values of QoS parameters taking into account contribution of their domains and then decide about their routing. In case of any changes, the routers advertise them to neighbours. Finally, EQ-BGP sets the roadmap of paths that are available for all e2e CoSs. The roadmap also provides values of QoS parameters that are guaranteed between each pair of source and destination prefixes.

Figure 6.6 shows an example of how QoS routing information is computed and advertised in the network using EQ-BGP. For the sake of simplicity, we assume a simple network consisting of three domains A, B and C, that support only one e2e CoS. Each EQ-BGP router is aware of the values of the QoS parameters that are assured inside its domain (Q_A, Q_B or Q_C depending on the domain) as well as on its corresponding interdomain link ($Q_{A \to B}$ or $Q_{B \to A}$, respectively). Those values should correspond to the maximum admissible load allowed by the admission control function. The actual values should be fixed during the network provisioning process taking into account details of domain configuration, used technology, provider policies, etc. The values of QoS parameters typically change at provisioning time scales, e.g. on the order of days or weeks, so route changes due to frequent variations of the QoS values are not expected.

Now, let us consider the case when Domain C advertises a new prefix, say $pref_c$. Then, the routing information is propagated toward Domain A through Domain B.

Figure 6.6 shows the routing tables of the border EQ-BGP routers along the path. During this process EQ-BGP routers aggregate the values of the QoS parameters taking into account the QoS contribution of particular domains as well as the inter-domain links on the path toward $pref_c$ advertised by Domain C. For example, domain A learns the e2e QoS path toward the destination $pref_c$, with QoS corresponding to $Q_A \oplus Q_{A \to B} \oplus Q_B \oplus Q_{B \to C} \oplus Q_C$ for considered CoS, wherein the operator $\oplus$ denotes QoS assembling function. Taking into account that QoS parameters used by the e2e CoSs can be treated as additive, we use a simple sum function.

The values of QoS parameters are advertised using the QoS Network Layer Reachability Information (NLRI) path attribute presented in Fig. 6.7. The attribute begins with the attribute header that contains flags, type indicator and the attribute length. The flags are used to inform routers that information carried in the QoS NLRI attribute is optional, nontransitive and complete. The main part of the attribute contains a number of structures describing particular e2e CoSs. Each structure covers

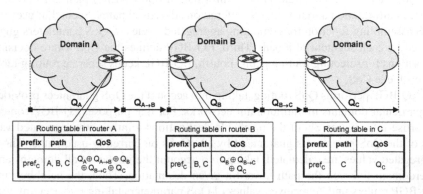

Fig. 6.6. Example of EQ-BGP operation

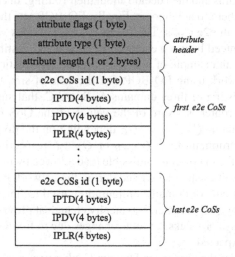

Fig. 6.7. Format of the QoS Network Layer Reachability Information path attribute

the e2e CoS identifier and three fields including IP Packet Transfer Delay (IPTD), IP Packet Delay Variation (IPDV) and IP Packet Loss Ratio (IPLR) parameters. Values of IPTD, IPDV are expressed in μsec, while IPLR is carried in the exponent form: $-1000 \cdot \log_{10}(IPLR)$.

EQ-BGP uses the QoS-aware decision algorithm. It allows the routers to compare the paths going toward a given destination and then to select "the best" one from the viewpoint of QoS objectives of particular e2e CoSs. The algorithm adds a new step in the routing decision process that evaluates the Degree of Preference (DoP) factor based on the values of QoS parameters carried in the QoS NLRI attributes. The degree of preference is used before the path length criterion. Therefore, EQ-BGP will first consider the QoS level offered by the available paths and if this criterion does not decide, the router will select the shortest path. The next decision steps are the same as in case of the BGP-4 protocol.

6.3.2 Invocation Process

This section presents the invocation process in the EuQoS system, explaining the signalling chain, the devices and functions triggered in each server involved in a session establishment.

6.3.2.1 Invocation in the Service Plane

The application invocation and signalling phase is used to trigger the application-to-application negotiation and then, if positive, to trigger the network invocation process described in Sect. 6.3.2.2.

Taking into account that some applications already have different application signalling, such as H323, SIP or any other ad-hoc protocols, EuQoS proposes a new application-level architecture that avoids the restriction of using EuQoS application signalling based on SIP as the only way to interact with the EuQoS network server. The key point of this approach has been to define a "QoS on-demand" service.

Two reference points are being defined to ask for the e2e QoS on-demand service:

- An interface provided by AQ-SSN to the EuQoS clients allows the clients to ask for an e2e QoS request. This interface is implemented using SOAP.
- The RM Service Access Point API (EQ-SAP) for trusted legacy terminals (e.g., as it is proposed in the Home Gateway Initiative) or for any other allowed entity.

It is important to note that this approach allows clients to ask directly for QoS parameter reservation to the EuQoS system (that means, the user asks for an e2e CoS for a set of flows, and the user provides its credentials to be authorised and charged) after obtaining the IP address and ports to be used by the callee side.

As explained in the general architecture description (Sect. 6.2.2), several scenarios can use this architecture. More details can be found in [131].

- EuQoS aware application using QoS-on-Demand service.

Table 6.1. Brief description of EuQoS main interfaces

	QoS on demand service	EQ-SAP
Service provider	AQ-SSN	RM
Service client	QCM and user administrator via Web interface	AQ-SSN and trusted terminals
Information exchange requirements	This service must support request–response transactions and shall provide a reliable delivery of the messages	This service must support request–response transactions and shall provide a reliable delivery of the messages
Information flows exchanged	Requests: • Perform Reservation • Modify Reservation • Terminate Reservation Responses: • QoS Answer to perform requests • Result of the reservation termination	Requests: • Perform Reservation Commit • Modify Reservation • Terminate reservation Responses • Resources available to reserve and modify requests • No response to terminate request. It is considered that the connection release is always successful

- QoS-on-Demand services used by administrators for legacy applications, via a Web interface.
- Trusted terminals, as home gateways, using EQ-SAP to reserve QoS.

In order to support these scenarios, the main goal of this new approach is to clearly specify the interfaces exposed by the AQ-SSN and RM, QoS on demand and EQ-SAP services, respectively. Table 6.1 sums up the main characteristics of these reference points.

6.3.2.2 Invocation in the Control Plane

A straightforward invocation process could be as follows:

- All domains involved in the EQ path must be asked to reserve the resources corresponding to the connection. This would require a high amount of signalling traffic and a high number of configuration on network equipment.
- The resources in each domain are reserved sequentially. This is not optimal if the setup time is a critical performance parameter, and would have a higher impact if the reservation of all the flows belonging to the same session would be also performed sequentially.

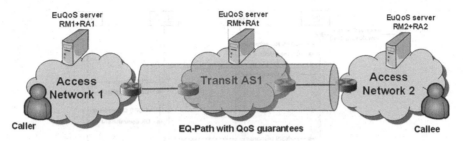

Fig. 6.8. Invocation scenario

To address the first problem, the hard model has been implemented in the EuQoS system (see Sect. 6.3.1.1). The configuration of transit domains is performed only during the provisioning process instead of during the invocation process. In this way, the signalling load is reduced and the configuration of network equipment in core networks that are supposed to aggregate the traffic from different access networks is not performed during the invocation process. If we consider the simple scenario shown in Fig. 6.8 to explain the invocation chain, the transit domain AS1 will not be asked to reserve resources during invocation process, since access networks 1 and 2 will see the EQ path as a link with a specific capacity.

Regarding the second problem, the invocation chain scheme has been designed to perform as many actions as possible in parallel.

When the AQ-SSN at the caller side receives the request to establish a new EuQoS session, it can ask the RM to reserve all connections from both directions (caller to callee side or callee to caller) in parallel, without waiting for the first QoS connection request response. The RM will process these requests in parallel triggering all the domains involved in the EQ path. The RM located at the caller side will receive all requests needed to reserve the resources for unidirectional flows.

In this scenario two cases can be distinguished, depending on the source IP address of the data flow:

1. The source IP address of the data flow belongs to the (caller) RM administrative domain. In this case the RM receives in the EQ-SAP interface the request to reserve resources for a flow whose IP address belongs to its administrative domain. In order to allow the parallel configuration of network equipment at the access networks, the RM forwards the requests to reserve resources to the next domain after performing the CAC algorithm specific for each technology. The RM effectively reserves the resources while other domains are performing the checking/configuration of their resources. In order to assure that the client has an e2e path with guaranteed QoS, each domain will only send back the confirmation response after receiving the confirmation of the reserved resources from its RA. The sequence of exchanged messages is shown in Fig. 6.9. As can be seen, this scheme allows configuring in parallel resources in both access networks. This is interesting, because if, for example, the first access network is UMTS (the time to establish a session is around 5–10 s) and the second is a WiFi do-

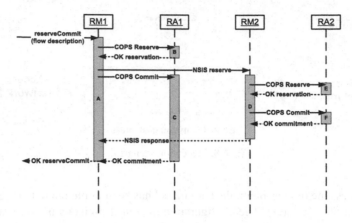

Fig. 6.9. Invocation sequence diagram

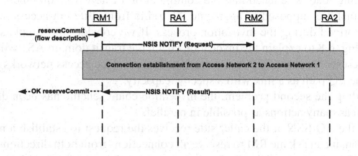

Fig. 6.10. Destination initiated scenario

main (this would require around 1–2 s), the time required to configure the WiFi equipment would not be added to the time to establish the UMTS session.

2. The source IP address of the data flow does not belong to the RM1 administrative domain. In this case the RM1 (caller side) must resend the request to the RM2 (located at the callee side) and be aware of the result of the reservation. In order to do that, the NSIS NOTIFY message will be used to transport the requests and responses between the access RMs, as shown in Fig. 6.10. The connection establishment from access network 2 to access network 1 follows the description presented in the previous case.

6.3.2.3 SomeTimes Per Flow Model

Taking into account the benefits and drawbacks of the loose and hard options mentioned earlier, an intermediate solution has been proposed, named SomeTimes Per Flow (STPF). The details about the STPF model can be found in [132]. The STPF assumes that the resources provisioned for a given CoS in considered domains are divided into two main parts, where one part is reserved only for handling the calls on the basis of the *hard model* scheme (as multidomains EQ links) while the second part is handled by the *loose model* scheme.

The resources designated to operate loosely per-flow can be used only when there are no resources available in the corresponding hard EQ link. As a consequence, the majority of the call requests should use the hard model, and will not use the full reservation scheme. The full reservation process is then used only for a certain percentage of calls. In this way, it is expected to get high resource utilisation while the required signalling traffic will be noticeably reduced.

6.3.3 Operation, Administration and Management

In order to guarantee the QoS commitment, the EuQoS system performs two actions: the first is admission control and the second is EQ path monitoring. This second goal is the main goal of the OAM process. Monitoring is done by means of measurement and fault management.

The measurement subsystem allows the EuQoS system to verify that EQ paths are not overbooked (i.e., the maximum allocated bandwidth corresponds, more or less, to the sum of reserved bandwidth). The fault management subsystem allows verification of the EQ path continuity and takes care of device, node and link failures. These two subsystems interact with the invocation process (so that the CAC adjusts the admission control threshold), and the provisioning process (in order to recompute the EQ path in case of node or link failure). This path protection can be improved by setting up some backup paths by means of a Fast Re-Route (FRR) mechanism when EQ paths are built with MPLS-TE in the hard model.

In order to monitor the provided QoS, the MMF/MMS functions of the EuQoS system monitor the QoS parameters (IPLR, IPTD and IPDV) and the used bandwidth per aggregate. In order to do that, different probes are distributed in each EuQoS domain and the information is reported to all functions involved in the invocation processes. Moreover, the MMF/MMS manages a set of thresholds for QoS parameters and global link utilisation. If any of these thresholds is overloaded, an alarm event is generated.

Moreover, for the loose model, the monitoring system will compare the actual EQ-BGP routes with the Service Level Agreement (SLA) information being managed by the TERO module. This will be done in order to check that the information agreed between different operators corresponds to the real usage of the network.

The final specification of the functionalities to be covered by the MMF/MMS subsystem of the EuQoS system are described in [133].

6.4 End-to-End Classes of Service in Heterogeneous Networks

This section describes the framework defined in the EuQoS system for providing at the application and at the network layers e2e QoS for heterogeneous multidomain networks. It presents how connections requiring QoS are established between communicating hosts attached to different access networks. Access networks can be built on different technologies such as xDSL, UMTS, LAN, WiFi, MPLS and satellite, and can be interconnected by many IP-based core domains. Furthermore, implementing the framework means to transfer packets while guaranteeing some QoS parameters, i.e. packet delay (IPTD), variation of the packet delay (IPDV) and packet loss ratio (IPLR). The proposed solution should assure that the optimal values of the above parameters are satisfied. The EuQoS approach establishes in the network a number of so-called Classes of Services (CoSs). Class of Service (CoS) is a service the network offers to traffic streams [14, 76, 134–136].

The rest of this section is organised as follows. Section 6.4.1 describes the implemented e2e CoSs in EuQoS, explaining their roles and their QoS objectives. Section 6.4.2 explains the main assumptions that have been made for QoS mechanisms and the algorithms required for implementing e2e CoSs in the underlying technologies. It focuses on the specification of generic CAC (Connection Admission Control) algorithms that is the key-element for providing QoS guarantees at the network level. Finally, Sect. 6.4.3 gives the basic approaches for providing e2e CoSs in each underlying technologies as IP interdomain links, xDSL, LAN/Ethernet, WiFi, UMTS, MPLS and satellite.

6.4.1 End-to-end Classes of Service in EuQoS

EuQoS assumes that a user can use six e2e CoSs (e2e CoSs)that differ in their QoS objectives. A specific CoS is used for handling packets generated by a given type of application as, for example, VoIP connections. Table 6.2 shows the complete set of the CoSs as proposed for the DiffServ architecture [20, 137]. In EuQoS, a subset of these CoSs has been implemented (marked in bold in Table 6.2), as follows:

- The Telephony e2e CoS belongs to the Real Time (RT) class and is mainly dedicated to handling VoIP, emitting streaming traffic of CBR or VBR type. This CoS requires strict QoS guarantees with respect to the selected values of IPTD, IPDV and IPLR.
- The RT Interactive e2e CoS: this class belongs to the RT class and is mainly dedicated for handling VTC (Video-Tele Conferences) as well as interactive games such as NEXUIZ [138] by emitting streaming traffic of CBR or VBR type. This CoS requires strict QoS guarantees with respect to assumed values of IPTD, IPDV and IPLR. This CoS and Telephony CoS differ in packet lengths (rather small for VoIP compared to VTC) and required bandwidth (again, smaller for VoIP) while the required QoS level is similar.
- The Signalling e2e CoS belongs to the RT class and is mainly dedicated for handling application, routing and network signalling traffic. This CoS provides strict guarantees with respect to assumed values of IPTD, IPDV and IPLR. This e2e CoS can guarantee fast connection setup times. More details about dimensioning this class are in [139].
- The Multi-Media (MM) Streaming e2e CoS belongs to the NRT (Non RT) class and is dedicated for handling streaming traffic (CBR or VBR) generated by VoD (Video on Demand) applications. This e2e CoS provides strict guarantees with respect to assumed values of IPTD and IPLR, but the value of IPDV is not critical.

Table 6.2. Mapping of EuQoS applications to classes of service

Treatment aggregate	End-To-End Service Class	QoS Objectives			EuQoS Applications				Medigraf			
		IPLR	Mean IPTD	IPDV	NEX-UIZ	VoIP	VTC	VoD	VTC	Collabo-ration	Data transfer	Chat
CTRL	Network Control	10^{-3}	100 ms	50 ms								
Real Time	Telephony	10^{-3}	100/350 ms (local/long distance)	50 ms		X						
	Signalling	10^{-3}	100 ms	U								
	MM Conferencing	10^{-3}	100 ms	50 ms								
	RT Interactive	10^{-3}	100/350 ms (local/long distance)	50 ms	X		X	X				
Non-Real Time / Assured Elastic	Broadcast video	10^{-3}	100 ms	50 ms								
	MM Streaming	10^{-3}	1 s non-critical	U				X				
	Low Latency Data	10^{-3}	400 ms	U								
	OAM	10^{-3}	400 ms	U								
	High Throughput Data	10^{-3}	1 s non-critical	U							X	
Elastic	Standard	U	U	U								X
	LowPriority Data	U	U	U								

- The High Throughput Data (HTD) e2e CoS belongs to the NRT class and is dedicated for handling elastic traffic generated by TCP-controlled applications (e.g., medical applications such as Medigraf [140]). As for MM Streaming, this CoS provides strict guarantees with respect to IPTD and IPLR, while the value of IPDV is not critical.
- The Standard e2e CoS provides best effort and it means that no guarantee is provided for the IPTD, IPDV and IPLR parameters, but the network allocates a given amount of bandwidth to this CoS.

The network will recognise that an IP packet belongs to a given e2e CoS by analysing the DSCP (Differentiated Services Code Point) field in IPv4 or the Type of Service (TOS) field in IPv6. The appropriate code in the packet is assigned by the user equipment and again by the first network element that handles the packet. Table 6.3 shows the DSCP codes/names corresponding to the e2e CoS in EuQoS, as proposed in [20].

Figure 6.11 shows the concepts followed for implementing the above-specified set of CoSs, regarded as globally known by the users (and the user QoS-aware applications). A user who wants to use a given application (VoD, VoIP, etc.) activates its

Table 6.3. DSCP codes/names for e2e CoSs in EuQoS (* xx ∈ {01, 10, 11})

e2e CoS	DSCP Name	DSCP Value
Telephony	EF	101110
Signalling	CS5	101000
RT Interactive	CS4	100000
MM Streaming	AF3x	011xx0*
High Throughput Data	AF1x	001xx0*
Standard	DF	000000

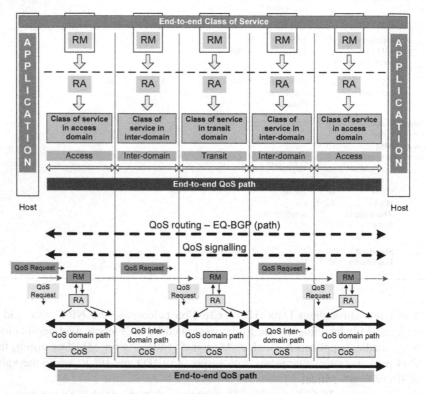

Fig. 6.11. Concept of e2e CoSs for implementation in EuQoS system

QoS and submits its QoS request to the predefined e2e CoS, according to the mapping given in Table 6.2. In EuQoS, possible paths are EQ paths, and when the path is established, the QoS request in sent to the RMs situated along this path. When an RM receives the QoS request, it communicates with its associated RA elements for checking whether the requested resources are available in the underlying network (see Sect. 6.3.2).

The simplest solution occurs when a given underlying technology supports, by itself, the same CoSs as EuQoS in terms of handled traffic profiles and QoS guarantees. For some underlying network technologies, however, there are not clearly specified CoSs that are compatible with the e2e EuQoS CoSs. So, new EuQoS-specific solutions have been investigated and implemented for providing packet transfer capabilities as requested by e2e EuQoS CoSs.

Depending on the capabilities of the network technologies, the proposed solutions are mainly based on providing an adequate Connection Admission Control (CAC) function to limit the QoS traffics, and on tuning the available QoS mechanisms (schedulers, shapers, policers, etc.) in the network elements (IP routers, access points in WiFi, LAN/Ethernet switches, etc.).

6.4.2 QoS Mechanisms and Algorithms for Specification of e2e Classes of Service

The ith ($i = 1, \ldots, 6$) e2e EuQoS CoS is designed to handle streams having a given traffic profile, i.e. to assure adequate packet transfer characteristics (maximum allowed values for $IPTD_{e2e,i}$, $IPDV_{e2e,i}$ and $IPLR_{e2e,i}$). Furthermore, the ith e2e CoS over a heterogeneous multidomain network needs a compatible $CoS_{j,i}$ for each domain j along the e2e path ($j = 1, \ldots, N$; N is the number of different domains along the path), also expressed by the above-mentioned three parameters, $IPTD_{j,i}$, $IPDV_{j,i}$ and $IPLR_{j,i}$. Due to the additive properties of IPTD, IPDV and IPLR[2], for each ith e2e CoS we have:

$$IPTD_{e2e,i} = \sum_{j=1}^{N} IPTD_{j,i},$$

$$IPDV_{e2e,i} = \sum_{j=1}^{N} IPDV_{j,i}, \qquad (6.1)$$

$$IPLR_{e2e,i} \cong \sum_{j=1}^{N} IPLR_{j,i}.$$

Note, that in (6.1) for a given e2e CoS we take into account only the parameters that are specified.

The general principles used to design CoSs mean: (1) to allocate resources for the considered class, (2) to apply QoS mechanisms (in network devices) for forcing required packet transfer characteristics, and (3) to limit the traffic submitted to these resources by an appropriate CAC.

Let us illustrate these rules by considering an e2e CoS that handles traffic streams described by a Peak Rate (PR) and requiring transfer characteristics not larger than the predefined values $IPTD_{e2e}$, $IPDV_{e2e}$ and $IPLR_{e2e}$. Let us also assume that after the provisioning process, the requirements for a given domain are the predefined maximum values of parameters IPTD, IPDV and IPLR.

---

[2] For two domains with $IPLR_1$ in domain 1 and $IPLR_2$ in domain 2, the resulting $IPLR$ is $IPLR_{1+2} = IPLR_1 + IPLR_2 - IPLR_1 \cdot IPLR_2$. In practical cases, $IPLR_{1+2}$ is around $IPLR_1 + IPLR_2$ as $IPLR_1 \cdot IPLR_2 \ll IPLR_1 + IPLR_2$. Therefore it can be considered as additive.

6.4.2.0.1 Example: Designing CoS with predefined maximum values of parameters IPTD, IPDV and IPLR. The CoS handles the traffic streams with declared PRs.

(1) *Allocation of resources*

The required resources for the CoS are usually represented by the link capacity (C) and an associated buffer (B). The CoS is designed for handling packet streams emitted by applications with similar traffic characteristics. Therefore, for the sake of simplicity, we can assume that the applications generate the packets with constant length (L). In this case, we can control IPDV by setting B and C, since

$$IPDV = \frac{LB}{C}. \tag{6.2}$$

Furthermore, the commonly known condition in the case when a number of packet streams is multiplexed on a single link is that the link utilisation should be less than 1. The condition for maximum link utilisation, say ρ_{max}, comes from constraints on IPLR or IPTD. The relations for IPLR and IPTD, derived from the analysis of the M/D/1/B [141] and M/D/1 (e.g., [142]), respectively, are

$$\rho_{IPTD} = \frac{2B}{2B - \ln(IPLR)} \tag{6.3}$$

$$\rho_{IPTD} = \frac{2(IPTD - T_{prop} - \frac{L}{C})}{2IPTD - 2T_{prop} - \frac{L}{C}}, \tag{6.4}$$

where T_{prop} represents propagation delay. Finally, we calculate ρ_{max} from

$$\rho_{max} = \min[\rho_{IPTD}, \rho_{IPTD}]. \tag{6.5}$$

The term (6.3) dominates in the most practical cases and (6.4) occurs only when the links have large propagation delays and rather low capacity C, e.g. for a case where $T_{prop} = 90$ ms, $C < 4.4$ MBps, $B = 10$ packets, $IPLR = 10^{-3}$, $L = 150$ Bytes and $IPTD = 100$ ms.

(2) *To apply available QoS mechanisms in devices for forcing required packet transfer characteristics*

The set of QoS mechanisms that are available in network devices differs depending on the underlying technology. Anyway, at least for now the reference QoS mechanisms are specified as PHB mechanisms in the DiffServ architecture. Assuring the requested packet transfer characteristics is based on the type of available schedulers. The preferred schedulers are Weighted Fair Queueing (WFQ) and Priority Queueing-Weighted Fair Queueing (PQ-WFQ), because they assure isolation between CoSs, i.e. guaranteeing isolated buffer size and a given percentage of the total link capacity. So, the traffic belonging to a given CoS is gathered in a dedicated queue.

(3) *Limiting the traffic submitted*

Limiting the traffic submitted to a given CoS can be accomplished by applying the following well-known formula for peak rate allocation [141]

$$PR_{\text{new}} + \sum_{i=1}^{K} PR_i \leq \rho_{\text{max}} C, \tag{6.6}$$

where PR_{new} is the peak rate of new connection requests while K is the number of running connections, each of PR_i ($i = 1, \ldots, K$). The CAC function is invoked during the invocation process in its setup procedure.

6.4.3 Implementation of e2e Classes of Service in Underlying Technologies

This section provides a very brief description of the technology specific CoSs, associated to e2e CoSs as specified by EuQoS. The approaches have been implemented and tested in the PAN-European testbed environment [127].

6.4.3.1 Interdomain Links

Interdomain links connect two peering ASs and have two unidirectional links, one for each direction. More precisely, the interdomain link for one direction begins at the output port at the egress Border Router (BR) in one domain and it terminates at the ingress BR of the peering domain. The Per Hop Behavior (PHB) mechanisms that are implemented in the egress BR, including schedulers such as PQ-WFQ or/and WFQ, can be used.

EuQoS defined four interdomain CoSs: (1) Signalling (S-CoS), (2) Real Time (RT CoS), (3) Non Real Time (NRT CoS), and (4) Standard (STD). Table 6.4 shows the mapping of EuQoS e2e CoSs (see Table 6.2) to the interdomain CoSs.

For interdomain, the CAC function is performed in the egress BR, at its output port. Each interdomain BR follows the DiffServ concept. This means that packets belonging to Telephony and Real Time interactive streams are treated by the router according to the same PHB as specified for the Real Time CoS, and packets belonging to Multi-Media streaming and High Throughput Data (HTD) are treated by the router according to the PHB defined for the NRT CoS. The details of the system analysis are in [143, 144].

Table 6.4. Mapping between EuQoS e2e CoSs and the interdomain CoSs

e2e Class of Service	Interdomain Class of Service
Signalling	Signalling (S-CoS)
Telephony Real Time Interactive	Real Time (RT CoS)
Multi-Media Streaming High Throughput Data (HTD)	Non-Real Time (NRT CoS)
Standard	Standard (STD CoS)

6.4.3.2 xDSL

In Digital Subscriber Lines (xDSL) networks, four possible network points are candidates to be the bottlenecks and need to be considered: the user xDSL modem (the gateway/Customer Premises Equipment CPE), the Digital Subscriber Line Access Multiplexer (DSLAM) Aggregation Module, aggregation switch(es) and IP edge node. However, in practice some simplifications can be made, depending on the specific characteristics of the network technologies and the capabilities of particular elements.

It must be clearly stated that the evolution of DSL technology results today in a range of DSL standards (ADSL, ADSL2+, SHDSL, VDSL2, etc.) with different bit rates and architecture. The major building blocks are DSLAM and the Broadband Remote Access Server (BRAS). The market demands cost-effective, differentiated multimedia services provided by DSL networks. This forces the most popular purely Asynchronous Transfer Mode (ATM) DSLAMs to be migrated to fully IP-aware appliances with Ethernet uplinks in the aggregation segment, making DSL architecture more flexible and scalable. For instance, for distributed and small groups of subscribers, IP-DSLAM may include the functionality of BRAS in one piece of equipment. Considering the access part of DSL, one may find customer equipment devices—which are very simple and limited in functionality—without QoS mechanisms, as well as fully configurable, DiffServ supporting, manageable gateways, mostly deployed for business customers.

In order to achieve CAC for any variant of DSL access network, the CAC algorithm proposed in Sect. 6.4.2 should be used for every IP-aware port with implemented QoS mechanisms. EuQoS considered the access and aggregation segments and focused on two network elements, the DSLAM (more precisely, the IP DSLAM, to implement the QoS mechanisms for IP traffic) and the IP edge node (BRAS). The proposed CAC algorithms for the above elements differ in their assumed type of CoSs provision. In the aggregation segment, we can apply a static partitioning of the link capacity between CoSs, as e.g. in the interdomain links, while for the access segment we need to focus on link capacity sharing.

6.4.3.3 LAN/Ethernet

In switched Ethernet, the basic mechanism for differentiating traffic is priority scheduling. According to IEEE 802.1Q [145] and 802.1p (part of the IEEE 802.1D [146]) standards, the MAC layer has specified eight priority levels, each for a different Ethernet CoS. The priority level of a Ethernet frame is marked in the three-bit priority field. It is important to remark that eight priority levels are not available in all devices and one can find equipment with four or even two priority levels. Table 6.5 shows the proposal for mapping the e2e CoSs into Ethernet CoSs in the case where four priority levels are available.

The implementation of e2e CoSs in LAN/Ethernet is not trivial, because the organisation of buffer management is based on a shared buffer architecture. The packets belonging to different CoSs share common buffer space. This space is for all

Table 6.5. Mapping between e2e CoSs and Ethernet CoSs

e2e Class of Service	Ethernet CoS	802.1p: values in priority field in Ethernet frame header
Signalling	Network Management	7 (highest)
Telephony, RT Interactive	Voice	6
	Video	5
MM Streaming,		
High Throughput Data	Controlled Load	4
	Excellent Effort	3
Standard	Best Effort	0
	Undefined	2
	Background	1

output ports. For providing isolation between CoSs and to control IPLR, it is proposed to explore the following additional features of an Ethernet switch:

- The ability to identify traffic flows based on information at layers 3 and 4, namely source and destination IP addresses, ports and transport protocol (for EuQoS flow identification) [147].
- The ability to perform data bit rate control on a per-flow basis [148, 149].
- The ability to perform random early packet discarding based on the queue size at the Ethernet output port (Weighted Random Early Detection (WRED) mechanism).

The CAC function is performed in two elements of the LAN/Ethernet access networks, in the Ethernet Switch (ES) output port and in the Edge Router (ER). The applied CAC algorithm follows (6.6).

6.4.3.4 WiFi

The EuQoS approach to providing e2e CoSs in WiFi technology is based on WiFi Multi-Media (WMM) extension [150] and exploits the Enhanced Distributed Coordination Access (EDCA) protocol defined in the extension. The EDCA protocol allows for differentiation of traffic using four so-called Access Categories (AC). However, the EDCA itself does not provide strict QoS guarantees as required for e2e CoSs. Then, our CoSs for WiFi use enhanced ACs with additional QoS mechanisms for: (1) provisioning of network resources dedicated for particular CoSs such as values of bandwidth, buffer size and parameters of the MAC protocol, (2) performing CAC, (3) conditioning the traffic generated by users (packets policing/shaping and marking), and (4) providing packet scheduling at the IP layer in access point (AP).

Table 6.6 shows the mapping between e2e CoSs and WiFi CoSs. The WiFi CoSs real time (RT), non-real time (NRT), signalling (SIG) and best effort (BE) are similar to the ones assumed for interdomain links (see Table 6.4).

The solution for WiFi WMM assumes that a single AP will handle traffic belonging to all WiFi CoSs (including Best-Effort traffic), and the EDCA algorithm provides traffic separation between the CoSs.

Table 6.6. Mapping between e2e CoSs and WiFi CoSs

e2e Class of Service	WiFi CoS (WMM AC)	QoS objectives[a]		
		IPTD [ms]	IPDV [ms]	IPLR
Telephony RT Interactive	Real Time (AC_VO)	5	15	10^{-4}
MM Streaming High Throughput Data	Non-Real Time (AC_VI)	10	–	10^{-4}
Signalling	Signalling (SIG)(AC_VI)	10	–	10^{-4}
Standard	Best Effort (AC_BE)	–	–	–

[a] Exemplary target values assumed in provisioning process

6.4.3.5 UMTS

For UMTS, the main recognised problem is the lack of open interfaces for controlling the specific QoS mechanisms. As a consequence, for EuQoS it has been decided to look at UMTS from two perspectives: (a) UMTS as a black box where available UMTS services are reused and (b) using an implicit, measurement-based, cell-load control approach that can be achieved by using traffic shaping for the connections with assigned low priority (non-EuQoS connections submitted to background CoS). This second approach also addresses the problem of defending the already established EuQoS connections against QoS starvation. This problem is typical of UMTS networks due to the frequent changes of radio channel conditions.

The first approach has been called Usage of built-in CAC from UMTS and the latter measurement-based Open GPRS Gateway Support Node (OpenGGSN) CAC.

6.4.3.5.1 Usage of built-in CAC from UMTS

The main goal of the proposal is to take advantage of the built-in CAC from UMTS, which enables decision-making based on cell load conditions (different among cells), and seamless resource reservation.

E2e CoSs are mapped to their corresponding UMTS traffic classes. Table 6.7 shows the proposed mapping, taking into account the desirable solution and the availability of commercial equipment.

6.4.3.5.2 Measurement-Based OpenGGSN CAC

Although currently available UMTS deployments provide CoSs with strict QoS guarantees with respect to the values of parameters IPTD and IPDV, such features cannot be fully exploited primarily due to some limitations in current operating systems of computer Terminal Equipment (TE), which are connected to UMTS by mobile phones (Mobile Terminal MT).

Table 6.7. Mapping between EuQoS and UMTS CoSs (THP—Traffic Handling Priority)

EuQoS e2e CoS	Ideal mapping to UMTS	Feasible mapping
Telephony	Conversational	Interactive (THP = 1)
Signalling	Background	Background
Real Time Interactive	Streaming	Interactive (THP = 2)
Multi-Media Streaming	Interactive (THP = 1)	Interactive (THP = 3)
High Throughput Data	Interactive (THP = 2)	Interactive (THP = 3)
Standard	Background	Background

Table 6.8. Mapping between EuQoS e2e CoSs and DiffServ MPLS CoSs

e2e Class of Service	DiffServ MPLS Class of Service
Signalling	CS5
Telephony	
Real Time Interactive	EF
Multi-Media Streaming	
High Throughput Data	AF
Standard	BE

The problem to solve is the preservation of already established sessions with a guaranteed quality in presence of dynamic changes of the radio channel. In this case, even for the admitted connections we need additional mechanisms such as continuous monitoring and prioritised treatment in order to maintain the assumed QoS level for them.

One feasible approach to prevent unexpected reconfiguration of resources is to reduce transmission rates to accommodate low-priority (non-EuQoS) users with worse radio channel characteristics. In any case, non-EuQoS users with better radio channel characteristics may maintain connections with unchanged bit rates if there are available resources. Some additional architecture components have been developed and deployed (protocol analyser with online session tracing and logging) to implement this function. To do this, the OpenGGSN basic functionality was improved by adding standards-compliant secondary Policy Decision Point (PDP) context management.

6.4.3.6 MPLS (DiffServ-TE)

The QoS enforcement in the hard model is based on a two-step approach. The first step consists of provisioning and reserving bandwidth for an EQ link, i.e. a Label Switch Path (LSP) of a given CoS. The second step consists of preventing an excessive amount of traffic to be routed through an LSP, which is accomplished by performing the usual CAC at the EQ link head-end before accepting the new session.

During the EQ link setup the bandwidth is guaranteed as follows:

- RSVP-TE reserves logical bandwidth for a given CoS. The remaining bandwidth for the CoS is automatically advertised by the TE-routing protocol.
- Each LSP of the same CoS shares the same queue, buffer and scheduler.

The PCE server compares the requirements of a tunnel against the remaining bandwidth of the CoS pool at each router as it performs the provisioning CAC. The bandwidth is maintained by the TE-routing protocol to protect the resource pool against overbooking.

On a link, four classes will have a guaranteed bandwidth allocation: Signalling, Real-Time, Non-Real-Time and Class Default.

Therefore, the QoS guarantee first provisions and reserves bandwidth for LSPs in a given CoS, and second protects the LSP against too many flows by performing usual CAC before accepting a new session.

6.4.3.7 Satellite

6.4.3.7.1 Scheme for Assuring QoS

The Satellite System provides an access network using the Digital Video Broadcasting—Satellite (DVB-S) and the Digital Video Broadcasting—Reverse Channel Satellite (DVB-RCS) standards to carry out IP-based applications over a geostationary satellite. The main concern in satellite communication is to make efficient use of the scarce and costly resources. The asymmetric nature of the satellite communication architecture involves different mechanisms to manage resource access.

Static and dynamic access techniques for satellites have been designed and integrated into the Demand Assignment Multiple Access protocol (DAMA) for the DVB-RCS standard, in order to ensure a high utilisation of the return link resources and offer QoS-oriented capacity assignment. DAMA access supports four main capacity assignment types to reach its objective:

- Continuous Rate Assignment (CRA): Static and fully guaranteed rate capacity.
- Rate Based Dynamic Capacity (RBDC): Guaranteed capacity up to the $RBDC_{max}$ ceiling rate, but this requires dynamic requests (on-demand capacity).
- Volume Based Dynamic Capacity (VBDC): The capacity is assigned when available in response to a request without any guaranty on assignment.
- Free Capacity Assignment (FCA): Automatic allocation of unused capacity, no guarantee and no requests are associated with this assignment type. Because of this automatic allocation, FCA type is not used in the EuQoS services.

Thus, the satellite lower layers are able to provide different types of service, while keeping efficient link resources utilisation.

The CAC algorithm performed by the satellite RA in EuQoS benefits from the DAMA access scheme, but also from the information provided by the Network Control Centre (NCC) concerning the agreement passed between the satellite terminal and the satellite system.

Table 6.9 summarises the mapping between RT, NRT and Standard CoSs and the DVB-RCS access classes.

Table 6.9. Mapping from EuQoS CoS to DVB-RCS access classes

DAMA Classes	EuQoS e2e Class of Service					
	Telephony	RT Interactive	Signalling	MM Streaming	High Throughput Data	Standard
CRA	X	X	X			
RBDC				X	X	
VBDC						X

6.5 EuQoS Enhanced Transport Protocol

6.5.1 Introduction

Past and new generations of transport layer protocols have been designed taking into account only a subset of the requirements of multimedia applications. These requirements are basically characterised by reliability and order constraints. Indeed, existing protocols have been designed to provide full order and full reliability (i.e., TCP and SCTP) or no order and no reliability at all (UDP and DCCP). Even if DCCP estimates network congestion by detecting packets out of order, it does not implement any mechanism to deliver packets in any particular order.

At the network layer, standard (Best-Effort) service is still the predominant network service in the Internet, but new network services are proposed, as in EuQoS. Additionally, emerging wireless, mobile or satellite technologies present different network characteristics that should be considered by transport protocol designers, which means, for instance, handling variable delay and packet loss rates induced by physical channels.

All these reasons led us to propose an EuQoS Enhanced QoS-oriented transport protocol, here noted as EQ-ETP, intended to provide optimised and differentiated e2e transport layer services for multimedia applications using the different available network layer CoSs.

Mechanisms implementing these transport layer services have to be designed such that they can respond to the various application requirements using the services provided by underlying heterogeneous networks. Moreover, an Enhanced Transport Protocol (ETP) should be designed within an extensible framework, aimed at integrating future mechanisms intended to satisfy new requirements and/or to operate under new networks.

The EuQoS Enhanced Transport Protocol is presented in detail in [127]. In the following, a brief overview of the different service compositions for the EuQoS network services is given.

6.5.2 Enhanced Transport Protocol Services for EuQoS

Enhanced Transport Protocols aim at fulfilling the multiple QoS requirements of multimedia applications over Best-Effort networks. EQ-ETP extends ETP for han-

Table 6.10. EQ-ETP service composition for the EuQoS traffic classes

	Streaming *e.g. VoD*	Non-Streaming *e.g. file transfer*
Telephony – RT Interactive	ETP [RC]	ETP [RC + EC]
MM Streaming – HTD	ETP [gTFRC]	ETP [gTFRC + EC]
Standard	ETP [TFRC + TC]	ETP [TFRC + EC]

dling multiple CoSs. As the corresponding protocols and solutions need to be deployed over different network services, they should be implemented using a dynamic architecture. A flexible and compositional architecture has been designed and implemented in ETP in order to achieve a polymorphic deployment of various internal mechanisms, suited to manage the multiple QoS requirements of applications over the various classes of services provided by EuQoS. This architecture allows QoS control and management mechanisms to be easily deployed and configured in order to efficiently work together.

The modular approach of ETP was defined in order to provide an effective way of satisfying a wide range of application requirements by adequately composing and fine-tuning different well-identified and designed transport layer building blocks (rate control, as well as shaping, congestion control, flow control etc.).

Given the nature of the EuQoS network classes of services, various possible compositions were developed for EQ-ETP in order to provide the most adequate transport layer services regarding the temporal requirements of both streaming applications and nonstreaming applications. These compositions are presented in Table 6.10 where RC is Rate Control, EC is Error Control and TFRC and guaranteed TFRC (gT-FRC) are congestion control mechanisms.

6.5.3 Services for Streaming/Nonstreaming Applications

In the following, the different EQ-ETP compositions for each of the EuQoS traffic classes are presented. Two possible combinations of these are possible, depending on the nature of the applications. Streaming applications, which transmit one or more multimedia flows, have specific requirements concerning error and time control, while nonstreaming applications (generally speaking FTP-like applications) require full reliability as their time constraints are of less importance than the ones of streaming applications.

6.5.3.1 Real-Time Classes of Service (Telephony, RT Interactive)

In case of Real-Time Classes of Service, the application respects the traffic profile it has issued a reservation request for, and reliability is guaranteed for the whole stream throughout the EuQoS system. In this context, as streaming applications are generally able to specify their bandwidth requirements accurately, the service composition is limited to a dynamic binding to the UDP protocol. Optionally, the operators might specify that a traffic shaper must be instantiated for shaping at the sending host. Thus, the load on the system routers is reduced. In this context, nonstreaming applications generally have no loss tolerance. As the application might have underestimated its resource requirements, the transport services are composed of a shaper coupled to a SACK based error control to provide full reliability.

6.5.3.2 Non-Real Time Classes of Service (MM Streaming, HTD)

In case of Non-Real Time Classes of Service, the application might exceed the traffic allowance for which it has issued a resource reservation. In such scenarios, the excess traffic competes with other flows for which it has to respect certain friendliness, in order to avoid network collapse caused by congestion. This is achieved by means of the gTFRC module [151] as described in Sect. 5.4.

In the case of a nonstreaming application, the zero loss tolerance is tackled by the addition of a SACK-based error control mechanism to ensure the correct and orderly delivery of packets.

6.5.3.3 Standard Class of Service (Best Effort)

In the Standard Class of Service, all traffic must be shaped according to a congestion-control algorithm in order to protect the network against congestion collapse. In order to improve the QoS provided to multimedia streams, a TC (Time Constraints) module will be used to offer fast retransmission mechanisms when the time dependence of the packets (VoD Scenarios) [152]. In these scenarios, as nonstreaming applications have total reliability requirements, a SACK-based error control is added to the composition. Furthermore, as time constraints are suitable for streaming applications, the TC module is not enabled for nonstreaming applications.

6.6 Multicast

If a data packet should be sent to more than one destination, the sender usually sends the same packet as many times as there are receivers interested in getting the data. Therefore, multiple point-to-point connections are established. This one-to-one communication paradigm is called unicast. In the early days of the Internet, when e-mail, FTP and remote host access were the main applications, there was no need for other paradigms. But the Internet has changed a lot since then. Particularly, the appearance of the Web changed the situation. Now, pictures, movies and audio/video streams are available over the network and their transmission uses up a significant portion of the available bandwidth. With today's technology it is possible to afford a unicast connection for everyone who wants to view a Web page. However, to send live audio and video data, which needs a huge amount of network resources compared with Web pages, it is not reasonable to have a single connection to each receiver.

The drawbacks of the unicast approach for these kinds of applications are evident. First, the source is required to hold a complete list of receivers and second, multiple identical copies of the same data flow over the same links. Instead, data to multiple destinations can be delivered using multicast [153]. Multicast allows the source to send a single copy of data, using a single address for an entire group of receivers. Routers between the source and receivers use the group address to route the data. The routers forward and duplicate data packets wherever a path to receivers diverges.

IP knows three basic addressing modes. A unicast packet is sent to one receiver, a broadcast packet is sent to all hosts of a subnet and a multicast packet is directed to a group of receivers. Unicast and broadcast can be seen as multicast communication with the group of receivers containing one or all hosts, respectively. A fourth mode is called anycast. This is a routing scheme that delivers the packet to the "nearest" (considering an appropriate metric) host out of a group of receivers.

The only difference between unicast and multicast addressing from the IP layer's point of view is the usage of special IP multicast addresses [154]. Unlike the unicast addresses, a multicast address is not assigned to a single host or network interface. The 32-bit address space of IPv4 (IP version 4) has been divided into five address classes A, B, C, D and E. The most significant bits of an address define its class. The multicast address class is sometimes referred to as class D. Unlike the address classes A, B and C the multicast address has no further structure. In case of the new IP version 6 (IPv6), all multicast addresses begin with the format prefix FF_{16} [155].

The Internet group management protocol (IGMP) [156] allows the hosts in the Internet to join and leave multicast groups. In order to reduce the amount of data sent over the network links, IGMP manages dynamic groups of multicast receivers. The group management is done by the routers. Therefore, every router remembers the hosts connected to its local interface(s), which are interested in receiving multicast data and the respective multicast group IDs. IGMP provides the functionality for hosts to tell the routers in which multicast groups they are interested. Now routers can exchange the information about the multicast packets they have to receive among themselves.

Another important group of multicast protocols is the group of routing protocols. These protocols allow the routers to exchange information about multicast groups and thus to build routes for each group. Examples for multicast routing protocols are protocol-independent multicast (PIM) [157, 158], distance-vector multicast routing protocol (DVMRP) [159] and multicast open shortest path first (MOSPF) [160].

IP-layer multicast has not been widely adopted by most commercial ISPs, and thus large parts of the Internet are still incapable of IP multicast more than a decade after the protocols were developed. As a result, the Multicast backbone (MBONE) was developed [161]. It consists of "islands" of multicast-enabled networks on the Internet, connected through different types of tunnels. This concept has some drawbacks, like the manual tunnel setup and the need for constant IP addresses. This is not feasible for the average Internet user. However, with the increasing acceptance of the Internet Protocol Television (IPTV) some providers have started to use multicast for the transport of live video streams, at least internally. It remains to be seen whether the support of IP multicast will be increased due to such new technologies.

6.6.1 Application Layer Multicast

Application layer multicast (ALM) is independent from the multicast support of the underlying network. The multicast forwarding functionality is implemented exclusively at end systems. Logically, the end systems form an overlay network, and the goal of application layer multicast is to construct and maintain an efficient overlay for data transmission. Since application layer multicast protocols cannot completely avoid the redundant transmission of data packets over the same link, they are less efficient than IP multicast. The advantages are that ALM systems do not require any modification of the underlying network components (e.g. routers) and can be implemented on the application layer without any special operating system support.

Figures 6.12 and 6.13 show the differences of the data flow in IP multicast and application layer multicast networks. The solid black lines identify the physical network connecting hosts and routers, while the dashed lines denote the data packet flow.

The IP routers in Fig. 6.12 forward the multicast packets from the sender to the receivers and duplicate the data if needed. The routers must therefore support the IP multicast protocol. In Fig. 6.13, the peer-to-peer (P2P) overlay connections are identified by a dotted and dashed line. In this environment no specialised routers are necessary. The packets are sent in unicast mode. The virtual data flow follows the overlay network structure, which does not necessarily correspond with the underlying physical connections. However, the data are only replicated in the end systems, which are interconnected using unicast (P2P) links. Therefore, some packets are sent over the same link more than once. The efficiency of the ALM heavily depends on the overlay network construction and routing. With an optimal overlay topology, application layer multicast can approximate the efficiency of IP multicast.

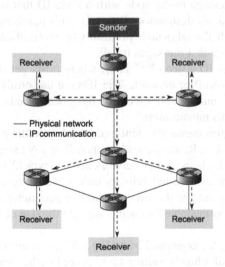

Fig. 6.12. IP multicast. The traffic is duplicated by the routers as needed

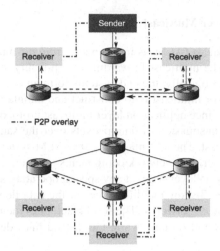

Fig. 6.13. Application layer multicast. Redundant data transmission cannot completely be avoided

6.6.2 Application Layer Multicast in the EuQoS System

Different ALM systems like Borg [162], VRing [163], Bayeux [164] or SplitStream [165] have been published over the past years. For the ALM support in the EuQoS system the combination Scribe/Pastry is used.

Pastry [166] is a scalable distributed object location and routing substrate for wide-area Peer-to-Peer applications. Nodes get an ID assigned when they join the Peer-to-Peer network. When a message needs to be sent to a certain ID, Pastry efficiently routes the message to the node with a node ID that is numerically closest to the ID of the message's destination. Pastry is self-organising, scalable and completely decentralised. It also takes node proximity (in terms of e2e delay) into account to minimise the distance that messages travel.

Pastry uses a large ID space (2^{128} IDs), where hosts get random IDs assigned when joining the Peer-to-Peer network. The IDs are uniformly distributed over the whole ID space. This random assignment of IDs does not take locality nor Quality of Service requirements into account.

Pastry reliably routes messages identified by a key to the peer with the numerically closest ID to the key. Routing uses less than $\lceil \log_{2^b} N \rceil$ steps on average, where N is the amount of nodes in the pastry network and b is typically a parameter with the value 4. Pastry guarantees eventual delivery unless $l/2$ or more nodes with an adjacent ID fail at the same time, with l, an even number parameter, being typically equal to 16. Pastry holds a routing table for each node with the size of $(2^b - 1)\lceil \log_{2^b} N \rceil + l$ entries.

The routing tables are organised into $\lceil \log_{2^b} N \rceil$ rows with each $2^b - 1$ entries. The entries of row n of a host's routing table point to other nodes, which share the same first n digits of their ID with the host itself, but the digit at position $n + 1$ has one of the $2^b - 1$ possible values different from the digit at position $n + 1$ of the host's

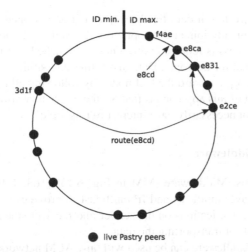

Fig. 6.14. Routing a message from peer *3d1f* to peer *e8cd*

ID. Each entry in the routing table consists of the node's ID and its corresponding IP address. Additionally, each node maintains a list of nodes (IDs and IP addresses) of the numerically closest hosts in its leaf set ($l/2$ entries for the larger and $l/2$ entries for the lower IDs). A message is routed to the closest (in terms of network latency) host found in the host's routing table whose ID matches the message's key prefix.

Figure 6.14 shows a simplified example of how Pastry routing works. A message with the key *e8cd* is routed from a peer with ID *3d1f* to the peer *e8ca*, which is numerically closest to the message key. On each hop from the source peer to the destination peer the message is sent to a peer whose ID matches more digits of the message key prefix than it matched at the hop before. For the first routing hop starting from peer *3d1f* the message is sent to peer *e2ce*, which shares the first digit *e* of the message key. At the second hop, the message is routed to the peer with ID *e831*, which shares the first two digits *e8*. Finally, it is sent to peer *e8ca*, which is the peer closest to the message key and shares the first three digits *e8c* with the key.

Scribe [167] builds on top of Pastry and is a large-scale decentralised Application Level Multicast infrastructure that supports a large number of groups and a potentially large number of members for each group. Scribe balances the load on nodes to achieve short delays and less link stress.

Any Scribe node can join any multicast group (or topic in Scribe terminology) at any time. For each topic, one node is designated to disseminate the topic data in the Pastry network. The node that is the root of the topic distribution tree has the ID numerically closest to the topic ID. Scribe offers best-effort delivery of the multicast data without guaranteeing that the order of the packets is maintained. The multicast or topic tree is built using a scheme similar to reverse-path-forwarding. A Scribe node, subscribing to a certain topic, sends a join message for this topic ID. This message is routed, using Pastry's routing mechanism, toward the topic's root. The next node, to which the join message is routed, remembers that the node sending the join message is interested in data for this topic. If this intermediate node, called a forwarder, has not already joined this topic, it will itself send a join message to the same topic. This process is repeated until a node is reached that has already joined the topic or is the root for the topic. Data dissemination within a topic is done from the root node of the topic toward the leaf nodes by following all reverse paths to the leaves. A side effect of this approach is that Scribe nodes forwarding messages for a certain topic may not necessarily have interest in this topic.

6.6.3 Multicast Middleware

The EuQoS Multicast Middleware (MM in Fig. 6.15) [168, 169] is a solution to bridge application layer multicast and IP multicast. It provides a standard IP multicast interface for the applications on the sender and receiver side and uses Application Layer Multicast for transporting the data.

The Multicast Middleware can be used with any ALM network, which offers the standard multicast operations (subscription to a multicast group, receiving and sending multicast data). The typical P2P ALM network tries to approximate the efficiency of IP multicast communication regarding link stress by using unicast communication. As discussed earlier, ALM is not able to totally avoid sending redundant data over the same physical link as IP multicast can.

The overlay network is usually built in a topology-aware manner. Therefore, peers that are "close" to each other in terms of communication latency are directly connected. The P2P links are constantly monitored, which allows reaction to failures in network communication or to failures of neighbour peers.

Eliminating the requirement for multicast support by the underlying network makes the use of Application Layer Multicast feasible for any kind of Internet users. The disadvantage of the ALM is the lack of standardisation. Each implementation has its own API and addressing scheme. This prohibits already existing multicast-aware applications from using the ALM.

The IP multicast interface for the applications is usually offered by the operating system. The operating system on the other side communicates with a multicast enabled router in the local network using IGMP as signalling protocol. Sending IP multicast traffic is not different from sending IP unicast traffic. The only difference is the reserved address range, which denotes different multicast groups (groups of multicast traffic receivers). On the link layer, multicast traffic is handled differently. For example, in Ethernet the IP packets with a multicast group as a destination address get an Ethernet multicast address assigned.

To provide an IP multicast interface for the whole system (including services integrated in the operating system's kernel), the Multicast Middleware uses a virtual Ethernet device (also known as TAP device—a software analogy of a wire tap). The TAP interface is a special kind of network interface, which is seen by the operating system as a normal Ethernet device. However, instead of forwarding the Ethernet frames to a hardware device, the TAP interface forwards the received Ethernet frames to a user-space process. On the other side, the TAP interface forwards all

Ethernet frames received from the user-space process as incoming frames to the operating system's kernel. TAP support exists for all major operating systems such as UNIX/Linux, MacOS X and WIN32.

Using a TAP interface and the Multicast Middleware makes processing of multicast traffic transparent to all applications. This includes the multicast functionality integrated in the operating system's kernel. This approach also does not require any modification of application code. Any IP multicast application can be supported transparently. Multicast traffic originating from an end system can be routed through the TAP device. This device forwards the packets (encapsulated in Ethernet frames) to a user-space process (the Multicast Middleware) for processing. The Multicast Middleware acts as a multicast router by implementing IGMP and transporting the multicast data.

IP multicast-enabled applications must subscribe to different multicast groups to receive video broadcast announcements and audio/video streams. The multicast group subscription is usually a system call, which instructs the operating system's kernel to send IGMP membership report messages to the IP multicast router. In our case, the IGMP membership reports are sent via the TAP interface to the Multicast Middleware. The Multicast Middleware interprets the IGMP membership reports and notifies the neighbour peers about the changes in the multicast routing table. This information (depending on the multicast routing protocol used in the overlay network) is propagated to other peers.

After a data packet has been sent by the application, it is forwarded by the operating system's kernel to the appropriate multicast-enabled network device (in this case the TAP device). The Multicast Middleware process receives the outgoing multicast traffic via the TAP device. The received multicast traffic is then encapsulated into application layer multicast messages. The IP multicast destination address of the packets is translated into ALM addresses to which the messages are sent. Figure 6.15 shows the message flow for sending and receiving data with the Multicast Middleware. The application (APP) is running on both end-systems for sending/receiving the data stream. It uses the IP multicast interface of the Multicast Middleware that hides the ALM layer.

After receiving an encapsulated IP multicast packet by ALM, the Multicast Middleware encapsulates the IP multicast packet into an Ethernet frame. The Multicast Middleware then sends the Ethernet frame via the TAP interface to the operating system's kernel for processing. The operating system's kernel delivers the data to the application.

For the multicast data transport, any ALM protocol may be used. However, the mapping of the IP multicast address space to the application layer address scheme might differ from one protocol to another.

Every IP multicast packet has a destination address out of the IP multicast address range. Most application layer multicast protocols implement their own addressing scheme. Depending on the protocol's addressing scheme this address range can be smaller, equal or larger than the IP multicast address range. In case of a larger or equal address range, multicast addresses can be mapped one-to-one to the application layer multicast addresses. For example, the IP multicast address range can be

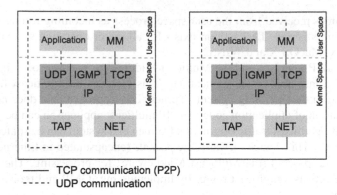

——— TCP communication (P2P)
- - - - UDP communication

Fig. 6.15. Sending and receiving data using the Multicast Middleware (MM)

mapped to a consecutive address range of the same size in the application layer multicast protocol's addressing scheme. In the case where the address range of the application layer multicast is smaller than the IP multicast address range, the IP multicast addresses must be projected to the application layer multicast address range.

IP packets can be encapsulated in Application Layer Multicast messages. If the length of an Application Layer Multicast message is larger than the IP packet length, the standard IP packet fragmentation can be applied to the packet in order to transport the packet through the overlay network. On reception of fragmented IP packets, the Multicast Middleware should be able to reassemble them and to deliver them to the TAP interface. The time to live (TTL) field of the transported packets should be reduced for each P2P hop. Packets with TTL=0 should not be forwarded.

6.6.4 Introducing QoS to Multicast Middleware

To satisfy the QoS requirements, the Multicast Middleware uses the EuQoS system to set up network-level QoS for the unicast links of the overlay network. Since the QoS requirements of the end systems within one IP multicast group can be heterogeneous, it is necessary that the multicast tree is built in such way that the QoS requirements and capabilities of end-systems are considered.

It is required that the QoS classes can be ordered and that they are independent of the path length. Such QoS classes can contain parameters such as bandwidth, jitter and maximum packet loss, but all the possible QoS classes must be comparable. Also note that in general there is no total order for a combination of such parameters and that the QoS parameter for maximum delay is not yet supported in the EuQoS system.

To provide QoS guarantees such as bandwidth or jitter in a multicast tree each e2e path from the root to a leaf node in the multicast tree must have a monotonically decreasing QoS requirement. Figure 6.16 shows an example of such a multicast tree. The path indicated as well as all other e2e paths of this multicast tree hold the following property: the QoS requirements (denoted by the thickness of the lines) are

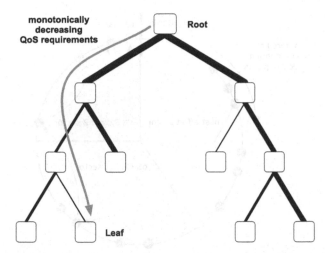

Fig. 6.16. Example of a multicast tree with monotonically decreasing QoS requirements from root to leaf nodes. Thickness of the lines represents the degree of the QoS requirement in terms of required bandwidth (thicker line = higher bandwidth requirement)

the same or decreasing when following the intermediate hops from the root node to a leaf node.

By analysing Scribe's multicast tree construction, it becomes clear that the constructed multicast tree does not necessarily hold this property. The reason for this is that the e2e path from a leaf to the root is more or less randomly chosen, due to random positioning of Pastry peers. Because Pastry's default ID assignment does not take QoS requirements of peers into account, the multicast trees constructed by Scribe are only by chance holding the described property. It is sufficient that only one link in an e2e path does not support this property to violate the QoS requirements for all nodes in the multicast tree below this link.

To enforce the construction of a QoS aware multicast tree using Scribe a dedicated Pastry P2P network is created for each multicast group. The reason for this is to have only peers interested in receiving the multicast data as potential forwarders. As a result, in this Pastry network only one topic exists. This topic ID is the highest possible topic ID. Since the QoS requirements of a peer can be higher than its QoS capabilities, the QoS class is chosen, which corresponds to the minimum of both.

As shown in Fig. 6.17, the ID space is partitioned into segments, one segment for each QoS class. Here, Best-Effort service is also considered to be a QoS class. The order of segments depends on the order of the QoS classes. The Best-Effort QoS class is located in the lowest segment and the highest QoS class is located in the highest segment. The assignment of IDs to joining peers depends on their QoS requirements/capabilities. The peer ID is randomly chosen within the corresponding segment of the ID space for the peer's QoS requirements/capabilities.

There are different possibilities for how large the segments should be. They do not necessarily have to be all of the same size and can, for example, decrease in size

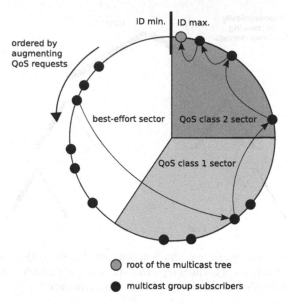

ordered by
augmenting
QoS requests

ID min.   ID max.

best-effort sector   QoS class 2 sector

QoS class 1 sector

root of the multicast tree

multicast group subscribers

Fig. 6.17. QoS aware distribution of peer IDs for Pastry

toward the root ID. The partitioning strategy has an impact on the construction of the multicast trees and therefore on how well and evenly balanced the overall traffic load will be distributed among the participating peers.

The routing path from a peer with a lower ID to a peer with a higher ID always contains peers with increasing IDs. Because the root node of the multicast tree has the highest possible Pastry ID, the routing should always use peers with increasing Pastry IDs for the hops on its path from leaf nodes toward the root node.

By assigning peer IDs proportional to the peer's QoS requirements, a construction of Scribe multicast trees, holding the decreasing QoS requirement property for each e2e path from the root to the leaves is ensured. For each node on the path from the root node to a leave node, the QoS requirement of the intermediate node is the same or lower than the one of its parent node.

6.7 Telemedicine Application

6.7.1 Telemedicine—the Case for Application-Driven QoS

The concept of utility, as a measure of the perceived value or benefit provided by QoS, is crucial to characterise the dependence of applications from QoS. For example, the utility of a standard mobile phone call is, up to a certain limit, relatively immune to QoS level variations—as long as end users are able to communicate in reasonable conditions. A certain level of QoS degradation is usually acceptable. Telemedicine applications are at the other end of the spectrum—near-perfect conditions are required by several application components (namely, real-time medical video), and there is minimal tolerance for fluctuations of quality as a result of network load. The widespread deployment of such applications over public IP networks is often hindered by the limited capability of service providers to guarantee the strict fulfilment of those requirements.

Given this wide range of application characteristics and requirements, a challenge for service providers is how to handle such diversity both satisfactorily and efficiently. In theory, QoS could be handled by providing the most demanding QoS level to all customers and applications at all times. Obviously, however, this would be economically unfeasible. Another solution could be the static allocation of specific QoS profiles to selected customers, thus ensuring that the required QoS treatment would be provided by the network to those customers in all circumstances. In either case, flexibility and cost effectiveness would be quite poor. The dynamic application-driven approach proposed by EuQoS described in the following provides a solution to this problem.

6.7.2 Overview of Medigraf

Medigraf is a real-time H.323-based telemedicine application including videoconference, collaborative facilities and an embedded multimedia repository to store patient data, medical images and reports. A typical Medigraf screenshot is shown in Fig. 6.18.

The application is used in several scenarios: performing remote cooperative diagnosis on a regular basis, providing remote specialised healthcare assistance, and enabling collaboration between healthcare professionals in several scenarios, such as emergency situations and remote online training. The application offers significant gains in terms of efficiency and cost minimisation, and is a valuable tool to provide specialised health care to populations in rural and sparsely populated areas, where the permanent availability of medical specialists is economically unfeasible.

The utility of the Medigraf application depends on the strict fulfillment of QoS parameters. In fact, proper medical diagnosis is not compatible with less than optimal QoS conditions. On the one hand, video quality is crucial to enable a correct medical diagnosis. On the other hand, e2e synchronisation of the application graphical elements requires stringent delay and jitter parameters.

Five basic traffic types are supported by Medigraf:

- Audio: used for audio communication. G.711 (PCMA, PCMU), G.728, G.722 and G.723 codecs are supported.
- Video: used for face-to-face communication and transfer of moving images acquired from specialised medical equipment (e.g. echocardiography). H.261, H.263 codecs are supported with CIF (352×288), QCIF (176×144) or SQCIF (128×96) resolution.
- Data: used for file transfer, typically medical images.
- Synchronisation: used for e2e synchronisation of graphical elements, e.g. pointers; requires strict compliance of e2e delay and jitter.
- Application control: only minimal values of loss and delay are tolerated.

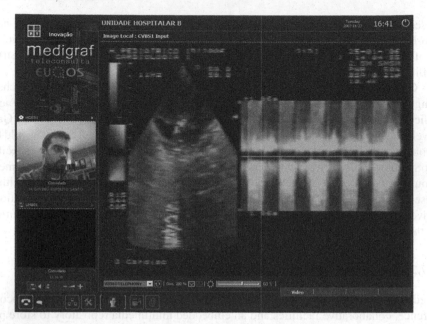

Fig. 6.18. Typical Medigraf screenshot

The difficulty of guaranteeing appropriate QoS conditions has been one of the issues affecting the deployment of Medigraf. In some cases, static prereservation of network resources in specific time slots has been the solution. Unfortunately, this approach is not scalable and, in many circumstances, not realistic. Most importantly, it is probably not viable in unplanned or emergency situations, which coincidentally constitute one of the scenarios in which Medigraf would be most valuable. Clearly, a solution capable of providing e2e guarantees on a dynamic "on-demand" basis would be an important added value to the application.

6.7.3 Medigraf Adaptation to EuQoS

One of the innovative aspects of the EuQoS solution for e2e QoS is the awareness and active participation of the application in the QoS control process. We call an application EuQoS-aware if it is capable of explicitly requesting network resources and actively participating in the QoS negotiation process by means of explicit signalling. This "EuQoS-awareness" requires the adaptation of the application or terminal to incorporate signalling capabilities, in order to interwork with the EuQoS system. Two basic scenarios can be considered to integrate applications in the EuQoS system, as illustrated in Fig. 6.19:

1. Adapted legacy application: this refers to an application that was enhanced with a software add-on named APP (see Fig. 6.19) to interwork with QCM. The approach followed in the case of Medigraf falls into this category, as described in the following.

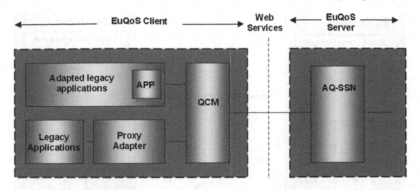

Fig. 6.19. Strategies for adaptation of applications

2. Proxy adapter: the strategy in this case is to leave the application untouched and use an external proxy adapter.

As explained in Sect. 6.2.2, QCM plays a pivotal role in the EuQoS architecture, as it provides a common standard interface between applications and the EuQoS system. Through QCM, applications are able to manage QoS-enabled sessions and handle session events coming from the EuQoS system.

A EuQoS-aware version of Medigraf has been used to demonstrate and validate the basic EuQoS concept of application-driven e2e QoS. The EuQoS application-driven approach provides Medigraf with the capability of requesting and controlling the network resources it needs on a dynamic basis. This provides a promising solution to enable the widespread use of medical applications over public IP network infrastructures.

The approach followed for adapting Medigraf is illustrated in Fig. 6.20. The original Medigraf application ("legacy" Medigraf) was extended with a set of functions provided by the APP module, to enable interworking with the EuQoS system through QCM.

APP incorporates the EuQoS awareness into the application and allows the communication with QCM; therefore, with the rest of the EuQoS system. This module was integrated into the application to enable the invocation of the QCM methods "performReservation" and "closeReservation".

Because Medigraf is natively based on H.323 signalling, a major design issue was how to deal with the coexistence of the legacy Medigraf H.323 signalling plane and the EuQoS signalling plane. To minimise the adaptation effort, it was decided to keep the H.323 plane untouched, moving the negotiation of QoS parameters to the EuQoS control plane and making sure that the result of the H.323 session setup (namely, codec characteristics, TCP/UDP port numbers) is consistent with the EuQoS control plane negotiation. The APP module must guarantee consistency and synchronisation between the two signalling planes, enforcing appropriate codec selection by means of hardware-specific functions, following the process illustrated in Fig. 6.21.

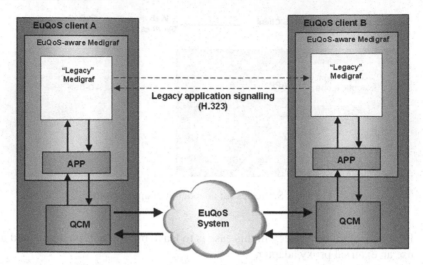

Fig. 6.20. Medigraf adaptation

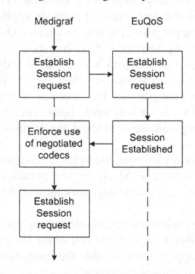

Fig. 6.21. Medigraf–EuQoS synchronisation

6.8 Conclusions

This chapter presented the global architecture developed in the EuQoS project for providing e2e QoS guarantees to Internet users. It addressed the problems of finding and providing e2e QoS paths between users connected through heterogeneous access network technologies.

A first prototype was designed and implemented on a real testbed composed of GÉANT and the NRENs in different countries, and using different access network technologies, in particular WiFi, LAN, xDSL, UMTS, satellite and MPLS.

The prototype implements all approaches and addresses all key problems, such as application negotiation, application QoS-on-demand capability, QoS- and technology-independent signalling, admission control, network provisioning, resource management and layered integration of coherent protocols. All this is provided using network technology independent and dependent solutions.

The evaluation revealed that the global architecture is quite general and is able to integrate both a large set of technologies and a large set of independent ways of providing QoS. The network technology independent virtual layer proved to be quite efficient in terms of designing, handling and abstracting all real technologies and all dependent technology choices.

Efficiency and scalability were proven, both in the access networks and in the core networks. This was especially so in the admission control function, solved in the latter case by defining and using MPLS-based tunnels using PCE.

Deduced from the framework architecture adaptability and the results obtained, it follows that the EuQoS system is sufficiently generic and is able to integrate a large set of solutions guaranteeing QoS in a unique e2e EuQoS architecture.

7

Summary and Outlook

Torsten Braun and Thomas Staub

The need for Quality-of-Service Support in the Internet is steadily increasing with the ever-growing number of commercial services transported via the Internet, such as Voice over IP, IP Television, etc. Clearly, users paying for those services do not tolerate bad quality. Initially, the Internet was not designed to support or even guarantee Quality-of-Service (QoS) in terms of throughput, delay, delay variation, packet loss, etc. There are two approaches to solve this problem. The first one is to either enhance existing and/or add new functions to the Internet protocol architecture. The second is to completely redesign the Internet protocol architecture in order to meet current and future requirements. EuQoS took the first approach by developing, implementing, integrating and testing a large set of mechanisms, protocols and software that extend the current Internet protocol architecture.

The goal of EuQoS was to combine existing and new components into a comprehensive system to guarantee end-to-end QoS, i.e., along the complete path between communicating end users, covering wired/wireless access networks, as well as backbone networks. The main components and its basics were introduced and described in this book. EuQoS started from the Differentiated Services architecture (introduced in the first chapter) that aims to provide service differentiation mechanisms in large-scale networks. A measurement and monitoring system was developed for EuQoS, which is based on recent standardisation activities described in Chap. 2. Data available from the measurement and monitoring system can be used by the resource management components of the EuQoS system. Another important component of EuQoS is traffic engineering and resource optimisation, which makes use of Multi-Protocol Label Switching (MPLS) introduced in Chap. 3. An end-to-end QoS solution requires that end systems and network devices exchange control and management information for proper configuration of network devices. This requires a set of signalling protocols on both application and network levels, such as the Session Initiation Protocol (SIP), and the Next Steps In Signalling (NSIS) protocol. For network device configuration and policy data exchange, the Common Open Policy Service (COPS) can be used. These signalling protocols, described in Chap. 4, serve different purposes and are all used by the EuQoS protocol architecture. Chapter 5 presents advances on transport layer protocols, in particular extensions of TCP, as well as advanced mechanisms for congestion and error controls. EuQoS has taken up existing proposed extensions and protocols for the Internet and developed additional new mechanisms. The existing and new mechanisms and protocols were integrated into a common architecture. In order to support end-to-end Quality-of-Service classes over heterogeneous access networks, sophisticated mechanisms were developed for a variety of access networks, such as Wireless LAN, Ethernet, DSL, UMTS, satellite networks and MPLS. Moreover, a solution to support QoS for multicast communications was developed and several applications were adapted to the EuQoS system.

EuQoS—a 6th Framework Programme (FP6) funded project—addressed the lack of QoS support in the current Internet by implementing the first approach mentioned at the beginning of this chapter. In order to achieve this, a relatively short-term solution was developed and implemented within a few years. The second approach, which is being pursued in recent activities that investigate the requirements of the future Internet, requires a rather long-term development. The most important programs fostering this approach are the FIND (Future Internet Network Design)/GENI (Global Environment for Network Innovations) programs in the U.S., and the Challenge 1 "Pervasive and Trusted Network and Service Infrastructures" within the EU FP7 ICT (Information and Communication Technologies) research program. While concrete results for these activities should become widely visible in the global Internet in about 10–20 years, the developed results from EuQoS can be implemented and introduced in the coming years.

A strong focus of EuQoS was the implementation, integration and testing of all the selected and newly developed components. A common pan-European testbed was established to deploy and test the EuQoS system. The project successfully demonstrated that the proposed system can be implemented and deliver QoS to a variety of multimedia applications. The project also contributed to standardisation activities, in particular the IETF and forums on next generation network architectures. Moreover, teaching material on QoS technologies was developed and is being used in e-learning courses maintained by several universities beyond the termination of EuQoS. This book complements this material.

Appendix A:
Implementing Protocols on Network Simulators

Thomas Staub, Jana Krähenbühl, and Torsten Braun

Summary. This chapter presents an overview of network simulation concepts, highlighting the importance of simulation as a technique for the evaluation of QoS mechanisms. Different network simulation types are explained and classified, and their possibilities and limitations are discussed. Furthermore, various representative network simulators are briefly described. The reader is also introduced to the widely used discrete and event-driven network simulator ns-2 through an explanation of its concepts, structure and message flow. Finally, a setup of a simple simulation and the implementation of a routing protocol for wired networks is shown step-by-step.

A.1 Main Simulation Terms and Concepts

Computer simulation describes the process of designing a model of an existing or theoretical system by executing the model on a computer system and analysing its output. Its advantages are manifold. In engineering, use of computer simulations in the design phase of a real system offers direct feedback for design decisions, without building a costly prototype. The engineer can evaluate different parameters by repeating the simulation several times, and he or she can change and evaluate parts of the model rapidly (i.e., fast prototyping). The gained experience about the model behaviour helps to deploy new technologies and improve existing ones. Simulation further supports the researcher in studying complex systems by offering different levels of abstraction. The whole system may be too complex, but at a higher abstraction level the processes can be analysed and understood. In the following, more details can be investigated using a top-down approach. Another advantage of simulation in research is the reproducibility of the testing results that cannot be guaranteed in real-world experiments, since too many unknown parameters influence the results. Moreover, simulation offers cost-efficient means for demonstration and training.

Simulations are commonly used in various research fields such as economics, social science, engineering and computer science, in areas ranging from flight simulators to earthquake analysis and weather forecasting.

A.1.1 Simulation Process

The simulation process is divided into three steps:

- Modelling
- Verification and Validation
- Experimentation and Analysis

Modelling starts with the definition of the problem. The objectives of the simulation and the tasks to be solved are set. The engineer identifies the system components to be modelled and the performance measures to be used. The model is formalised by creating, e.g., a flow chart of the model's behaviour. This formalisation is then translated into a simulation program.

Verification guarantees that the simulation behaves as expected by means of debugging and analysis. Validation ensures that there are no significant differences between the behaviour of the simulation model and the real system. Simulation models are often approximations or abstractions from reality. Validation is the method to show that these approximations or abstractions are justified. Before validating the required simulation, it is necessary to point out the basic situation: small-model simulations can be compared with real-world experimentation, while large models simulate well-known phenomena. During experimentation alternate models are developed, the simulation is executed with different parameter sets and different models. The results of different simulation runs are then statistically analysed.

A.1.2 Simulation Types

Computer simulations are divided into two main categories: discrete and continuous simulations [170] (see Fig. A.1). In continuous simulations the quantities are represented by continuous variables, whereas in discrete simulation systems quantities of interest are represented by discrete-valued variables.

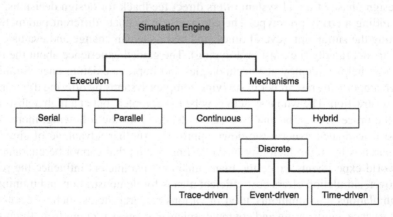

Fig. A.1. Types of simulation [170]

The dynamics of a discrete simulation can be considered as a sequence of events at discrete time points. As a third type of simulation, the Monte Carlo simulation is related to discrete-event simulation, which is commonly used to model stochastic systems. "Monte Carlo methods are a widely used class of computational algorithms for simulating the behaviour of various physical and mathematical systems, and for other computations", [171]. Monte Carlo simulators usually make use of random numbers to model nondeterministic parts in order to simulate the system. They calculate their results by repeating a random sampling a high number of times. The law of large numbers is often used as the justification for the correctness of the results.

Continuous simulations are implemented as a set of differential equations. The simulation program solves all the equations periodically by numerical evaluation.

For large-scale simulations, hybrid approaches have emerged as viable solutions, where important parts are implemented as discrete simulations and other less important parts as continuous simulations. Hybrid simulation strategies save significant amounts of computing resources compared to discrete simulations [172].

The different simulation types can be executed either in parallel or serially. The parallel execution of simulations provides shorter execution times, but increases the complexity of the implementation of the simulation model, as well as its verification.

A.2 Network Simulation

The rapid changes and growth of computer networks have spurred a lot of development in protocols and algorithms. New requirements in security, mobile networking, policy management and QoS support issues have become necessary. The main strength of simulations lies in the ability to imitate complex, real-world problems and to analyse the behaviour of a complex system.

The simulation of a general computer network is a challenging task and not easy to handle. The main problem is the fact that a computer network is composed of many nodes such as routers, switches and hosts, making the modelling part of the simulation process a nontrivial task. There are certain decisions to make at the beginning of the simulation process:

1. What are the facts that the simulation should show or prove?
2. Which are the important parts that should be investigated?
3. Which simulator provides the best possibilities to model the system?
4. Is the simulation accurate enough in order to use the results for research?

There are a lot of different methods to simulate computer networks, such as the parallel/distributed and the serial execution of simulation, or the tracking method of packets in fluid, packet and hybrid simulation models.

A.2.1 Parallel/Distributed versus Serial Execution of Simulations

Parallel or distributed simulation refers to the execution of simulation programs on multiprocessor systems or networks of workstations. The primary goal of parallel/distributed simulations is to obtain higher performance. The following further goals can be achieved through parallel/distributed simulations:

- Reduced execution time: By subdividing a large simulation into small simulation parts, the execution time can reduced by a factor equal to the number of processors.
- Fault tolerance, reliability: Multiple processors are used as backup systems.

There are different kinds of parallel/distributed simulations. We distinguish between replicated trials, parallel simulations and distributed simulations. In the replicated trials case, several independent simulations run concurrently on different processors. The processors can be in one computer or distributed over several machines. As a simulation is usually executed with several random sets, this is a very common case. In parallel simulations, a single simulation runs on multiple processors. The processors are tightly coupled, e.g., in a multiprocessor machine. For distributed simulations, a single simulation runs on a collection of distributed processors. The processors are loosely coupled, e.g., in a computation cluster.

A.2.2 Packet-Level, Fluid-Based and Hybrid Model Simulation

Discrete-event or packet-level simulations are used extensively for protocol design and evaluation. They represent a system by a collection of states and a set of events that describe state changes. The simulator has information about each packet generated and is aware of the path that the packet has to cover. Each packet is tracked individually on each link, in each queue and at each data source and sink. Packet losses are computed deterministically.

In the fluid model approach, network traffic is modelled as flows, which behaves like a fluid flowing through pipes. There are no discrete packet instances. A fluid simulator keeps track of the fluid rate changes at traffic sources and network queues. The flows are characterised by a set of mathematical models (often differential equations). Since a large number of packets are abstracted as one single flow, the computational overhead is expected to be reduced compared to the more detailed packet-level simulation. Due to the higher abstraction level, fluid models are less accurate, but far more efficient than packet-level models and therefore enable the simulation of larger topologies not otherwise possible. The fluid approach is often used to show bottlenecks in large networks. A known problem in fluid models is the ripple effect. It describes the situation where the propagation of rate changes leads to rate changes in other flows, which then need to be propagated [173] limiting scalability [174]. The arrival of new flows at the node cause a change in the departure rate of other flows from this node. This is propagated and amplified throughout the whole network. Advantages and disadvantages of packet-level and fluid-based simulations are shown in Table A.1.

Hybrid models try to combine the advantages of the both models, the packet and the fluid model. A hybrid model has better computational efficiency than the packet-level model, but is more accurate than the fluid-based model. Parts of the scenario

Table A.1. Comparison of packet- and fluid-based simulation models

Simulation Model	Advantage and Disadvantages
Packet-Based	+ finite changes of state
	+ trivial mathematical models
	+ exact analysis for event
	+ exact modelling of circumstances
	− limitation of size of the simulation
	− high memory and processor consumption
Fluid-Based	+ computational efficiency
	− reduced accuracy
	− high loss of information
	− lot of estimated or average values
	− ripple effect

that are required in detail are simulated in packet-level, others that influence the result, but of which their own behaviour is not required in full detail, are modelled as flows. This reduces the computational complexity of the model and therefore allows the calculation of larger network topologies.

A.2.3 Simulation Speedup

A big issue in network simulation research is to find more efficient simulation techniques to speed up simulation processes (see Fig. A.2).

Simulation can be accelerated either by using computers with more computational power (faster CPU, multiprocessor system), new and faster simulation algorithms, or by modelling in a more abstract way (e.g., fluid or hybrid models), which reduces the complexity of network simulation.

A.2.4 Network Simulation in Research

In the past few years, the large scale of deployed networks make real-world experiments and their mathematical analysis very difficult. Even if analytical methods are available, network simulation is often used to validate the analysis. Furthermore, requirements in network research such as security, mobile networking and Quality-of-Service have changed a lot. In addition, simulation has become an important utility to cope with miscellaneous problems in network research.

Simulations provide methods to investigate newly developed protocols and their behaviour, performance and interaction with other protocols, validation, feasibility and to remove points of uncertainty. They offer a simple and cost-saving technique to evaluate design alternatives in different system configurations. Network simulators are often used if real-world systems are not available for testing. This emerges if network systems are busy or in security mode, which does not allow testing the required scenarios. Even if a test network is available, simulation provides more

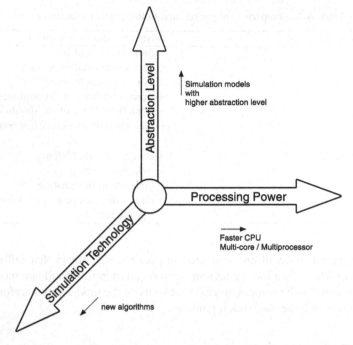

Fig. A.2. Accelerated simulation [175]

Table A.2. Comparison of reality and simulation

	Simulation	Real-World Experiments
Reproducibility	+ easy	− difficult
Network Traffic	− simulated	+ real
Simplification	− high abstraction	+ no abstraction
Scenario creation	+ easy	− complex
Scalability	+ high	− minor
Costs	+ cheap	− costly
Duration	− different	+ real time

flexible validation of new protocols (e.g., different scenarios, multiple error cases). Simulation results are reproducible, since in contrast to real-world experiments there are no unknown interactions with the environment (e.g., influence of a railway's high-voltage current on wireless experiments).

Table A.2 briefly compares simulation versus real-world testing.

A.2.5 Simulation for Education Purposes

Network simulation has obvious advantages over a real network for education purposes. Educational tasks can potentially cause some problems in a real network and therefore harm the network operation or at least require a new initialisation of the network by the tutors. In a simulated environment the learner has the freedom to experiment, and if errors occur he can revert the simulation to the initial state prepared by the tutors. This reduces the effort of the learner as well as the tutors. Moreover, the tutors may prepare the training with different scenarios which the learners can load during the exercises.

A.3 Network Simulators

Commonly used network simulators support multiple protocols and therefore provide substantial benefits such as:

- improved validation of existing protocols
- an infrastructure for developing new protocols
- easier comparison of results

The focus of this chapter is on the ns-2 network simulator. Nevertheless, some other network simulators are now briefly described in a more abstract way.

A.3.1 GloMoSim and Qualnet

GloMoSim [176] is a scalable, discrete-event simulation library that supports studies of large-scale network models up to millions of nodes, using parallel and distributed execution. The primary use of GloMoSim is the simulation of wireless and wired network systems. GloMoSim is a library for the C-based parallel discrete-event simulation language PARSEC (Parallel Simulation Environment for Complex Systems). GloMoSim is implemented based on the OSI layered approach. The standard API specifies parameter exchanges and services between neighbouring layers. A number of protocols are available at each layer, and models of these protocols or layers can be used at different levels of detail. GloMoSim is freely available.

QualNet [177] is a commercial product from Scalable Network Technologies. It shares the PARSEC language as well as the layered architecture emulating the OSI layer model with GloMoSim. Compared with GloMoSim, QualNet provides a wider range of models and protocols for both wired and wireless networks (local, ad hoc, satellite and cellular) and has a better support for mixed (wired and wireless) network simulations. QualNet is delivered with a very good analysis and visualisation tool. It provides trace and statistic file output. A further advantage is the rapid GUI-based model design.

A.3.2 JiST/SWANS

JiST is a discrete-event simulator using the standard Java virtual machine. The JiST system architecture consists of four distinct components: a compiler, a byte code rewriter, a simulation kernel and a virtual machine. JiST programs are written in plain unmodified Java and then compiled to byte code using a regular Java language compiler. The compiled classes are then modified, via a byte code-level rewriter, to run over a simulation kernel and to support simulation time semantics. The entire simulation runs within a standard Java virtual machine (JVM).

SWANS [178] is an extension to JiST for wireless network simulations. SWANS is composed of independent software components that form a complete wireless network following the OSI model. It offers capabilities comparable to the ones of ns-2 and GloMoSim. Performance comparisons show that SWANS is able to handle larger network topologies than its competitors, ns-2 and GloMoSim.

A.3.3 Scalable Simulation Framework (SSF) and SSFNet

Scalable Simulation Framework (SSF) [179] is a public domain framework for discrete event simulations. It offers a simulation kernel implementing different simulation technologies for Java and C++ models. User-created modules communicate with the simulation kernel by the SSF API (Application Programming Interface) either for Java or C++. For module configuration SSF uses its own language, the Domain Modeling Language (DML).

SSFNet [179] provides open-source Java models for network simulation. It includes models for several protocols (e.g., IP, TCP, UDP, BGP4, OSPF) and network components such as hosts, routers and links. Furthermore, several support classes enable the realistic modelling and simulation of multiprotocol and multidomain Internet scenarios.

A.3.4 OMNeT++ and OMNEST

OMNeT++ [180] (Objective Modular Network Testbed in C++) is an object-oriented modular discrete-event simulator built on C++ foundations. It offers C++ simulation class library and GUI support (editing and animation). OMNeT++ provides component architecture for models. Components (modules) are programmed in C++ and then assembled into larger components and models using a high-level NEtwork Description language (NED).

The INET Framework on top of OMNeT++ contains implementations of IPv4, TCP and UDP protocols and some application models. The list of protocols implemented by INET is growing.

Moreover, wireless simulations are supported by the Mobility Framework (MF). As MF focus on simulations on the lower layers, some protocols have been ported to INET for simulations involving the whole network stack.

OMNet++ is freely available for academic and noncommercial use. Commercial users have to buy a license of the OMNEST simulation environment which is the commercial derivative of OMNet++.

A.4 The Network Simulator ns-2

The network simulator ns-2 [181] is an object-oriented discrete-event simulator and includes a large number of applications, protocols, different network types, network elements and traffic models. The development is part of the Virtual InterNetwork Testbed (VINT) project [182]. The project aims at building a network simulator that offers innovative methods and tools. The central concept of ns-2 is to unify the effort of network simulation research.

ns-2 is well-suited for packet switched networks and is used mostly for small-scale simulations of queuing algorithms and transport protocol congestion control. It provides support for various implementations of TCP, routing, multicast protocols, link layer and MAC.

A.4.1 The Language Concept

Rather than using a single programming language that defines a monolithic simulation, ns-2 incorporates a more modular programming model using a two-language concept.

Two class hierarchies exist. Besides C++ for the implementation of the core parts, the interpreted language Tcl is used for scripting configuration and control of the simulation run. On the one hand, tasks such as low-level event processing or packet forwarding through a router, require high performance and efficiency. These tasks are best served by an implementation in a compiled language such as C++, called the compiled hierarchy. C++ is fast to run, but slow to modify. On the other hand, the interpreted scripting language Object Tcl (OTcl)), called the interpreted hierarchy, provides flexible and interactive ways to define particular network topologies, dynamic configuration of protocol objects, the specification and placement of traffic sources, etc.

In a nutshell, C++ implements the simulation kernel and the core parts of high-performance primitives. The OTcl scripting language expresses the definition, configuration and control of the simulation. It represents the glue between the individual network components implemented in C++.

A.4.2 Hierarchical Structure

The simulation is configured, controlled and operated through the interface provided by the Tcl class *Simulator*. This main class provides methods for creating and setting up the topology, selecting the scheduling method, and managing the simulations.

Topology elements are created with the basic components *node* and *link*. A node models a router or host that can transmit and receive packets through its interfaces (see Fig. A.3). Interface, address and port mapping are done by classifier objects. A unicast node (default node) has an address classifier that does unicast routing and is a port classifier. A multicast node has an address classifier that separates the multicast and unicast packets. Moreover, it includes a multicast classifier that performs the multicast routing. Another basic component is the Agent that represents the endpoint component of a node, where application packets are constructed or consumed.

A link represents another major component in ns-2 and is characterised via delay and bandwidth. Links are built as connector objects. The data structure represents

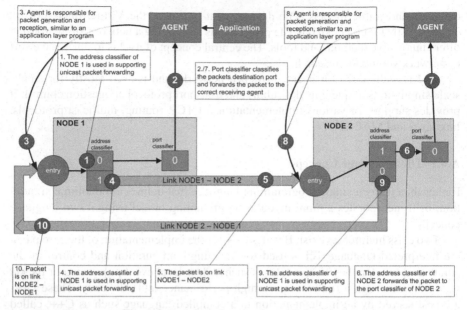

Fig. A.3. Packet cycle on node and link in ns-2

a link by queue connector objects. The connectors receive packets, calculate their treatment according to a predefined function, and then either send the packets with a calculated delay to the next connector or drop them.

A.4.3 First Steps—Simulation Script Template

The execution of a simulation in ns-2 requires a simulation script written in OTcl. Some basic commands required by every simulation are shown in the first script (Listing A.1). It does not execute any simulation process yet, but provides a basic template for future use.

Every ns-2 simulation script starts with the creation of a new instance of the Simulator class (see line 1 in Listing A.1). Afterwards, the format and output direction of trace files is set by declaring the file names of the traces (lines 4, 8 in Listing A.1). Moreover, the simulator is set to trace all events into the two different formats (lines 5, 9 in Listing A.1).

The simulation run-time is set by invoking the simulator instance to execute the finish procedure after a certain number of seconds (line 11 in Listing A.1). The finish procedure (lines 13–20 in Listing A.1) closes the trace files and clears the trace buffer. In addition, the Network Animator (nam) is started and the ns application is exited.

After the complete definition of the simulation model the simulator is executed. (line 22 in A.1).

Listing A.1. ns-2 Preliminaries

```
1   set ns [new Simulator]

3   # Open Trace File
    set tracefile [open out.tr w]
5   $ns trace-all $tracefile

7   #Open the NAM Trace File
    set namfile [open out.nam w]
9   $ns namtrace-all $namfile

11  $ns at 125.0 "finish"

13  proc finish {} {
        global ns tracefile namfile
15      $ns flush-trace
        close $tracefile
17      close $namfile
        exec nam out.nam &
19      exit 0
    }
21
    $ns run
```

A.4.4 Nodes, Links and Traffic

The next steps generate a small network topology for the simulator ns-2. The topology contains four nodes: one node is a router and two nodes send data to the fourth through it (see Listing A.2).

- **Nodes:** Lines 22–26 in Listing A.2 create four instances of class Nodes.
- **Links:** Lines 28–31 in Listing A.2 create three instances of class duplex-link connecting the nodes with 10 ms propagation delay and a capacity of 10 Mb/sec for each direction. To define a unidirectional link instead of a bidirectional link, *simplex-link* should be used instead of *duplex-link*. An output queue of a node is defined in the link. The output queues for node n0-n3 are defined as DropTail queues. Other queue objects derived from the base class Queue are Fair Queuing(FQ), Stochastic Fairness Queuing (SFQ), Deficit Round-Robin (DRR), Random Early Detection (RED) and Class Based Queueing (CBQ) (see Chap. 7.3 in the ns manual [183]).
- **Transport Protocols and Traffic Sources:** The transport protocols Transport Control Protocol (TCP) and User Datagram Protocol (UDP) are already defined in ns-2. Furthermore, multiple traffic sources exist such as Constant Bit Rate or File Transport Protocol (FTP).
  TCP is a connection-oriented protocol. It uses acknowledgements created by the destination to know whether packets are received or not. The TCP connection is

defined in line 34 in Listing A.2 and is connected to node n0 in line 35. TCP's parameters with fixed default values can be changed as an example in line 37 where the standard packet size of 1000 bytes is changed to 552 bytes. When the TCP connection has been defined, a FTP application is set up on top of it (lines 39–41). The next lines (43–47) define the behaviour of the destination node of the TCP connection. The TCPSink agent has an active role in the protocol. It generates acknowledgement packets. By line 47 the two agents are connected to each other.

Similar to the TCP setup, lines 49–64 in Listing A.2 create **UDP** traffic between node n1 and node n3. Since UDP is a connectionless protocol, it is enough to generate a Null agent in line 62 as the traffic sink. A CBR source with a packet size of 1000 bytes and a transmission rate of 200 packets per second is selected as the application. The random option in line 59 is a flag indicating whether or not to introduce random noise additionally to the scheduled transmission.

Start and end times for the FTP and CBR application are set in lines 66–69 of Listing A.2. Afterwards, the simulator instance is started by the command run. The simulation script can now be executed.

Listing A.2. ns-2 Nodes Links and Traffic

```
   set ns [new Simulator]
2
   # Open Trace File
4  set tracefile [open out.tr w]
   $ns trace-all $tracefile
6
   #Open the NAM Trace File
8  set namfile [open out.nam w]
   $ns namtrace-all $namfile
10
   $ns at 20.0 "finish"
12
   proc finish {} {
14    global ns tracefile namfile
      $ns flush-trace
16    close $tracefile
      close $namfile
18    exec nam out.nam &
      exit 0
20 }

22 #Create four nodes
   set n0 [$ns node]
24 set n1 [$ns node]
   set n2 [$ns node]
26 set n3 [$ns node]

28 #Create links between the nodes
```

```
     $ns duplex-link $n0 $n2 1Mb 10ms DropTail
30   $ns duplex-link $n1 $n2 1Mb 10ms DropTail
     $ns duplex-link $n3 $n2 1Mb 10ms DropTail

32
     #Create a TCP connection on n0
34   set tcp0 [new Agent/TCP]
     $ns attach-agent $n0 $tcp0
36   $tcp0 set fid_ 1
     $tcp0 set packetSize_ 552

38
     #Setup a FTP over TCP connection
40   set ftp0 [new Application/FTP]
     $ftp0 attach-agent $tcp0

42
     #Setup
44   set sink0 [new Agent/TCPSink]
     $ns attach-agent $n3 $sink0

46
     $ns connect $tcp0 $sink0

48
     # Setup a UDP connection
50   set udp1 [new Agent/UDP]
     $ns attach-agent $n1 $udp1
52   $udp1 set fid_ 2

54   # Setup a CBR over UDP connection
     set cbr1 [new Application/Traffic/CBR]
56   $cbr1 attach-agent $udp1
     $cbr1 set packetSize_ 1000
58   $cbr1 set interval_ 0.005
     $cbr1 set random_ false

60
     # Setup a Null Agent
62   set null1 [new Agent/Null]
     $ns attach-agent $n3 $null1
64   $ns connect $udp1 $null1

66   $ns at 1.0 "$ftp0 start"
     $ns at 4.0 "$ftp0 stop"
68   $ns at 0.5 "$cbr1 start"
     $ns at 4.5 "$cbr1 stop"
70   $ns run
```

A.4.5 Wireless Networks

Wireless simulation models consist of *MobileNodes* (see Fig. A.4). Thus, a *Mobile-Node* is the basic Node object with enhanced functionalities for wireless communication and node mobility. A mobile node can receive and transmit packets to/from a

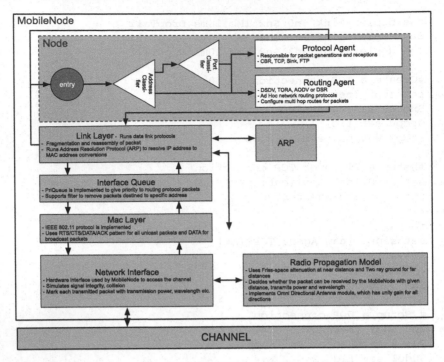

Fig. A.4. MobileNode architecture

wireless channel. In addition, it can move in a given topology. As a major difference between MobileNode and Node, a MobileNode is not connected by links to other mobile nodes. ns-2 has further various modules added to support node mobility and wireless networking:

- **Ad-hoc Routing** (Dynamic Source Routing (DSR), Ad-hoc On-demand Distance Vector (AODV), Destination-Sequenced Distance-Vector Routing (DSDV))
- **MAC 802.11** denotes a set of Wireless LAN standards.
- **Radio Propagation Model** is an empirical mathematical formulation for the characterisation of radio wave propagation. Currently, the ns-2 distribution contains the free space, two-ray ground reflection and shadowing models.

A.4.5.1 A Wireless Simulation Scenario

Although the scripts for wired and wireless simulation scenarios are quite similar, there are some changes required to establish a wireless simulation model. This includes the setup of the topology, additional parameters for wireless nodes, the General Operations Director (GOD) component, and the nodes' mobility. First, the topology has to be set by the area parameter (see lines 24 and 25 in Listing A.3) as an instance of the class Topography. The wireless nodes in ns-2 are called MobileNodes.

They require more parameters to be set than a normal wired node (lines 39–52 in Listing A.3). A MobileNode is generated with all the given values of ad-hoc routing protocol, network stack, channel, topography, propagation model, with wired routing turned on or off and tracing turned on or off at different levels (router, MAC, agent). The General Operations Director (GOD) element is introduced to support wireless network simulations. It stores the smallest number of hops from one node to another and is automatically generated by the scenario file (lines 36–37 in Listing A.3). Furthermore, the mobility of the nodes has to be defined in the scenario. Ns-2 provides the Mobile Movement Generator to simplify this task. Detailed instructions can be found in the ns-2 manual ([183], Chap. 16). The next step is to set up the traffic for the simulation. The easiest way to do this is with the Traffic Generator, another supporting tool of ns-2.

Listing A.3. ns-2 Wireless Scenario

```
   set opt(chan)    Channel/WirelessChannel
 2 set opt(prop)    Propagation/TwoRayGround
   set opt(netif)   Phy/WirelessPhy
 4 set opt(mac)     Mac/802_11
   set opt(ifq)     Queue/DropTail/PriQueue
 6 set opt(ll)      LL
   set opt(ant)     Antenna/OmniAntenna
 8 set opt(x)       670  ;# X dimension of the topography
   set opt(y)       670  ;# Y dimension of the topography
10 set opt(ifqlen)  50       ;# max packet in ifq
   set opt(seed)    0.0
12 set opt(tr)      694demo.tr ;# trace file
   set opt(nam)     694demo.nam ;# nam trace file
14 set opt(adhocRouting) DSDV
   set opt(nn)      3          ;# how many nodes are simulated
16 set opt(cp)      "traffic.file"
   set opt(sc)      "movement.file"
18 set opt(stop)    200.0    ;# simulation time

20 # create simulator instance
   set ns_ [new Simulator]
22
   # topology
24 set topo [new Topography]
   $topo load_flatgrid 670 670
26
   # ns trace
28 set tracefd [open wireless_scenario.tr w]
   $ns_ trace-all $tracefd
30
   # nam trace
32 set namtrace [open wireless_scenario.nam w]
   $ns_ namtrace-all-wireless $namtrace 670 670
34
   # create god
36 set god_ [create-god 3]

38 # Mobile Node configuration
   $ns_ node-config -adhocRouting $opt(adhocRouting) \
```

```
40              -llType $opt(ll) \
                -macType $opt(mac) \
42              -ifqType $opt(ifq) \
                -ifqLen $opt(ifqlen) \
44              -antType $opt(ant) \
                -propType Propagation/TwoRayGround \
46              -phyType $opt(netif) \
                -channelType Channel/WirelessChannel \
48              -topoInstance $topo \
                -agentTrace ON \
50              -routerTrace OFF \
                -macTrace ON
53  for {set i 0} {$i < 3} {incr i} {
        set node_($i) [$ns_ node]
55      #disable random motion
        $node_($i) random-motion 0
57      $node_($i) topography $topo
    }
60  #Load movement file
    source movement.file
63  #Load traffic file
    source traffic.file
66  # Define node initial position in nam
    for {set i 0} {$i < 3 } { incr i} {
68      $ns_ initial_node_pos $node_($i) 20
    }
71  for {set i 0} {$i < 3 } {incr i} {
        $ns_ at 150.0 "$node_($i) reset";
73  }
    # Tell ns/nam the simulation stop time
76  $ns_ at 150.0 "$ns_ nam-end-wireless 150.0"
    $ns_ at 150.0 "$ns_ halt"
79  # Start your simulation
    $ns_ run
```

A.4.6 Implementing Protocols with ns-2

The implementation always starts with a formal description of the protocol, e.g. in the form of a pseudo code, a flow chart, sequence diagrams or another graphical representation. In the following, the packet format is specified and the protocol algorithms are implemented. As an example, a step-by-step implementation of a simple QoS-aware link state routing protocol is shown. Please note that the code is not complete and should only show you how to proceed. The protocol implementation procedure is based on [184] and on existing implementations of link state and distance vector routing in the ns-2 package.

A.4.6.1 Description of QoS-Aware Link State Routing (QLS)

QoS-Aware Link State Routing (QLS) is a simple routing protocol based on link state routing using RTT as the QoS metric for the individual links. The main concept of link state routing is the distributed calculation of next best hops on a network connectivity graph structure at each router. Every router broadcasts its link state. These link state advertisements are distributed to all nodes in the network. As a result, every node has a network connectivity map describing the whole network topology and may then calculate the best next hop for each destination. In our case, the individual nodes calculate the next hops using a variant of Dijkstra's shortest path algorithm. It considers the round trip time (RTT) as the cost of an individual link. RTT is determined by periodic measurements. The network connectivity is exchanged using periodic link state advertisements messages. Our protocol requires the following steps:

- Creation of network connectivity map
  - RTT measurements: Each node periodically sends Probe messages to its neighbours, which include their creation time as a time stamp. The nodes receiving the Probe message reply with Probe ACK messages. At the reception of a Probe ACK message, the nodes add the replying node including the link costs to its neighbourhood table. The entries includes the TTL of the Probe / Probe ACK message as a simple QoS parameter.
  - Link state advertisement (LSA): A link state advertisement message containing source address, direct neighbours as well as a sequence number is periodically sent throughout the network.
  - Generation of network map: The network map is generated by iteration over all received link state advertisement messages.
- Routing table calculation
  - Calculation of shortest path tree: Dijkstra's shortest path algorithm is executed at each node in order to calculate the shortest path tree. The root element of the tree (level 0) is the node itself.
  - Route table setup: In order to fill the routing table, the shortest path tree is traversed and for each neighbour node the best next hop on level 1 is written to the routing table.

A.4.6.2 Formal Description of QLS

The flow chart in Fig. A.5 shows the behaviour of the QLS agent. The agent periodically sends Probe messages for RTT measurements. If the QLS agent receives such a Probe message, it replies with unicast Probe ACK message including the information of the received Probe message. Upon reception of a Probe ACK message, the node calculates the RTT and adds the replying node to its neighbourhood table. Then it sends a new link state advertisement (LSA) message. Nodes receiving a LSA message, check its freshness by sequence numbers, add the included data to their topology table, and forward the LSA. If the LSA is an old one, it is simply dropped. The format of the three QLS messages is shown in Fig. A.6

A.4.6.3 Preparations

In order to start the implementation of a new routing protocol for ns-2, some general preliminary steps have to be taken. Simple protocol implementations usually consist

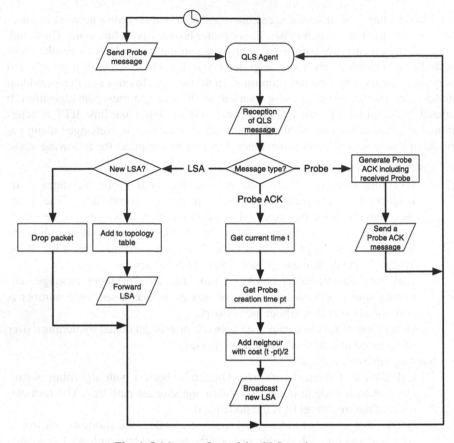

Fig. A.5. Message flow of the QLS routing agent

of a basic C++ class and a new packet header. For the QLS example, the following four files are compiled into ns-2:

- **qls.h** is the header file where all necessary timers and the routing agent are defined.
- **qls.cc** includes implementation of the routing agent.
- **qls_packet.h** declares all routing packets.
- **qls.tcl** integrates the new QLS agent in the ns-2 OTcl environment.

The new routing agent is implemented as a subclass of the Agent class. The ns-2 manual describes Agents as follows: "Agents represent endpoints where network-layer packets are constructed or consumed, and are used in the implementation of protocols at various layers." ([183], Chap. 10). The Agent class is linked to the Tcl interface, so you can control your agent through simulation scripts written in Tcl.

Moreover, the new protocol uses a new packet type defined in qls_packet.h, which represent the format of the packet generated through the routing agent.

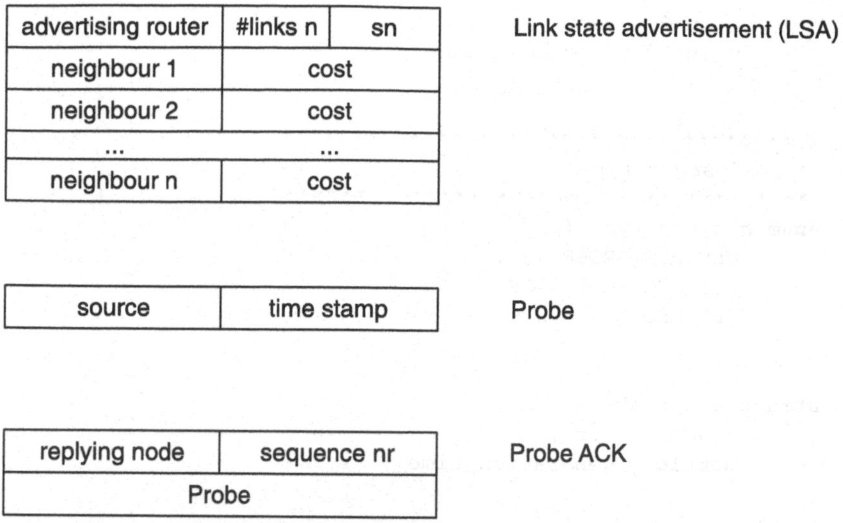

advertising router	#links n	sn
neighbour 1	cost	
neighbour 2	cost	
...	...	
neighbour n	cost	

Link state advertisement (LSA)

source	time stamp

Probe

replying node	sequence nr
Probe	

Probe ACK

Fig. A.6. Format of the QLS messages: LSA, Probe and Probe ACK

A.4.6.4 Implementing the New Packet Types for QLS

The packet type definition contains all data structures, constants and macros related to our new packets. Listing A.4 provides the complete source code. The new packet header for the QLS routing protocol (hdr_qls_pkt) is defined in lines 50–67 in Listing A.4. In order to access the information in the new packet, *offset()* and *access()* have to be defined (lines 59–62). The packet header then is bound to the OTcl interface by subclassing the PacketHeaderClass with QLSHeaderClass in lines 73–79.

Listing A.4. QLS Packet Type (qls/qls_packet.h)

```
   #ifndef __qls_pkt_h__
2  #define __qls_pkt_h__

4  #include "common/packet.h"

6  #define MAX_LINKS_LSA 6
   #define QLS_HDR_LEN sizeof(qls_msg_type)\
8        + sizeof(qls_probe) \
         + sizeof(qls_probe_ack) \
10       + sizeof(qls_lsa)

12 /***************************************
    * QLS linkstate respresenting one link
14  * (neighbor, cost, sequence number)
    ***************************************/
16 struct QLSLinkState {
         u_int8_t neighbor_;
```

```
18          u_int8_t cost_;
            u_int32_t sequenceNumber_;
20    };

22    /**************************************
       * QLS packet types
24     **************************************/
      enum qls_msg_type {
26          QLS_MSG_PROBE = 0,
            QLS_MSG_PROBE_ACK = 1,
28          QLS_MSG_LSA = 2
      };
30
      struct qls_probe {
32          nsaddr_t src_;
            double   generation_time_;
34    };

36    struct qls_probe_ack {
            nsaddr_t src_;
38          double generation_time_;
      };
40
      struct qls_lsa {
42          nsaddr_t advertising_router_;
            u_int16_t sn_;
44          struct QLSLinkState link_state_[MAX_LINKS_LSA];
      };
46
      /**************************************
48     * Header QLS packet
       **************************************/
50    class hdr_qls_pkt {
      private:
52          qls_msg_type type_;
            qls_probe probe_;
54          qls_probe_ack probe_ack_;
            qls_lsa lsa_;
56
      public:
58          static int offset_;
            inline int& offset() {return offset_;}
60          inline static hdr_qls_pkt* access(const Packet* p){
                  return (hdr_qls_pkt*)p->access(offset_);
62          }
            inline qls_msg_type& type() {return type_;}
64          inline qls_probe& probe() {return probe_;}
            inline qls_probe_ack& probe_ack() {return probe_ack_;}
66          inline qls_lsa& lsa() {return lsa_;}
```

```
   };
68
   int hdr_qls_pkt::offset_;
70 /***************************************
    * PacketHeaderClass for QLS
72 ***************************************/
   static class QLSHeaderClass : public PacketHeaderClass {
74 public:
        QLSHeaderClass(): PacketHeaderClass("PacketHeader/QLS",
            sizeof(hdr_qls_pkt))
76      {
                bind_offset(&hdr_qls_pkt::offset_);
78      }
   } class_rtProtoQLS_hdr;
80 #endif
```

A.4.6.5 The Routing Agent—Header File

The header file *qls.h* (see Listing A.5) declares the timer for neighbourhood probing in lines 24–32, helper classes in lines 37–73 and the QLS routing agent in lines 79–118.

Listing A.5. Header file for the routing agent (qls/qls.h)

```
   #ifndef ns_qls_h
2  #define ns_qls_h

4  #include "common/packet.h"
   #include "common/agent.h"
6  #include "common/ip.h"
   #include "qls/qls_packet.h"
8  #include "common/node.h"
   #include "common/timer-handler.h"
10 #include "linkstate/ls.h"
   #include <map>
12 #include <list>
   #include <string>
14
   using namespace std;
16
   #define CURRENT_TIME Scheduler::instance().clock()
18
   class QLS; //forward declaration (required for timer)
20
   /***************************************
22  * Timer for Neighborhood probing
    ***************************************/
24 class QLS_ProbingTimer : public TimerHandler {
   public:
26      QLS_ProbingTimer(QLS* agent) : TimerHandler(){
                agent_=agent;
28      }
   protected:
```

```cpp
30          QLS *agent_;
            virtual void expire(Event* e);
32   };

34   /***************************************
      * Helper classes
36    ***************************************/
     typedef std::list<QLSLinkState> QLS_LS_List;
38   typedef std::list<nsaddr_t> Path_List;

40   class Path {
     protected:
42          int cost_;
            Path_List path_;
44   public:
            const string toString(){
46                  string temp = "";
                    temp += cost_;
48                  std::list<nsaddr_t>::iterator i;
                    for(i=path_.begin(); i!= path_.end(); i++){
50                          temp += *i;
                    }
52                  return temp;
            }
54          Path_List getPath() {return path_;}
            u_int16_t getCost() {return cost_;}
56          void setPath(Path_List path) {path_=path;}
            void setCost(u_int16_t cost) {cost_=cost;}
58   };

60   class Tokenizer : public std::list<int> {
     public:
62          Tokenizer (const char * str, const char * delim)
                    : std::list<int> () {
64                  for ( char * token = strtok ((char *)str, delim);
                        token != NULL; token = strtok(NULL, delim) )

                        {
66                          push_back ( atoi(token) );
                    }
68          }
     };
70
     typedef map<nsaddr_t,QLS_LS_List, less<int> > QLS_Topo_Map;
72
     typedef map<nsaddr_t, Path, less<int> > Routes;
74

76   /***************************************
      * The QLS Routing Agent
78    ***************************************/
     class QLS : public Agent{
80
            friend class QLS_ProbingTimer;
82
     public:
84          QLS();
            int command(int argc, const char*const* argv);
```

```
86          void recv(Packet* p, Handler*);
            nsaddr_t getNodeAddr() { return nodeAddr_; }
88          void establishRoutes() {
                Tcl::instance().evalf("%s_install-routes", name()
                    );
90          }

92  protected:

94          typedef LsMap<int, ns_addr_t> Peers;
            Peers peers_;
96
            nsaddr_t nodeAddr_;
98          u_int16_t sn_;
            QLS_ProbingTimer* probingTimer_;
100         QLS_Topo_Map* topology_;
            Routes* routes_;
102         double probingInterval_;

104         void initialize();
            void computeRoutes();
106         void lookup(nsaddr_t destinationNodeId);

108         // Tx and Rx methods
            void sendProbe();
110         void sendProbe(ns_addr_t destination);
            void sendProbeACK(Packet* p);
112         void sendLSA();
            void recvProbe(Packet* p, Handler*);
114         void recvProbeACK(Packet* p, Handler*);
            void recvLSA(Packet* p, Handler*);
116
            void setNeighborLinkCost(nsaddr_t n, double cost);
118  };

120
     #endif // ns_qls_h
```

A.4.6.6 The Routing Agent—Source File

The source file *qls.cc* implements the behaviour of the QLS routing agent (Listing A.6). The QLS agent and its methods are defined and the class is bound to the corresponding OTcl class. Lines 29–225 implement the QLS agent with receive and send methods. The QLS agent class is bound to the OTcl class (*Agent/rtProto/QLS*) in lines 7–15.

QLS::recv(Packet* p, Handler* h) is the central method of the QLS agent (line 73–95). Every packet that the QLS agent receives is handled by this method. The packets are dispatched to the responsible methods according to their QLS type. The content of the packet is accessed by the *access()* method of the particular header.

Communication between C++ objects and OTcl space requires additional bindings between the two hierarchies. There exists the binding of member variables, the OTcl interface of C++ classes, and calling of OTcl methods by C++ classes.

C++ member variables can be bound to OTcl variables by the commands *bind()*, *bind_time()*, *bind_bw()*, and *bind_bool*. For example, the probing interval is bound to a OTcl variable for flexible configuration in line 37. The OTcl interface of a C++ class is implemented in the method *command()*. The QLS agent defines the OTcl interface methods *lookup*, *initialize*, *probe-neighbors* and *computeRoutes* in lines 44–69 besides the ones of the class Agent. If the OTcl command is executed successfully, the method returns a *TCL_OK*. Results can be passed to OTcl by writing them into *Tcl::instance().result(".....")* (see *lookup method* in line 113 of Listing A.6). Moreover, OTcl methods can be invoked by first getting a reference to the TCL instance (*tcl*), calling the methods by the evaluation functions, and then retrieving the result with *tcl.result()* (e.g., lines 119–126).

Listing A.6. Source file for the routing agent (qls/qls.cc)

```
 1   #include "qls.h"
     #include "qls_packet.h"
 3
     /***************************************
 5    * TCL Class constructor
     ***************************************/
 7   static class QLSClass : public TclClass {
     public:
 9        QLSClass() :
                  TclClass("Agent/rtProto/QLS") {
11        }
          TclObject* create(int argc, const char*const* argv) {
13              return (new QLS);
          }
15   } class_rtProtoQLS;

17   /***************************************
      * Implementation of Timer expire
19    * methods
      ***************************************/
21   void QLS_ProbingTimer::expire(Event *e) {
          agent_->sendProbe();
23        resched(agent_->probingInterval_);
     }
25
     /***************************************
27    * Implementation of QLS Agent
      ***************************************/
29   QLS::QLS() :
          Agent(PT_QLS) {
31        probingTimer_ = new QLS_ProbingTimer(this);
          sn_ = 0;
33        // Variable binding C++ <-> OTCL
          // (bind() -> int, float, double,
```

```
35      // bind_time() -> time, bind_bw() -> bandwidth
        // bind_bool() -> boolean
37      bind_time("probingInterval", &probingInterval_);
   }
39
   /****************************************
41  * Command defines functions which can
    * be called from TCL space
43  ***************************************/
   int QLS::command(int argc, const char*const* argv) {
45      if (argc == 3) {
            if (strcmp(argv[1], "lookup") == 0) {
47              int dst = atoi(argv[2]);
                lookup(dst);
49      // lookup results are passed to TCL space by tcl.
           resultf()
                return TCL_OK;
51          }
        }
53
        // initialize QLS agent
55      if (strcmp(argv[1], "initialize") == 0) {
            initialize ();
57          return TCL_OK;
        }
59      if (strcmp(argv[1], "probe-neighbors") == 0) {
            probingTimer_->resched(0.0);
61          return TCL_OK;
        }
63      // Start the route computation
        if (strcmp(argv[1], "computeRoutes") == 0) {
65          computeRoutes();
            return TCL_OK;
67      }
        return (Agent::command(argc, argv));
69  }

71  /****************************************
    * Handles the packets received by QLS
73  ***************************************/
   void QLS::recv(Packet* p, Handler* h) {
75      struct hdr_cmn* ch = hdr_cmn::access(p);
        struct hdr_ip* ih = hdr_ip::access(p);
77      struct hdr_qls_pkt* qls = hdr_qls_pkt::access(p);

79      if (ch->ptype() == PT_QLS) {
            ih->ttl_--;
81          switch (qls->type()) {
```

```
                    case QLS_MSG_PROBE:
83                         recvProbe(p, h);
                          break;
85                  case QLS_MSG_PROBE_ACK:
                          recvProbeACK(p, h);
87                        break;
                    case QLS_MSG_LSA:
89                         recvLSA(p, h);
                          break;
91                  default:
                          fprintf(stderr, "Unknown QLS packet type");
93                        break;
             }
95       }
    }
97


99  /****************************************
     * Compute the current routes using
101  * Dijkstra's algorithm
     ****************************************/
103 void QLS::computeRoutes() {
            // To be implemented
105 }


107 void QLS::lookup(nsaddr_t dest) {
            map<nsaddr_t, Path>::iterator destItr;
109     destItr = routes_->find(dest);
            if (destItr == routes_->end()) {
111             Tcl::instance().resultf("%s", "");
            } else {
113             Tcl::instance().resultf("%s", destItr->second.
                    toString().c_str());
            }
115 }


117 void QLS::initialize() {
            // get nodeAddr from OTcl space
119     Tcl & tcl = Tcl::instance();
            tcl.evalf("%s get-node-id", name());
121     const char * resultString = tcl.result();
            nodeAddr_ = atoi(resultString);
123
            // add routing peers from OTcl space
125     tcl.evalf("%s get-peers", name());
            resultString = tcl.result();
127     int nodeId;
            ns_addr_t peer;
129     for ( Tokenizer tokenizer(resultString, " \t\n");
```

```
                    !tokenizer.empty(); ) {
131                  nodeId = tokenizer.front();
                     tokenizer.pop_front();
133                  peer.addr_ = tokenizer.front();
                     tokenizer.pop_front();
135                  peer.port_ = tokenizer.front();
                     tokenizer.pop_front();
137                  peers_.insert(nodeId, peer);
                 }
139
     }
141
     /*************************************
143   * Tx methods
      *************************************/
145  void QLS::sendProbe() {
          Peers::iterator iter;
147       for(iter = peers_.begin(); iter != peers_.end(); iter
              ++) {
                  ns_addr_t peer = iter->second;
149               sendProbe(peer);
          }
151
     }
153
     void QLS::sendProbe(ns_addr_t destination){
155       Packet *p = Packet::alloc();
          struct hdr_cmn *ch = hdr_cmn::access(p);
157       struct hdr_ip *ih = hdr_ip::access(p);
          struct hdr_qls_pkt *qls = hdr_qls_pkt::access(p);
159
          ch->ptype() = PT_QLS;
161       ch->direction()=hdr_cmn::DOWN;
          ch->next_hop_ = destination.addr_;
163       ch->prev_hop_ = this->addr();

165       ih->saddr() = this->addr();
          ih->daddr() = destination.addr_;
167       ih->sport() = port();
          ih->dport() = destination.port_;
169       ih->ttl_ = 2;

171       qls->type()= QLS_MSG_PROBE;
          qls->probe().src_= this->addr();
173       qls->probe().generation_time_ = CURRENT_TIME;;
          target_->recv(p);
175  }

177  void QLS::sendProbeACK(Packet* p) {
```

```
        struct hdr_cmn *ch = hdr_cmn::access(p);
179     struct hdr_ip *ih = hdr_ip::access(p);
        struct hdr_qls_pkt *qls = hdr_qls_pkt::access(p);
181
        ch->ptype() = PT_QLS;
183     ch->size()=IP_HDR_LEN+QLS_HDR_LEN;
        ch->direction()=hdr_cmn::DOWN;
185
        ih->saddr() = getNodeAddr();
187     ih->daddr() = qls->probe().src_;
        ih->sport() = RT_PORT;
189     ih->dport() = RT_PORT;
        ih->ttl_ = 2;
191
        qls->type()= QLS_MSG_PROBE_ACK;
193     qls->probe_ack().src_= getNodeAddr();
        qls->probe_ack().generation_time_= qls->probe().
            generation_time_;
195
        target_->recv(p);
197 }
    void QLS::sendLSA() {
199     // To be implemented
    }
201
    /**************************************
203  * Rx methods
     **************************************/
205 void QLS::recvProbe(Packet* p, Handler*) {
        sendProbeACK(p); // reply to probe
207     Packet::free(p);
    }
209 void QLS::recvProbeACK(Packet* p, Handler*) {
        struct hdr_qls_pkt *qls = hdr_qls_pkt::access(p);
211     double cost = CURRENT_TIME - qls->probe_ack().
            generation_time_;
        setNeighborLinkCost(qls->probe_ack().src_, cost);
213     sendLSA();
        Packet::free(p);
215
    }
217 void QLS::recvLSA(Packet* p, Handler*) {
        // To be implemented
219 }
221 /**************************************/
    void QLS::setNeighborLinkCost(nsaddr_t n, double cost){
223     // To be implemented
    }
```

A.4.6.7 Integration of the New Protocol in ns-2

Integration of the new protocol requires some changes in OTcl files. The new agent *Agent/rtProto/QLS* has to implement two procedures and several instance procedures of its OTcl superclass (see Listing A.7). It defines the procedures *init-all* (lines 9–38) and *compute-all* (99–101). In *init-all* QLS routing is set up on all nodes in the simulation. The procedure *compute-all* is left empty as the computation of the routes is done on each node individually. The instance procedures *init node* (lines 41–61), *compute-routes* (lines 64–67), and *install-routes* (lines 69–97) initialise the QLS agent on the node, compute the routes and install them. The *init* instance procedure is the constructor of the OTcl class. In order to call the methods from the superclass, the command *next* is used (e.g., line 43).

Listing A.7. Ns-2 integration of QLS routing agent by a Tcl source file

```
1   Agent/rtProto/QLS set preference_ 120
    Agent/rtProto/QLS set UNREACHABLE [rtObject set unreach_]
3   Agent/rtProto/QLS set INFINITY [Agent set ttl_]
    # set default value for bound time variable (real value =
        seconds,
5   # m = milli-seconds, n = nano-seconds, p = pico-seconds)
    Agent/rtProto/QLS set probingInterval 1000m
7
    # Initialize QLS on all nodes
9   Agent/rtProto/QLS proc init-all args {
            set nodelist [[Simulator instance] all-nodes-list]
11
            eval rtObject init-all $nodelist
13
            foreach node $nodelist {
15                  set proto($node) [[$node rtObject?] add-proto QLS
                        $node]
            }
17          foreach node $nodelist {
                    foreach nbr [$node neighbors] {
19                      set rtobj [$nbr rtObject?]
                        if { $rtobj != "" } {
21                          set rtproto [$rtobj rtProto? QLS]
                            if { $rtproto != "" } {
23                              $proto($node) add-peer $nbr [$rtproto
                                    set agent_addr_] [$rtproto set
                                    agent_port_]
                            }
25                      }
                    }
27          }

29          foreach node $nodelist {
                    set rtobj [$node rtObject?]
31                  if {$rtobj != ""} {
```

```
                              set rtproto [$rtobj rtProto? QLS]
33                            if {$rtproto != ""} {
                                      $rtproto initialize
35                            }
                      }
37            }
       }
39

       # Initialize QLS on node
41     Agent/rtProto/QLS instproc init node {
              # call the init procedure of the superclass
43            $self next $node

45            $self instvar ns_ rtObject_ ifsUp_ rtsChanged_ rtpref_
                    nextHop_ \
                      nextHopPeer_ metric_ multiPath_
47            Agent/rtProto/QLS instvar preference_

49            set ns_ [Simulator instance]
              set UNREACHABLE [$class set UNREACHABLE]
51            foreach dst [$ns_ all-nodes-list] {
                      set rtpref_($dst) $preference_
53                    set metric_($dst) $UNREACHABLE
                      set nextHop_($dst) ""
55                    set nextHopPeer_($dst) ""
              }
57            set ifsUp_ ""
              set multiPath_ [[$rtObject_ set node_] set multiPath_]
59
              $self startProbing
61     }


63

       Agent/rtProto/QLS instproc compute-routes {} {
65            $self computeRoutes
              $self install-routes
67     }


69     Agent/rtProto/QLS instproc install-routes {} {
              $self instvar ns_ ifs_ rtpref_ metric_ nextHop_
71            $self instvar peers_ rtsChanged_
              $self instvar node_ preference_
73
              set MAXPREF [rtObject set maxpref_]
75            set UNREACHABLE [rtObject set unreach_]
              set rtsChanged_ 1
77
              foreach dst [$ns_ all-nodes-list] {
79                    if { $dst == $node_ } {
```

```
                     set metric_($dst) 32
81                   continue
              }
83            set path [$self lookup [$dst id]]
              if { [llength $path ] == 0 } {
85                   # no path found in QLS
                     set rtpref_($dst) $MAXPREF
87                   set metric_($dst) $UNREACHABLE
                     set nextHop_($dst) ""
89                   continue
              }
91            set cost [lindex $path 0]
              set rtpref_($dst) $preference_
93            set metric_($dst) $cost
              set nhNode [$ns_ get-node-by-id [lindex $path 1]]
95            set nextHop_($dst) $ifs_($nhNode)
       }
97   }

99   Agent/rtProto/QLS proc compute-all {} {
         # Proc methods are not inherited from the parent class.
101  }


103
     Agent/rtProto/QLS instproc get-node-id {} {
105      $self instvar node_
         return [$node_ id]
107  }

109  Agent/rtProto/QLS instproc get-node-addr {} {
         $self instvar node_
111      return [$node_ addr]
     }
113
     Agent/rtProto/QLS instproc add-peer {neighbor agentAddr
         agentPort} {
115      $self instvar peers_
         $self set peers_($neighbor) [new rtPeer $agentAddr
             $agentPort $class]
117  }


119
     Agent/rtProto/QLS instproc get-peers {} {
121      $self instvar peers_
         set peers ""
123      foreach nbr [lsort -dictionary [array names peers_]] {
             lappend peers [$nbr id]
125          lappend peers [$peers_($nbr) addr?]
             lappend peers [$peers_($nbr) port?]
```

```
127        }
        set peers
129    }

131    Agent/rtProto/QLS instproc startProbing {} {
        set random [new RNG]
133        set probingStartTime [$random uniform 0 2]
        [Simulator instance] at $probingStartTime "$self_probe-
            neighbors"
135
    }
```

After finishing the protocol implementation, there are some changes required to ns-2 in order to integrate the new protocol.

The QLS implementation introduces the new packet type **PT_QLS**, which has to be defined in *<nsrootdirectory>/common/packet.h* as well. The packet type has to be added into the structure *enum_packet_t* as it is done in Listing A.8 on line 7. In the same file on line 19, the string definition for trace files for this packet type can be set.

Listing A.8. Required changes in ns-2 packet.h

```
enum packet_t {
2       PT_TCP,
        PT_UDP,
4       PT_CBR,
        (...)
6       // QLS packet
        PT_QLS,
8       // insert new packet types here
        PT_NTYPE // This MUST be the LAST one
10   };

12   (...)

14   p_info() {
        name_[PT_TCP]= "tcp";
16       name_[PT_UDP]= "udp";
        name_[PT_CBR]= "cbr";
18       (...)
        name_[PT_QLS]="QLS";
20       name_[PT_NTYPE]= "undefined";
    }
```

Afterwards, additional changes have to be made in the Tcl files of ns-2. First, the new packet type is added. Then, the default values for bound variables are set. These changes are necessary for proper functioning of the new protocol. The Tcl interpreter has to know the new functionalities written in C++, as it is done in Listing A.9. The new packet header has to be added to the common ns-2 packet in the file *tcl/lib/ns-packet.tcl* in order to be accessible.

Listing A.9. Required changes in ns-2 (tcl/lib/ns-packet.tcl)

```
1 foreach prot {
        (...)
3 # Routing Protocols:
        NV
5       rtProtoDV
        rtProtoLS
7       SR
        Src_rt
9       QLS   # QoS aware Linkstate Routing (QLS)
        (...)
11 } {
        add-packet-header $prot
13 }
```

A default value has to be provided for all bound variables. Default values are either defined in tcl/lib/ns-default.tcl or in the tcl files of the new protocol, e.g. in *qls/qls.tcl* (line 6 in Listing A.7).

Listing A.10. Required changes in ns-2 (tcl/lib/ns-lib.tcl)

```
1 (...)
   if {[ns-hasSTL] == 1} {
3 source ns-nix.tcl
   (...)
5 source ../qls/qls.tcl
   (...)
```

Then, the qls.tcl file has to be added to *tcl/lib/ns-lib.tcl* (see Listing A.10). In our case, it is included in the section for protocols that require C++ Standard Template Library (STL).

Listing A.11. Required changes in ns-2 Makefile.in

```
   # Makefile.in
2
   OBJ_STL = diffusion3/lib/nr/nr.o diffusion3/lib/dr.o \
4  (...)
      qls/qls.o
6
   NS_TCL_LIB_STL = tcl/lib/ns-diffusion.tcl \
8  (...)
      qls/qls.tcl
10
   OBJ_CC = \
12 (...)
14 NS_TCL_LIB = \
   (...)
```

The last step in the protocol implementation is the integration of the new agent into the ns-2 build system. The *Makefile.in* of ns-2 is adapted as shown in Listing A.11. The C++ and the OTcl code is included in the make process. The files are added to *OBJ_STL* and *NS_TCL_LIB_STL* variables as the C++ STL are used. Otherwise, the code has to be added to *OBJ_CC* and *NS_TCL_LIB*. After applying the changes to *Makefile.in*, a new *Makefile* can be generated and the source code is compiled by the following commands:

```
1  [ns-2]$ ./configure
   [ns-2]$ make clean
3  [ns-2]$ make depend
   [ns-2]$ make
5  [ns-2]$ make install
```

The QLS routing agent is now available in ns-2 simulation scenarios. The new routing protocol can be enabled after the definition of the nodes by the command *rtproto* (see Listing A.12). This sets QLS routing for all nodes.

Listing A.12. Usage of the new QLS routing protocol

```
1  set ns [new Simulator]
   Node set multiPath_ 1
3  set n0 [$ns node]
   (...)
5  $ns rtproto QLS
   (...)
```

A.4.7 Advice for Running ns-2 Simulations

There are several pieces of advice for performing simulations with ns-2. The most important one is the removal of unused packet-headers. In ns-2, different protocols add packet headers. By default, all these headers are added to every packet, e.g. a TCP packet contains headers of TCP, IP, QLS, ARP etc. A packet then contains a lot of unnecessary data for protocols not used even once in the simulation scenario. This consumes enormous unnecessary amounts of memory per packet and decreases the scalability of ns-2. Therefore, it is strongly recommended that you remove all headers of unused protocols. This can be done as follows. First, all headers are removed. Then, only the required headers are added again (see Listing A.13). Further details can be found in "Selectively Including Packet Headers in Your Simulation" in the ns manual ([183], Chap. 12).

Listing A.13. Remove all headers and add only the required

```
   remove-all-packet-headers
2  add-packet-header QLS ARP CBR IP
```

In addition, the size of trace files may be reduced by the following two methods:

• Avoid *trace-all*. Take a look at the other trace possibilities in the ns manual [183].

- Directly use command shell tools (e.g., awk, sed, perl) through a UNIX pipe instead of first writing the file. This can be simply done by modifying the trace file target in the simulation file.

```
set tracefile [open "| command_shell_tool >
    preprocessed_tracefile.tr" w]
$ns trace-all $tracefile
```

A.4.8 Analysing Methods

Trace files are the basic input for all analyses. The simple text file can be processed by various programming languages, which are able to read text files, like awk, sed, Perl or Java.

Different values like End-to-End Delay, Routing Overhead, etc., may be retrieved from the trace files. The retrieved values provide the basis for further processing like graphical representation. The values can, for example, be plotted with gnuplot, xgraph, etc.

Appendix B:
Network Emulation Focusing on QoS-Oriented Satellite Communication

Laurent Dairaine, Mathieu Gineste, and Hervé Thalmensy

Summary. The rapidly growing Internet architecture is causing most recent computer applications to integrate parts of distributed functionalities—such as transport layer services, transport protocols and other services—to meet user's needs in terms of functionalities and Quality of Service (QoS). Emulation platforms are a classic way to conduct protocol and applicative experiments to check if user and QoS requirements are met. They complement the simulation and real network experiments, since they enable us to use real implementation of protocols or applications without having a real network deployed for the experiments. This chapter presents the emulation approach in the context of networking experimentation: First, the different possible uses of dynamic emulation in the context of networking and protocol engineering are presented. Then, requirements for a general network emulation framework are proposed. Furthermore, different network emulation platforms and tools implementing the general framework are exposed; we describe how to use them in the context of protocol engineering and discuss their advantages and disadvantages. Finally, the emulation of wireless systems is challenging, due to many parameters that affect the behaviour of the channel. Satellite emulation, a subset of wireless emulation, has unique characteristics concerning access to the resource that combines static and dynamic assignment. As an example, the emulation of a QoS-oriented satellite system is detailed in a final section.

B.1 Network Emulation Basics

B.1.1 Introduction to Network Emulation

Rapid growth in Internet network support is leading to distributed computer applications, which not only make use of transport layer services by well-known transport protocols such as TCP or UDP, but also have to implement specific application and/or transport protocols in a way to meet user's necessities in terms of functionalities and QoS requirements. But these applications, and particularly their distributed components, have to be carefully tested to determine whether they perform well, are reliable and robust. This involves the expensive task of testing and debugging the produced software that is expected to run on distributed computers, interconnected by either a large area network such as the Internet, or by specific network technologies like wireless or satellite networks.

Nowadays, end users' requirements and competition between software development companies have continuously shortened the development process. But even if the time-to-market decreases, a company cannot release a product if it has not been fully tested and certified to meet clients' expectations in terms of services, QoS and reliability. If the client is disappointed in the product, he or she will switch to products offered by other companies. These are the reasons why companies need a quality lab that allows the rapid testing of their products under various conditions. There are two classical ways to achieve these tests: simulation and live testing.

Event-driven simulation is a powerful tool to achieve economical and fast experimentation. Its main specifications rely on an ad-hoc model working with and using a logical event-driven technique to achieve the simulation. The modelling techniques allow simplifying the problem under study in order to concentrate on the most critical issues. In addition, the model execution is linked to logical time, not real time. Depending on the complexity of the model, logical time can be related to real time. For example, it is possible to simulate a logical hour in few real-time milliseconds or a logical second in several real-time days. Due to both characteristics, no real implementations involving man-in-the-loop are directly possible in such simulations. Thus, a reliable link between the tested protocol model and the real implementation has to be accomplished in such a way as to ensure that the offered services and performance results between the simulation model and the experimental implementation protocol are consistent.

Another classical way of testing and debugging distributed software is to use real technology. This technique is generally expensive and time-consuming. The software can be tested on an ad-hoc testbed using real equipment and implementing a specific technology. This approach is particularly expensive in the context of large area networks, but also in specific technological conditions such as satellite networks. Moreover, it is sometimes impossible to implement this testing method, because the technology support is not available (e.g., developing an application over a new satellite transmission technology). This high experimentation cost is due not only to the technology costs involved, but also to the distributed man-in-the-loop manipulations and synchronisation it requires. Furthermore, it has limited value due to the inherent discrepancies between a particular test network and the much broader range of network imperfection that will be encountered by the software users. Another possibility for experimenting with real technology is to use, when possible, the target operational network, e.g. the real Internet. However, lack of control on the network experimentation conditions makes it very difficult to achieve and reduce measurements and obtain the relevance of test results.

More recently, progress in high-speed processing and networking has fostered the rapid development of network emulators. Network emulation is used to conduct experiments implementing real protocols, distributed applications and network models. This enables the network emulator to create a controlled communication environment, which can produce specific target communication behaviour in terms of QoS. Therefore, network emulation reproduces not only real underlying network architecture, but also artificial network impairments aimed at testing the characteristics of the experimental protocol. These tools represent a network service and reproduce the network performance dynamics. This approach is considered to be efficient and useful for simulations and live experiments, because it mixes real-time aspects of the experiment, real and simulated functionalities and emulation models. It provides a means of experimentation using real data and a network model.

B.1.2 What is Network Emulation?

In the most general sense, an emulator is designed to mimic the functions of a system on another system that is potentially totally different—the two different systems should then behave similarly. In software engineering, as shown in Fig. B.1, the same real software can be executed in the same way and without any modification, either in the real system environment or in an emulated environment with a system emulator acting exactly like the real system.

B.1.2.1 System Emulation and Virtual Machines

A perfect system emulator would offer the same services (functional properties) and the same performance level (nonfunctional properties) as the reproduced system. In electrical engineering, the word "emulation" traditionally means a very low-level reproduction of real-life electrical signals. For example, professional microprocessor emulator software comes with a processor-shaped connection, which you can actually plug in to a motherboard and run instructions with it. But emulation can be folded into a larger set of applications, for instance various levels of computer systems. Network emulation is an example of a system emulator, where the system is a

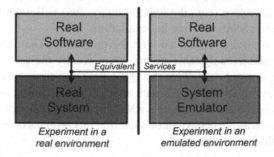

Fig. B.1. Experiment in real or emulated environments

computer network offering various communication services and is based on a set of well-known protocols.

An example of a system emulator is the VMWare product [185]. The VMware Workstation is desktop virtualisation software for software developers/testers who want to streamline software development, testing and deployment. The VMware Workstation enables users to run multiple x86-based operating systems, including Windows, Linux, FreeBSD, and their applications simultaneously on a single PC in fully networked, portable virtual machines.

The VMware Workstation works by creating fully isolated, secure virtual machines that encapsulate an operating system and its applications. The VMware virtualisation layer maps the physical hardware resources to the virtual machine's resources, so each virtual machine has its own CPU, memory, disks, and I/O devices, and is a full equivalent of a standard x86 machine. VMware can be installed on the host operating system and provides broad hardware support by inheriting device support from the host.

The main purpose of the VMware Workstation is to streamline software development and testing, which enhances productivity by e.g. configuring and testing desktops and servers as virtual machines before deploying them to production, and facilitating computer-based training and software demos by deploying classroom material in virtual machines. The VMware workstation also provides virtual networks, allowing the connection between the virtual workstation and the real world. Thus, it is possible for the virtual workstation to communicate with the real host, in which the virtual machine is executed with external real machines, using the physical interface of the host executed. Finally, several virtual machines can also communicate with each other using a virtual network inside the real machine. It is also possible to emulate various virtual networks by interconnecting different virtual machines. Therefore, it is more likely to build a realistic network architecture that implements various subnets with switches, interconnected by virtual hosts implementing the routing functionality.

The VMWare networking capability provides a realistic and functional interface, which allows real pieces of software such as operating systems including networking code (IP, TCP, etc.) and any applications to be executed. It is then possible to build a complex distributed architecture with numerous real implementations of protocols and test the functional characteristics of this system in a Best-Effort environment. Furthermore, performance (e.g., throughput, delay, etc.) will mainly depend on the capacity of the real machine hosting the emulation.

No real-time control is associated with the emulation. The nonfunctional characteristics of the emulated systems are not supported by the software. The system does not provide a way to represent the QoS characteristics of the target network (and the system), even simplest ones such as a given probability of packet loss, or a simple delay between the end-systems. Of course, more complex network emulation scenarios—such as the behaviour of a satellite link with particular atmospherical conditions—would not be supported.

B.1.2.2 Network Emulation

While the system emulation allows users to reproduce system behaviour on hardware architecture (like Linux on Windows, or hand-held video game systems on computer), network emulation enables network behaviour to be reproduced in a controlled testbed. The primary aim of using such emulation tools is to achieve experiments with real applications as well as protocols and provide them with a support ability to evaluate their functional (does the protocol work?) and nonfunctional properties (how does the protocol performs in particular network conditions?).

The network behaviour can reproduce real technologies (e.g., wireless, satellite link or network interconnections) as illustrated in Fig. B.2, where the satellite link behaviour is reproduced by a simple emulation box.

Network emulation is used as a method to test nonfunctional properties of real implemented protocols. It means that emulation tools must provide a way to introduce network impairments such as delay, packet loss and bit errors according to a model to test the protocols and applications properly. Another important issue in network emulation is to provide a way to produce a predefined possible behaviour to test and stress the experimental protocol under a specific condition.

In the particular but very common case of level-3 IP service emulation, the resulted QoS is mainly dependent on external factors, such as underlying technologies, interconnection topology, network traffic, etc. Thus, IP network service emulation could offer a "perfect" QoS channel to a 100% loss channel depending on the underlying protocols and many other external factors. This leads to a large set of possibilities in the emulation experiments. The level-3 service emulation is able to produce an end-to-end QoS channel that could focus on:

- Artificial QoS:

The emulator implements processing that aims to test the experimental protocol on specific QoS conditions, not imperatively related to any technology. This processing allows the user to test and stress its experimental protocol in a target QoS condition, aiming to point out errors or bugs that could be difficult to produce in a noncontrolled environment. This can be useful, for example, at the transport level to study the impact of various packet drops in a TCP connection (e.g., the SYN/ACK, etc.), or at the application level to study what happens if a particular block of the "Intra" picture is delayed.

- Realistic QoS:

Fig. B.2. Experiment in (a) operational real environment and (b) emulated environments

The emulator implements a process that aims to reproduce the behaviour of a specific network architecture as accurately as possible. This type of emulation allows the user to test their protocols over an existing network or internetwork without using a real test bed with all related technologies (e.g., a wireless network, a satellite network, Ethernet Gigabit network, or any interconnection of such technologies).

B.1.3 Why Use Network Emulation?

What types of users are potential customers of an emulation system? Various types of customers with their own aims provide different use cases for emulation systems. Emulation platforms can help at various stages of protocol research and development. Examples are:

- at the research stage to study the existing solutions and to help the design of new protocols and applications;
- at the conception and development stages to study advantages and drawbacks of new proposed solutions compared to the existing ones;
- at testing and study of performance stage to test, benchmark and evaluate the protocols and application; and
- at the final stages, to demonstrate the effectiveness of new solutions by a real demonstration.

B.1.3.1 Network Emulation at Research and Design Stage

The application and protocol that researchers are working on is for existing or future network solutions. Therefore, a testbed that can help study different cases is required. The emulation can then be used for:

- Precise study of a protocol or an application under specific network conditions to find outside effects, limitations, bugs or any problems. The advantages of this protocol can also be investigated. These studies will help in proposing new solutions, possibly based on existing ones.
- Comparison of several protocols under specific network conditions to see the advantages and drawbacks of each.
- Comparison of several protocols under realistic network conditions (e.g., satellite network QoS) to reveal the limitations of a solution over some QoS.

B.1.3.2 Network Emulation at Conception and Development Stage

The designer and implementer needs to study his or her current development to see whether it is reliable and efficient. Different tests can be designed, for example:

- Testing the behaviour of the solution under specific network conditions to find new solutions that can be used to detect potential bugs. Moreover, the test can also be used to investigate the advantages of the new solution under conditions where another solution is deficient.

- Testing the behaviour of the developed solution when a parameter (e.g., delay) is involved. This can help to design charts with the ideal conditions for the solution.
- Testing the behaviour of new solutions under specific network conditions to see whether it can be used on every network or if it cannot be released over a specific technology.
- Doing comparison charts between several protocols and applications, including the new one, to show the pros and cons of the new one.

Live testing would be definitely too complicated and expensive to meet all these conditions. The test phase would therefore be too long, or the tests could be incomplete.

B.1.3.3 Network Emulation at Testing and Performance Evaluation Stage

The end of the testing and development process will be part of the support phases, leading to the following experiments:

- Product testing over a realistic end-user network condition to see whether the product can be released to the public. This test is very important to ensure the service provided is adequate with regard to user or application requirements.
- Debugging a product to find why it is not working on a specific network or under specific conditions. It can also provide the proof that the product is well designed for the network, but that several bugs are present under specific end-user computer configurations.

B.1.3.4 Network Emulation When Demonstrating Software

Demonstration is an important activity to facilitate adoption of the application or the protocol. The protocol and application designer must often demonstrate the efficiency of the proposed solution. In the context of distributed application and protocols, the demonstration is organised in the lab environment. Obtaining an ad-hoc underlying network behaviour for the lab requires the help of the network emulator tools. The resulting behaviour can either emulate an operational real network technology or a specific condition to show particular efficiency of the software being tested.

In this context, the first type of user could be an end-user, involved in a final application test or in the reception of specific software. The users need to be able to evaluate the main use so that the network supervisor is able to plan the development of his/her network and to see the consequences of a faulty link or an increased capacity link on his/her network.

B.1.4 Requirements for Emulation Systems

The main issue regarding network emulation is to achieve experiments with protocols. An experiment is any process or study that results in the collection of data where the outcome is unknown [186]. An experimenter is the actor conducting the experiment.

The term network emulation will be restricted to situations in which the user has control over some of the networking conditions under which the experiment takes place. This yields a new definition of an emulation experiment. An emulation experiment can be defined as deliberately imposing processing on the set of packets exchanged by distributed software in the interest of observing the resulting response. This differs from an observational study, which involves collecting and analysing the behaviour without changing existing conditions.

The various cases of emulation previously introduced into the different stages of protocol design and developments lead to the following set of functional needs:

- Protocol or application testing: the emulation should be used to test a system under development, or an existing system with specific network conditions to reveal bugs, performance problems, deadlocks or advantages. Therefore, modification can be performed on the product.
- Protocol performance analysis: the emulation should provide means for the system under development to be tested and compared to other systems, under specific network conditions or realistic network parameters to draw performance and comparison charts.
- Demonstration: the emulation platform will be used to show that the system under development is working under specific conditions and so be well-suited according to user need.

B.1.4.1 Functional Requirements

Considering the high-level needs of network emulation, several requirements for the network emulator can be defined. Note that all these requirements are not necessarily required for all uses of emulation.

- Controllability: The delay, loss or modification of packets must be achieved by using an emulation model that can totally be controlled. The model aim is to produce a specific set of impairments to either mimic real network architecture or to introduce a possible QoS scenario.
- Accuracy: The packets that have been computed to be dropped should be deleted. The remaining packets have to be delivered according to modification of the transmission delay calculated from the emulation model.
- Transparency: The emulation system should be used with minimal (or no) modification to the tested protocol or application. Moreover, it should offer an interface typically used in the protocol's context, for example, sockets for Internet applications.
- Flexibility: A large variety of methods should be provided to the experimenter to be able to compute and measure packet impairments. These methods should be adapted to either the development of an emulation model linked to real networking technologies, or to the development of a specific emulation model intended to stress a particular aspect of the tested protocol.

- Extensibility: The emulation should be able to facilitate further development of a new emulation model. The new model should be used to achieve particular requirements associated with the experiment.
- Scalability: Scalability can be a very important factor, especially in the context of specific protocol testing such as high-speed or multicast protocols.
- Dynamics: The QoS in the communication area is evolving rapidly with various limitations, depending on the underlying technology being used. In wireless environments (due to a variety of physical effect on the signal) and also in the context of wired networks (due to congestion, physical link failure, routing update, etc.), communication conditions may evolve. The emulation system should provide a way to test applications and protocols in evolving and different QoS conditions.
- Reproducibility: Experiment conditions that are developed to be carried out for testing or comparison between protocols should be reproducible to achieve fair comparisons and provide deterministic performance results.

B.1.4.2 Requirements on Packet Impairments

The basic action that the emulation system has to provide is to introduce QoS impairments on flows generated by the tested protocol. The impairments that can happen in a network are basically packet latency (delay), packet loss and packet modification.

The four main components of latency are propagation delay, transmission delay, processing delay and queuing delay (see Chap. 1).

The packet modification is mainly due to two possible sources. The transmission system can introduce bit errors due to fading or any signal-level problem. This bit error could be transmitted to higher layers, if no error control mechanism is used in the lower layers. This is not a common case, but various studies at network and application level address this strategy and the gain that could be produced in a particular networking scenario. Another much more common type of packet modification is packet segmentation, which can happen in the network due to the necessary adaptation of transmission units in a heterogeneous networking environment. Furthermore, packet duplication is also a possible packet modification that can (rarely) happen in the network.

Packet loss is due to various situations in the network. First, as stated in the previous paragraph, media transmission can produce bit errors that usually imply packet loss at a higher level, due to the loss of (checksum-based) detection techniques and associated protocol behaviour. Another important source of packet loss is due to buffer congestion. Buffer congestion can appear in many active network elements such as in a network router, but also in a link layer bridge or end-systems.

These impairments are the basic emulation actions that happen in a network. The impact of all these packet-level actions is very important in higher protocols. Producing and controlling these impairments is a way to efficiently evaluate the functional and nonfunctional properties of these protocols and distributed applications. For testing purposes, these impairments can be produced to accurately stress a particular situation of loss, delay or packet modification. Similarly, for reproducing a global networking behaviour, these packet emulation actions are required.

B.1.5 Network Emulation System Approaches

Various approaches have been proposed to implement the general network emulation framework proposed in the previous section. In this section we will discuss each component in more detail.

B.1.5.1 Traffic Shapers

Once the experiment flows are constituted by the classifier, the emulation processor will add impairments to the packets; for example, delay them, drop some of them and shape the flows to meet a given flow rate. A scheduler has to be implemented to manage the different existing queues.

Two approaches can be designed for the emulation controllers. The first one is when the emulation controller is implemented in a single computer (centralised approach) that represents the whole network. The second way to build an emulation processor is to use a distributed system (distributed approach) such as a grid, each computer having its own emulation processor and model, and representing a slice of the targeted network.

B.1.5.1.1 Centralised Approach

ONE [187] was a research project at Ohio University's Internetworking Research Group. It provides basic emulation of a network cloud between two interfaces, using a single computer running under the Solaris system. It does not manage several flows, so the user must provide a general model. It implements the following functionalities: bandwidth, buffer storage size, output queue size, RED algorithm, bit error rate and the delay.

Dummynet [188] integrates an emulation processor, working in the operating system kernel. It intercepts the packets between the network layer and the application layer and is able to delay them. It simulates/enforces queue and bandwidth limitations, delays, packet loss and multipath effects by inserting two queues between the protocol layers, namely rq and pq. When a packet arrives, it is put into the rq queue that is bound and has its own policy (FIFO, RED for example). The packets are moved from rp to pq (which has a FIFO policy) at the given bandwidth. Once in pq, the packets are delayed by the amount of time specified. It can be placed on users' workstations or on FreeBSD machines acting as routers or bridges. It is controlled by ipfw and some sysctrl commands. The user has to create pipes to classify the packets and then configure Dummynet to process the packets following these settings: bandwidth, queue size, delay and random packet loss. Dummynet also allows the user to create dynamic queues. All the packets matching the pipe rule will go in the same queue. With the "mask" option, users can define more flows that will be split into different queues applying the same impairments. Each pipe is associated with one or more queues. Each queue has its own weight, size and discipline. A variant of Weighted Fair Queuing, named WFQ2+ is used to schedule the different queues of a single flow.

Although Dummynet was initially designed to study TCP performance, NistNet [189] was designed from the beginning as a network emulator. It integrates an emulation processor and also works in the system kernel. It neither classifies the packets, nor the rate control. NistNet can apply the following effects on the flows: packet delay, both fixed and variable (jitter); packet reordering; packet loss, both random and congestion-dependent; packet duplication, and bandwidth limitations. The advantages of NistNet compared to Dummynet are mainly the statistical delay distribution it offers.

Netem [190] was developed on the basis of NistNet, which is not compatible with the 2.6.x version of Linux kernels. Netem is an emulation Linux queuing discipline, integrated into the Traffic Control (TC) module. It is only an emulation processor and does not include a classifier (i.e., see the various classifiers proposed by TC). Once TC has classified the packets into different classes, Netem impairs the flows. Finally, TC takes care of the queuing discipline and the transmission of the packets. Netem can provide the following effects on the packets: variable delay, choice of delay distribution, packet loss rate, packet duplication, packet reordering and flow differentiation. As it is based on TC, the user can choose all the other queuing disciplines and the shapers available for this tool.

EMPOWER [191] is an emulation project based on its own emulation processor. Each network node implements a Virtual Device Module (VDM). This module receiver is mapped to a network port and receives an egress flow, diverted from the IP operating system layer. Once in the VD module, the flow passes through six submodules, representing a different effect: MTU sub module, Delay submodule, Bandwidth submodule, Loss submodule, Bit error submodule and finally out-of-order submodule. The flow goes through the submodules in the order previously mentioned. Once the last submodule has passed, the flow is redirected to the underlying network port and transmitted. While in the bandwidth submodule an on/off heterogeneous traffic can be injected in the VD to study their impact on the experimental flow.

B.1.5.1.2 Distributed Approach

Besides these solutions integrated in the kernel, another way to perform the emulation processing is to use a computer grid. A computer grid [192] is an association of a wide variety of geographically distributed computers, storage systems, databases and data sourcing interconnected via a network. Several applications—like parallel calculus—have been using grid computing, but it can also be used for emulation. These systems provide a way to implement a testbed as a configurable topology and a large amount of computers is provided. Some of the computers on the grid become an emulation processor and are connected to end-system computers with real links. Using a low-level emulator in certain nodes enables us to produce bottleneck links. The whole grid behaviour can then represent a target network behaviour. These systems reproduce a real network and take into account side effects such as routing. We will present two different grid computing systems.

Emulab [193] is a grid computing oriented emulator. Emulab provides integrated access to three disparate experimental environments: simulated, emulated and wide-area network testbeds. Emulab unifies all three environments under a common user interface and integrates the three into a common framework. This framework provides abstractions, services and name spaces common to all, such as allocation and naming of nodes and links. By mapping the abstractions into domain-specific mechanisms and internal names, Netbed masks much of the heterogeneity of the three approaches.

The Emulab emulation testbed consists of three subtestbeds (nodes from each can be mixed and matched), each having a different research target:

- Mobile Wireless: Netbed has been deployed and opened to public external use, a small robotic testbed that will grow into a large mobile robotic wireless testbed. The small version (5 motes and 5 stargates on 5 robots are all remotely controllable, plus 25 static motes, many with attached sensor boards) is in an open area in our offices.
- Fixed 802.11 Wireless: Netbed's Fixed Wireless testbed consists of PC nodes that contain 802.11 a/b/g WiFi interfaces, and are scattered around a building at various locations on multiple floors. Experimenters can pick the nodes they want to use, and as with other fixed nodes, can replace the software that runs on the nodes all the way down to the operating system.
- Emulab Classic: a universally available time- and space-shared network emulator, which achieves new levels of user-friendliness. Several hundred PCs in racks, combined with secure, user-friendly Web-based tools, and driven by ns-compatible scripts or a Java GUI allow remote configuration and control of machines and links down to the hardware level. Packet loss, latency, bandwidth and queue sizes can be user-defined. Even the OS disk contents can be fully and securely replaced with custom images by any experimenter. Netbed can load up to a hundred disks in less than two minutes.

Grid 5000 [194] is a French project. It aims to interconnect geographically distributed clusters with high-speed links using Renater's network. Grid'Explorer is included in this project. This is a smaller grid designed to emulate network conditions. It will contain three components: 1000 nodes PC Cluster, an Experimental Condition Data Base and a tool set (emulators, simulators).

PlanetLab [195] is more a resource overlay network than a grid computing emulator. In this system, the Planetlab nodes are located across the world and linked using real Internet links. The nodes do not perform impairments on the packets arriving as they are interconnected using a real network. As PlanetLab implements real routers and real network protocols, this emulation platform is totally transparent to the user. The main criticism of PlanetLab is that it only reproduces a small slice of the Internet. It allows experiments to be conducted over computers linked by the research network (which is different from the commodity/commercial Internet).

The major drawbacks of these platforms are their low availability and their very high costs. Indeed, building a grid requires a large free space to store all the nodes and considerable funds to buy the different computers. Once a grid has been set up, it is usually shared in order to use it at maximum capacity. Reserving a grid is usually compulsory and it can sometimes take a long time to get a slot. The question of the grid administration has also to be solved. If the computers are geographically distributed, each site can administrate their own computers or a global administrator can be nominated.

B.1.5.2 Emulation Models

The emulation processors are a feasible way to process the experimented traffic. They must be controlled by the way of emulation models. Various levels of complexity in the emulation models are possible, depending on the aim of the whole experiment. There are three ways to obtain a network model: ad-hoc model (static or dynamic), trace-based model or by using a simulator.

B.1.5.2.1 Emulating QoS Parameters

An ad-hoc model is a set of parameters that are static during the whole experiment; in this case, describing the network we want to emulate. It can be useful to reproduce artificial QoS. The parameters are the ones previously defined: delay, loss rate, BER etc. With an ad-hoc model, the users design the network the way they want and get the QoS they need. With this type of ad-hoc model, the network offers the same quality of service throughout the experiment. It can be useful to test all the possibilities of a product or to compare it to other already existing products. In order to set up these models, some GUIs are offered to the user by the emulation processor. For example, NISTNet comes with a GUI while a PHP script has been developed to control Netem.

Ad-hoc models can also evolve according to external events, e.g., time. In reality, the QoS offered by a network is not the same during the night than during the day for example. Time-oriented models allow the user to define the network and to enable to evolve with time. For example, the delay will increase during high network utilisation. This can be useful to test a new product in different conditions or to schematically represent a general behaviour. The tester will be able to validate the product under several conditions and compare it to the other solutions. The Net Shaper [196] project uses time-oriented emulation. In this case a daemon is executed and is waiting for the new model to be applied to the emulation processor. The daemon was able to successfully receive and treat up to 1000 messages per second.

The events can also be driven by randomly generated events. In this case, the artificial QoS offered by the network would not be driven by time, but by an algorithm. The algorithm could represent, for example, a node failure randomly occurring or, in the case of a mobility impact study, the algorithm could modify the QoS offered, depending on where the user is located. The EMPOWER project [191] uses this kind of emulation in the wireless section. In this case, a VMN (Virtual Wireless Node) is added and is associated with an event table where randomly generated mobility events are listed. A time-stamp is also associated with the events. The incoming flows are impaired according to this event table.

A last event driven ad hoc model is the script driven model [197, 198]. In this case, a script describes what the emulator processor should do (e.g., impair the flow differently, transmit another packet, reply to this packet, etc.) when it receives a packet. It is useful to study experimental protocols and determine their reactions under several conditions.

B.1.5.2.2 Virtual Nodes Approach

In this approach, the global network behaviour is produced by virtually reproducing the network topology and components. All nodes constituting the target network to be emulated are implemented either on a single centralised system or distributed on various distinct systems usually connected by high speed networks. Virtual links are used to connect these nodes according to the topology of the target network. Real protocols such as IP or routing protocols can also be implemented in the virtual node system. This approach can be implemented in a system (several virtual nodes co-exist in the centralised system) or over a distributed system such as a grid. Of course, in this type of architecture, the classical strategy to produce realistic behaviour is to introduce real traffic into the emulated network to produce congestion, etc.

IMUNES [199] is an example of the centralised virtual node approach and proposes a methodology for emulating computer networks by using a general purpose OS Kernel partitioned into multiple lightweight virtual nodes, which can be connected via kernel-level links to form arbitrary complex network topologies. IMUNES provides each virtual node with a stack that is independent of the entire standard network, thus enabling highly realistic and detailed emulation of network routers. It also enables user-level applications to run within the virtual nodes.

At the user level, IMUNES proposes a very convenient interface that enables the target emulated network to be defined, defining the virtual nodes and their software and links as well as the impairments parameters.

Another comparable approach is the Entrapid protocol development environment [200] that introduces a model of multiple virtualised networking kernels and presents variants of the standards BSD network stack in multiple instances that run as threads in specialised user processes. Other similar approaches include the Alpine simulator [201] project and Virtual Routers [202].

This approach is often considered the only means to achieve realistic emulation of complex network topology. It enables the target network to be specified accurately and realistic behaviour—as a direct effect of real traffic and protocol implementations running in the system—to be produced. Nevertheless, the major problem of this approach is scalability. How can one implement a core network router in a single machine? What if a realistic network contains several dozens of network elements? How can one manage the number of necessary flows to produce realistic conditions in a centralised manner? These questions are very difficult to answer, in particular in the context of a total centralisation, but are real problems in distributed systems like grids. Moreover, most of the emulation experiments do not require such an approach to be implemented. What is really needed by most protocol experiments is the notion of channels interconnecting the various protocol entities that are under testing with either a realistic or a specific behaviour.

B.1.5.2.3 Trace-Based Approach

The trace-based approach is another way to obtain realistic behaviour according to a given network infrastructure. By using different probes on the real network, or even on a modelled network (e.g., with a discrete-event simulator) it is possible to get the different parameters aiming to reproduce the network behaviour.

The trace-based approach consists of recording the performance of a real (or a simulated) network, and then use these traces to drive the emulation processor impairments. Virtual Routers [203] provide an appropriate methodology for the trace-based approach. It consists of three complementary phases:

- Collection: in this phase, an experimenter with an instrumented host takes measurements. In the case of a wireless network, the experimenter can be mobile and traverse a path. During the collection, packets from a known workload are generated. The mobile host records observations of these packets. By performing multiple traversals of the same path, one can obtain a trace family that captures the network quality variation on that path.
- Distillation: The distillation phase transforms a collected trace into a form suitable for the next phase. For each time instant, the distillation examines the performance of the known workload and produces a set of parameters for a simple network performance model. By composing these, distillation produces a concise, time-varying description of the network performance.
- Modulation: in the modulation phase, the system under test is subject to network impairment driven by the previous network performance model.

The parameters associated with the end-to-end channel are, for example, delay, loss rate, packet reordering or packets duplicated [203]. The user must have probes on the end-user stations that are used to record the dates the packets arrive or leave the station. Once this is done, the results are transmitted to a controller that evaluates the delay and the mean loss rate, given the network model. This enables the user to obtain a dynamic network profile. Depending on the limitations of the trace (over a month, or over an hour) we obtain general or specific network conditions. The trace-based approach has one major drawback: it cannot reproduce all the conditions that a network can encounter. The trace-based approach is not a panacea. A single trace can capture only a snapshot of the varying performance along a particular path. Moreover, the traces cannot offer precise reproducible results because network processes are nondeterministic, and the same situation at another time could have produced additional impairments.

B.1.5.2.4 Simulation-Based Approach

Using a simulator, like a discrete-event simulator, is a very common way to conduct experiments in networking (see Appendix A). The key characteristics of Discrete Event Simulations are:

- Events occur at specific moments in time.
- Polling is done to find the time of the next event.

- Time does not increment by fixed amounts. Time jumps to the time of the next event.

An event occurs any time the state of the simulation needs to be updated. This happens, for example, when a packet is created, when it is sent from one node to another, or even during the processing of a packet in a node (if required).

Event-driven simulators provide a very convenient and very useful way to model networks. The idea here is to provide the ability to use the simulator capacity to drive the emulation processor. This cooperation is achieved at a price of having to undertake several modifications on the original tool. The simulator has to work in real time and needs to capture and generate real data packets. Figure B.3 depicts the general model of discrete-event simulator aided emulation.

NS [204] is a widely used discrete-event simulator (see Sect. A.4). The international networking research community has greatly contributed to the models and tools used in this simulator. An extension of this tool, nse [205], allows integration between modelling capacity with the impairments implemented in real time and applied to live traffic.

Of course, various modifications have been designed to enable such utilisation. First, the event-driven scheduler has to be replaced with a real-time scheduler. In the case of emulation, the simulator does not have to jump onto the next event once the last event has been processed. It is crucial to process the events synchronously in real time. This real-time synchronisation is an important limitation of the tool's capacity. For example, if too many events occur at a given time, the simulator still has to process them at the right time, not before and not after. Then, the simulator can come into a "livelocked" state if a packet arrived while it delays the last event. Obtaining a very accurate real-time clock is nearly impossible and that causes the simulator to misbehave under heavy traffic conditions. Another drawback is that if a large delay is applied to the packets, large memory systems are required to store all the events to be treated.

Another task to perform to get NS working is to interface it with real traffic. Indeed, to "route" packets through the simulator, NS uses its own representation of the network, totally different from the IPv4 or IPv6 world. When a packet arrives, two possibilities can be considered: the real IP address can be mapped to the NS address or NS could be modified to understand IP addresses. The first possibility is

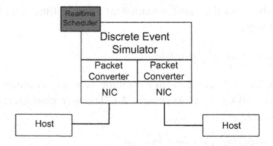

Fig. B.3. Using discrete-event simulator to provide emulation behavior

implemented. Finally, NS also has to be modified to the process of capturing and injecting real data and the packets going through the network. For this task, NS provides a network object that can understand UDP/IP, raw IP and frame-level data. To capture UDP/IP and raw IP packets it uses the standard socket API while using the Berkeley Packet Filter to intercept the frame level packets.

Nse can perform emulation in two different modes: opaque and protocol. In the opaque mode, the packets are passed through the computer without being interpreted. NS implements an emulation processor allowing the real packets to be dropped, delayed, reordered or duplicated depending on the simulation results. Opaque mode is useful in evaluating the behaviour of real-world implementations not interfering with the model.

In the protocol mode, packets are interpreted by the ns model. The real packets are translated into simulation events and take part in the simulation just like any other internal event. The simulated protocols can then react depending on the real packet. An inverse function allows the simulator to convert internal packets into real ones and inject them into the network. The protocol mode can be used for end-to-end application testing, protocol and conformance testing. Since the protocol mode includes a protocol agent understanding the headers, it enables the users to drop packets depending on header flags.

This approach is theoretically very powerful with respect to the modelling possibilities it may offer. Nevertheless, the major drawback of this approach is the scalability problem, which requires extensive system memory and CPU speed to handle the potentially large number of packets on the network. Other approaches using simulation for emulation have been developed to improve the scalability of the virtual network. For example, in IP-TNE (Internet Protocol Traffic and Network Emulator) [206] the use of parallel discrete-event simulation and simulation abstraction such as fluid simulation are addressed to improve the simulation. Various models can be applied in order to configure the emulation processors. Each model has its advantages and drawbacks, depending on the experiment the user wants to conduct. In all cases, getting an exact representation of the reality is a difficult task to implement.

B.1.5.2.5 Active Emulation Approach

This section outlines the concept of active network emulation. We will see how active emulation can be a realistic way to emulate complex network behaviour, and an application of this concept will be presented in the next chapter to emulate a satellite link.

Some networks produce network dynamics that may require complex models and mechanisms to be emulated. The complexity of this type of emulation often comes from the highly dynamic behaviour of the protocols used in such networks. Protocols react depending on internal factors like their own mechanisms and external factors (such as the traffic crossing the network). For instance, satellite networks, in particular access schemes such as DAMA, propose three main different types of traffic assignment techniques that may be combined. Some of them depend on the traffic characteristics, while others do not. Since the behaviour of this access scheme is not predictable in advance, dynamic configurations of the emulation system are required. The only way to have sufficient realistic emulation behaviour is to react in real time on the emulation model, according to various factors and including the experimental traffic. In this sense, emulation needs to be active: the traffic will modify the configuration of the emulation and consequently the resulting modifications will have an effect on the traffic crossing the emulator. Considering this emulation problem, several techniques might be used to emulate a satellite link.

In the context of low-level protocol developments, satellite emulation systems can be based mostly on real protocol implementations (e.g., DAMA, adapted routing protocols, etc.), using a wire emulation model to avoid the use of a real air interface. The protocol's complete behaviour and signalling is then actually implemented while only the physical link is emulated, introducing geostationary end-to-end delay, and possibly loss models. Such systems are often very accurate in the emulation service they provide, but are also very complex and expensive to develop and maintain when protocols evolve. In the context of end-to-end communication, protocol experimentations do not need such low-level emulation.

The active emulation approach is an alternative [207]: Instead of reproducing access to the satellite link according to a heavy implementation of low-level protocol behaviour, only resulting effects on data transfer are emulated by way of a proper emulation model. This results in a simple and practical implementation that can be thus combined with more complex emulation scenarios (e.g., for emulating a wider network including a satellite link) or operational networks. To achieve this goal, the emulation model must react in real time to various external events such as time or processed traffic, leading to the concept of active emulation. The advantage compared to the first type of emulation is that it provides an "in-a-box" solution, integrating an emulation processor and a potentially complex and realistic emulation model (not limited to satellite links) into an easy-to-deploy system.

B.1.5.3 Implementation

The emulation platform can be implemented in different layers, ranging from the hardware layer up to the application layer.

B.1.5.3.1 User Space Implementation

Random events and programming facilities in user space have been the reason for many emulators being developed at this level. The major challenge is that even a more contemporary, but user-friendly GUI, and a greatly tweaked application need to be developed to solve the problems. In these architectures, the software has to intercept the packets in the network stack to then process and reinject them. It can either trick the operating system into making it believe that it is in the network stack, or it can intercept the packets and inject them using its own sockets, enabling us to add further services on the classical sockets. Some projects dynamically configure the emulator running in the operating system stack. Although the packets are not captured, the modules in the network stack are constantly modified.

User space offers lots of services, programming tools and libraries that facilitate building complex network emulation models. One of the major requirements of such implementations is to have access to packets that usually cross the system where the user space emulator is implemented. Various possibilities exist to capture those packets, such as Raw IP socket, Libpcap and libnet or Divert socket.

The main advantage of the user-level implementation is the flexibility of services and development that it offers in comparison to kernel space. The two main drawbacks of user-level implementations are:

- At least one packet copy exists between the system kernel and the user space, affecting the performance of the processed streams.
- User-space processes can be interrupted. It basically means that a higher priority task can be scheduled instead of the emulation task, with all the timing and processing.

NS Emulation, including its Emulab front end and the Ohio-Network-Emulator ONE, is an example of emulators implemented in user space.

B.1.5.3.2 Kernel Implementation

Network emulation is time critical. As stated in the general requirements of network emulation, the delay impairment must be achieved as precisely as possible and user-level implementations might fail on this real-time task. A possible alternative to implement the emulation processor is to do it in the operating system kernel to optimise its performance. In this context, various emulators, such as dummynet or NISTnet, are implemented between the Ethernet and IP layers.

Packet interception is completely hidden from user-space programs and any user-space software using the standard UNIX communication interfaces (sockets, raw sockets) will be affected by the specified network properties. The overhead introduced by the additional layer a packet has to pass is crucial, because packet data has not to been modified or copied to different memory areas (unlike with user space approaches). Communication through interfaces with NETShaper is required.

The kernel-based solutions offer a powerful set of possibilities that are cheap to develop and do not introduce much overhead in the packets. The major drawbacks of these solutions is that they are limited to the precision of the operating system clock and that if the operating system is highly loaded, some clock ticks can be missed, impacting the platform performance. Furthermore, development of applications within the operating kernel is harder than on the application layer. The developer has fewer tools and functions to program, and he or she has to be careful with the memory management and the stability of the software. It is highly probable that if the module crashes, the kernel crashes too.

Most of emulation systems like dummynet or NISTNET are implemented in the kernel to provide high performance. The implementation of the emulator on a real-time operating system might be a potential solution to the problem, which needs further investigation.

B.1.5.3.3 Hardware Implementation

An emulation implemented with hardware (e.g., FPGAs) can possibly perform better. The emulator needs to be set up based on the parameters given by the user. It processes the flow with limited software overhead. This approach has the advantage of minimising the processing time of each packet, but it is also less flexible, harder to design and more expensive to develop than using software included in the operating system network stack. The emulator can also be implemented with dedicated hardware like a network processor, but the software is harder to develop than under regular X86 architectures, even if the flows are treated more efficiently.

B.2 Case Study: Emulation of QoS-oriented Satellite Communication

B.2.1 Introduction

Among the large set of network types considered into the EuQoS project, a geostationary satellite link is particularly interesting for experiments, due to the particular QoS services it offers. The satellite link targeted is based on the widely spread DVB-S standard for the Forward link (from the Hub Station toward the Satellite Terminal) and DVB-RCS standard for the Return link (from the Satellite Terminal toward the Hub Station) [208]. This satellite access network has to be provided in order to make the corresponding experimentations when a satellite link is part of the end-to-end communication. Due to the high cost of satellite resources, experimentations involving this particular access network will be conducted on an emulated satellite link. In order to develop this emulation platform, the characteristics of the satellite link will be first presented.

The main issue in satellite communications, and more particularly on the satellite return links—which will be the particular subject of this use case—is to make efficient use of the precious transmission resources, which are scarce and costly. Recent techniques based on dynamic bandwidth assignment enable a high efficiency of the return link usage. Emerging protocols, such as DAMA (Demand Assignment Multiple Access) integrates a combination of these existing protocols in order to both ensure a high utilisation of the return link resources and to offer QoS-oriented capacity assignment types. This access scheme is targeted at the satellite access network experiment presented by this case study.

B.2.2 DVB Satellite Communications

DVB-S and DVB-RCS are standards used to carry out IP-based applications over geostationary satellites: **DVB-S** (Digital Video Broadcasting-Satellite) is used to transport data over the forward link (from the gateway earth station to the numerous satellite terminals). **DVB-RCS** (DVB-Return Channel System via Satellite) is used to transport data over the return link and specify the access scheme to the return link (from the satellite terminal to the gateway earth station). This standard allows resources to be efficiently shared between great numbers of Satellite Terminals (ST) accessing the return link. We will now see in detail how access and resource allocation is managed by the protocol and how we can take advantage of it to introduce QoS differentiation on this kind of link.

The satellite user terminal receives a standard DVB-S transmission generated by the satellite hub station (the gateway). Packet data may be sent over this forward link in the usual way: DVB-S [209] defines several ways to encapsulate data packets into an ISO MPEG-2 Transport Stream [210], but the common practice for IP datagrams encapsulation is to use the DSM-CC sections through an adaptation layer protocol, named Multi-Protocol Encapsulation (MPE) [211]. DVB-RCS standard [208] is associated to the use of AAL5/ATM, but can also use MPEG2-TS Stream.

To get an idea of the availability and requirements of QoS in the targeted satellite system, here is a description of how the DVB-RCS system works:

A Return Channel Satellite Terminal (RCST) receives general network information from the DVB-RCS Network Control Centre (NCC), sent over the forward link, to get control and timing messages.

All data transmissions by the RCST over the return link are controlled by the NCC. This dynamic resource admission control assures optimal use of the costly resources of the satellite.

Dynamic resource control consists of assignment of resources (slots) to STs based on their requests to the NCC and limit values negotiated during connection establishment. The assignments are conditioned by the availability of resources within defined return channels. The assignment is the responsibility of the MAC Scheduler (in the NCC), which implements a Demand-Assignment Multiple Access (DAMA) protocol.

The uplink scheduling consists of processes taking place in the scheduler and in STs: First, STs calculate capacity request required for the current traffic and send it to the NCC. Then NCC calculates and sends the overall assignment to every ST of the satellite system taking into account current load of the system as well as requests and limitations of specific ST. Finally, the capacity is distributed within terminals to end-users and their applications (depending on ST MAC queuing architecture and service discipline).

The Service Level Agreement (SLA) between the terminal and the hub specifies guarantees on different classes of access to the Return Link of the satellite. These classes are defined in the DVB-RCS standard as capacity allocation of a different type [208].

The DAMA implementation of DVB-RCS uses a combination of static and dynamic allocation techniques in order to ensure a set of QoS guarantees as well as high bandwidth efficiency. The return link scheduler supports three main capacity assignment types to reach this objective, described as follows:

- **Fixed rate** (Continuous Rate Assignment—**CRA**). The CRA assignment type is a guaranteed rate capacity, fully provided for the duration of the connection between a ST and a Satellite System, without any DAMA request. The delay associated with this capacity assignment is fairly constant and reduced to the propagation delay of the satellite link.

- **Variable Rate** (Rate Based Dynamic Capacity—**RBDC**). This traffic assignment is based on requests that depend on the average rate of incoming data on the ST. This assignment type can be guaranteed (up to RBDCmax ceiling rate) or not, but always on demand. The rate assignment is valid for a certain period of time: after the timer has expired, capacity is not assigned anymore except if a request was done in the meantime. Sustained traffic will be doing periodic requests, thus avoiding expiration of timers. In this case, the delay associated to this capacity assignment, after the initial requests, will be equal to the propagation delay.

- **Best effort** (Volume Based Dynamic Capacity—**VBDC**). This traffic assignment is based on requests that indicate the volume of data in the ST buffers. The capacity is assigned when available in response to a request, without any guarantee on assignment. The delay for traffic using this capacity assignment type can be long (if capacity is not available) and may vary considerably. A guaranteed VBDC capacity can also be defined by setting a minimum value for VBDC (MinVBDC) per ST. VBDC capacity up to MinVBDC will be granted (when requested), in every superframe.

The return access scheme of the satellite is able to provide different types of service. However, QoS differentiation cannot be done without architectural solutions at the upper layers. The next section presents a brief overview of these solutions as well as the QoS-oriented architecture targeted for the emulation.

B.2.3 QoS Support for Satellite Network Systems

In the satellite networking context, the interaction between the IP Layer where the QoS might be set, and the lower layers where the traffic is finally prioritised, is of major importance. QoS techniques and architectures for satellite networks have been widely studied in the literature and the standardisation of these QoS architectures are in progress. [212, 213] propose to use DiffServ architecture [14] on both the forward and return links. This architecture is well adapted to the return link due to the different classes-of-service of the DVB-RCS capacity allocation. The satellite system, in this study, is assumed to be an access network to the Internet for end-users. Thus, as a boundary node, the ST is the most important component regarding QoS support on the Return Link. It has to implement traffic conditioning/policing functions, in addition to packet classification and per-hop forwarding/scheduling according to a packet's Class-of-Service, as illustrated in Fig. B.4.

The proposed mapping and admission control based on these recommendations are as follows:

The end-to-end QoS architecture deployed in EuQoS system integrates DiffServ and includes signalling mechanisms for admission control as well as resource pre-reservation. In order to meet the DiffServ forwarding requirements, the IP classes of service need to be appropriately mapped into MAC QoS classes and then into DAMA capacity categories supported by the Scheduler. Here we consider that **RT** traffic is

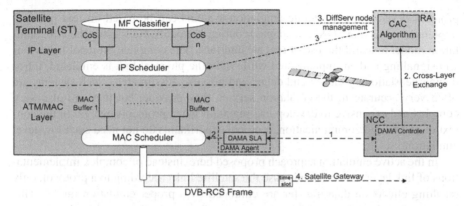

Fig. B.4. QoS-oriented architecture of the satellite terminal in EuQoS

directed to the highest priority MAC buffer DVB-RT using CRA capacity. **NRT** traffic is redirected to a medium-priority MAC buffer DVB-VR using RBDC capacity. **Elastic** traffic is redirected to the lowest priority MAC buffer DVB-JT using VBDC and the remaining capacity. The admission control is done by the Resource Manager (RM) and Resource Allocator (RA) depending on the available satellite resources on the return link. This information is passed from the Network Control Center (NCC) of the Satellite System to the RA. A Service Level Agreement (SLA) is passed at logon between ST and the satellite system's NCC. The bandwidth guaranteed for high priority classes (CRA, RBDC) in this SLA, are generally restricted due to their cost. Thus, to avoid the waste of high-priority capacity, admission control is based on the remaining satellite resources and limitations per end-user. If bandwidth is available for a specific IP CoS (RT or NRT) in relation with remaining satellite resources in the corresponding DAMA class, the flow is admitted, if the user is under its contract limitation. No per-flow admission control is done for the elastic CoS type, but its global rate is limited to the remaining bandwidth not used by high-priority traffic. This ensures full resource use while limiting congestion in the ST. This QoS architecture, including differentiated services and admission control, enables a flow to use a satellite access class on the return link without any interference with concurrent traffic. Thus, a prioritised flow is able to use CRA or RBDC access class, and will not be delayed by Best-Effort traffic that would rather use VBDC capacity when available. However, the prereservation of resources realised by the QoS architecture is different from the actual allocation done by the satellite system with internal requests. Indeed, reservations could be prereserved on the control plane, but the connection could finally fail. Thus, immediate allocation of resource in a satellite environment is not feasible due to its cost.

B.2.4 Emulation of a DVB-S, DVB-RCS Satellite System

Emulation platforms are a classical way to achieve protocol experiments, particularly in the expensive and complex satellite environment. In the context of low-level protocol developments, satellite emulation systems can be based on real protocol implementations (e.g., DAMA, adapted routing protocols, etc.), using the wire emulation model to avoid the use of real air interface. The complete protocol behaviour and signalling is then implemented while only the physical link is emulated, introducing geostationary end-to-end delay, and possibly loss models. Such systems are often very accurate in the emulation service they provide, but they are also very complex and expensive to develop and maintain when protocols evolve. In the context of end-to-end communication, protocol experiments do not need such low-level emulation.

In the active emulation approach proposed here, instead of complex implementations of link layer access (in this case the satellite link) according to a protocol, only resulting effects on data transfer are emulated by a proper emulation model. This leads to a simple and powerful implementation that can be thus combined with more complex emulation scenarios (e.g., for emulating a wider network including a satellite link) or operational networks. To achieve this goal, the emulation model must react in real-time to various external events such as time or processed traffic, leading to the concept of active emulation. The advantage compared to the first type of emulation is that it provides an "in-a-box" solution integrating an emulation processor and potentially complex and realistic emulation model (not limited to satellite links) into an easy-to-deploy system.

B.2.4.1 Integration of an Emulated Satellite Link and the EuQoS System

Figure B.5 presents a simplified scenario of the target satellite system previously described, integrated into the EuQoS architecture.

The satellite system presented in Fig. B.5 is emulated by a single physical component, the Emulation System. The Emulation System is managed by an emulation controller, configured by an experimenter through predefined scenarios. This emulation controller also integrates the Resource Allocator specific to the satellite system

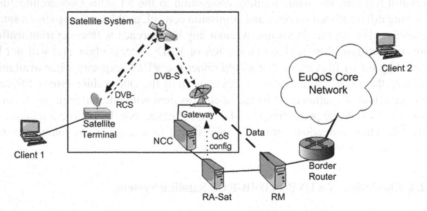

Fig. B.5. Simplified target satellite system

implementation that also influences the Emulation System (configuration of over-all resources and admitted flows). This RA-Sat manages the technology-dependent QoS provisioning specified by the RA-Controller through the EuQoS standard inter-face. The RA-Sat provides information to the RA-Controller on the current status of satellite system utilisation.

The Resource Manager of the satellite system is running on the same machine as the RA-Controller and manages Admission Control to the Satellite System. Two sets of modules are accessing the Emulation System:

- The first one represents the satellite Resource Allocator modules defined in Eu-QoS, namely:
    1. The Connection Admission Control algorithm specific to the satellite link.
    2. The underlying Network Configuration module, that needs to configure the satellite link (here the satellite emulator) upon traffic admission or release.
- The second one corresponds to the scenario-based emulation control. Scenarios are defined by the experimenter (using XML files) in order to specify and emulate concurrent cross-traffic on the satellite terminal as well as overall load of the satellite system.

To access simultaneously the satellite link emulation, these two sets of modules use a common class instantiated for each satellite access class. Then, these objects send messages to the Emulation Control module.

The Impairment System is able to apply impairments to the traffic concerning three types of parameters:

1. the delay experienced,
2. the bandwidth limitation,
3. the loss model.

Messages sent by the satellite RA and scenario control modules through access class objects are translated into control messages sent to the impairment system. These control messages have an impact on the bandwidth allocated to the traffic and the packet loss model experienced by the traffic crossing the emulator. Concerning the delays applied, messages do not modify them; the delay variations reflect the intrinsic behaviour of the access scheme and are not influenced by external events other than real data (for instance, admission of flows or cross-traffic emulation), in the case of satellite emulation.

The behaviour of each Class-of-Service of the EuQoS System in the satellite context is preconfigured in this Emulation Control module. The Classes-of-Service behaviour for the return link is directly linked with the Satellite Access classes con-sidering the proposed mapping.

An emulation control and impairment system can produce basic behaviour that can be composed to produce more complex behaviour including interaction with the traffic crossing the emulator leading to the "active" aspect of this architecture. The composition of such basic impairment modules may correspond to a specific behaviour of a network, used to evaluate a protocol in this context, or to produce a target technology, such as the QoS-enabled satellite link. The emulation control is also in charge of managing information on the traffic. The impairment system finally applies rules to interfaces in order to configure the impairments on the traffic as needed. It is also in charge of providing in real time required information about the traffic to the emulation control, such as sequence number of packets, packets' size or any kind of useful information for emulation control modules in order for them to take some decisions on the evolution of the emulation and thus to apply appropriate rules to the ongoing traffic. The concept of active emulation corresponds to the dynamic configuration of the impairment system depending on information gathered in real time from the data crossing the system; on the opposite, passive emulation could refer to emulation models where scenarios are defined in advance, independently of the traffic crossing the impairment system. A traffic shaper is then in charge of applying constraints on traffic crossing the emulator in accordance with the current configuration. A detailed description of this active impairment framework and emulation control is described in the next section.

B.2.4.2 Active Emulation of DVB-RCS Access Scheme

As presented earlier, three main IP Classes-of-Service are used to provide different levels of QoS in the EuQoS system. A distinct emulation of these three classes needs to be achieved for the satellite system, on forward and on return links. We will detail how these access classes are emulated using the active emulation concept after a description of the impairment framework and emulation control.

B.2.4.2.1 Impairment Framework and Emulation Control

The impairment system that will be used to produce the QoS-enabled satellite behaviour uses a framework based on the experimentation channel (EChannel). The EChannel component offers a target QoS to the System under Test (SuT). The EChannel is defined as a data path providing particular QoS impairments to the SuT. The actual EChannel QoS will be here associated with the DVB technology.

The Experiment Channel, illustrated in Fig. B.6, intends to produce the final target behaviour in terms of QoS for the experimentation. This resulting behaviour can implement a very simple behaviour, such as constant end-to-end delay or a more complicated one such as the behaviour of an end-to-end path constituted by various underlying network technologies. To allow the implementation of such an arbitrary complexity, the EChannel is built by the composition of Experimentation Nodes (ENodes) having a programmable action on the traffic. Each ENode is an active component that offers the necessary communication ports to achieve the internal communication of experiment packets. The nodes are individually parameterised using an additional communication port (pConf). Finally, a specific spying port called pSpy may be used to give information about the ongoing processed traffic to an external management module. The communication and spying ports (pConf and pSpy) enable active emulation. InputTap and OutputTap are input and output interfaces ensuring the packet capture and reinjection into the physical network.

As illustrated in Fig. B.7, the experimentation node is divided into two main parts to differentiate the actual impairments to achieve and the controlling process: the

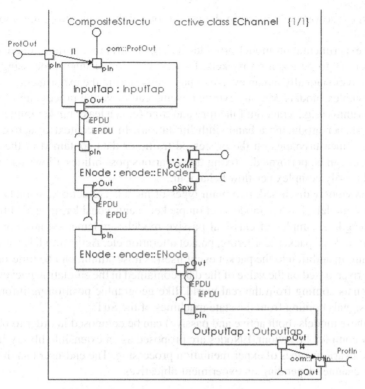

Fig. B.6. The Experiment Channel is a way to produce a target behaviour

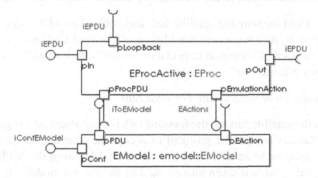

Fig. B.7. The experimentation node is composed of an experimentation processor and experiment model

emulation processor is impairing the packets while the emulation model is deciding how each packet will be processed, having access to various information (i.e., length of packet, capture time, internal packet fields, external ports etc.). When a packet enters into the ENode, the processor asks the model what to do with it. The model can be arbitrarily complex, but needs to reply to the processor which really processes the packet. The various actions in the processor are delaying, dropping, modifying etc.

The experimentation model provides an abstract representation aimed at specifying actions to be taken on packets. Experimentation channel processing can be defined either statically or can evolve dynamically during the experiment.

In complex models, various external events can drive the processing of packets like algorithms (e.g., a random function) and time (e.g., a leaky bucket implementing a traffic shaper producing a bandwidth limitation). In the context of active experimentation, measurements on the processed traffic or data contained in the packets themselves can be performed. Mixing those various possibilities allows us to implement arbitrarily complex per-flow behaviour.

As previously discussed, two main types of models are defined, namely passive and active models. Passive models act on packet events considering arrival time and packet length. Examples of classical passive models implemented are, e.g., delay, jitter, packet loss, packet reordering, packet alteration etc. Active models can react to any stimuli in addition to the packet event itself. Those stimuli can be time-driven or packet-driven based on the value of the data contained in the emulation packet, or any other signals coming from the real world, like geographic positioning information, or even signals coming from the state machines of the SuT.

All these models (both active and passive) can be composed in order to obtain an arbitrary complex behaviour. ENodes are proposed as an extensible library intended to provide various types of experimentation processing. The end-user can then compose the channel depending on experiment objectives.

B.2.4.3 Emulation Details of the Satellite System in EuQoS Architecture

We will now detail the way the satellite link and each Class-of-Service is emulated using the active emulation concept. Emulation of Forward Link access is presented first. Then emulation of various access classes of return link as well as combination of these classes is presented.

B.2.4.3.1 Emulation of the Satellite Forward Link

The access to the satellite link on the forward link is centralised on the gateway. This implies that there is no specific protocol to access the channel, but just a classical allocation of resource to an aggregate and an encapsulation in the MPEG2/DVB-S frame. The encapsulation is taken into account by the control modules to set the total bandwidth allocated for each Class-of-Service and to update this bandwidth at the time the flows are admitted.

The Forward link is proposed as a simple experiment channel integrating a constant delay, a throughput shaper and a loss rate ENodes. For each Class-of-Service the same delay, corresponding to the link crossing, is experienced on the forward link and thus needs to be emulated by the impairment system. In lower priority classes, additional delay might be experienced due to larger buffers. The delay experienced to cross a geostationary satellite link is around 250 ms, this is the delay applied to packets crossing the Forward Link in **RT**, **NRT** or **Elastic Classes**.

The differences between these classes are the assigned buffer sizes, implying different delay and losses for the traffic:

For **RT class**, the buffer size is reduced to the minimum, because the traffic of this class does not admit additional delay. Flows are admitted if the required bandwidth is available in the class. This requires that the input traffic rate is lower or equal to the output traffic rate.

For **NRT class** the buffer size is reduced, but not as much as for the RT class, because the traffic admitted in this class is more prone to fluctuations, and thus the buffer needs to absorb potential bursts. Besides, the delay is not the main issue of this Class-of-Service.

The **Elastic Class** is able to take advantage of resources unused by the other classes and is tolerant to delay. Thus, the buffers need to have rather large dimensions in order to efficiently use the potential resource unused by other classes.

The bandwidth impairment for each Class-of-Service depends on a static consideration: the agreement considered between the satellite terminal and the satellite system's NCC (including guaranteed resource for each access class) as well as on a dynamic consideration: the flows admitted in the class. A simple configuration through high-level modules is possible in order to set this bandwidth limitation on the throughput ENode. The applied loss model is the same for all Classes-of-Service and depends on the loss model defined in the scenario (based on weather conditions).

B.2.4.3.2 Emulation of the Satellite Return Link

The emulation of the return link is more complex than for the forward link. Several Satellite Terminals access the link simultaneously. Thus, a more complex access scheme has been defined to share efficiently the resource between them. The emulation of on-demand capacity allocation types requires the usage of active emulation.

Depending on the traffic assignment type to emulate, predefined QoS parameters, such as delay and throughput, are initially set by control modules, in order to emulate propagation delay or bandwidth limitations. Some QoS parameters are then set in real time in order to emulate signalling process, cross-traffic and satellite load, and take into account admission of new flows. The signalling protocol is not implemented, but only its resulting effect on the traffic.

The emulation control is based on the experimentation channel defined in the impairment framework to perform impairment decisions. The spying and communication ports of emulation nodes enable communication about ongoing processed traffic and to apply real-time impairment decisions taken.

The experiment channel implementing the return link uses a more complex ENodes composition than the forward link, especially for on-demand access classes. An active ENode has to dynamically compute the bandwidth limitation, delay and packet loss rate values to apply to the set of ENodes, which actually impair the flows according to the initial configuration of the satellite link emulation and the information about ongoing network traffic. Depending on the initial configuration corresponding to the predefined type of contract, several types of traffic assignment classes will be available and accordingly instantiated in the emulator. Depending on the traffic assignment types and the ongoing traffic, the active ENode will initially set some values for the parameters such as delay and throughput, and will take the decision to modify these values in real time. This will be done in order to produce the delay introduced by the signalling process, depending on the resources delivered to a particular Satellite Terminal.

The three main IP Classes-of-Service of the EuQoS framework are mapped to the three access classes of DVB-RCS as follows:

- **RT Class** is mapped to the CRA allocation type. This access class offers a guaranteed bandwidth permanently allocated (without signalling) during the entire connection. Delay for the traffic using this class is then reduced to propagation delay.
- The **NRT class** is mapped to the RBDC allocation type. The capacity allocated to this class is on demand and requested based on the data rate entering the ST buffers.
- The **Elastic class** is mapped to the VBDC allocation type. The capacity allocated to this access class is on demand, and requested based on the data volume in the ST buffer.

The emulation of the RT Class is similar to the forward link and uses a simple experimentation channel composed of three ENodes:

- The first ENode emulates a constant delay of 250 ms that is applied to packets, according to the propagation delay.
- The second ENode is a throughput shaper. The bandwidth impairment depends on the SLA passed between the ST and the Satellite System's NCC as well as the admission of real flows by the Resource Allocator or emulated ones.
- The third ENode emulates the loss rate. The loss model depends on the defined scenario (based on weather conditions).

The experimentation channel used for NRT and Elastic classes are based on the model of active emulation. Active emulation is required for on-demand traffic, because the behaviour of experimentation channel depends on the traffic injected by the SuT. In particular, the signalling part of this protocol has a nonnegligible effect on the delay and bandwidth experienced by the traffic reaching a satellite return link. Figure B.8 shows the used experimentation channel.

As shown in Fig. B.8, four passive ENodes and one active ENode have been composed together in this particular experimentation channel. Packets that are conveyed through the return link EChannel cross the four ENodes. Each ENode is responsible for a particular aspect of the on-demand access class behaviour. All together, they emulate the signalling protocol and the return link access behaviour:

- The first ENode emulates the interval of time between two capacity requests that are sent from the satellite terminal toward the NCC. A spying port is placed on this node to measure the volume and rate of incoming traffic and send this information to the emulation control (the active ENode).

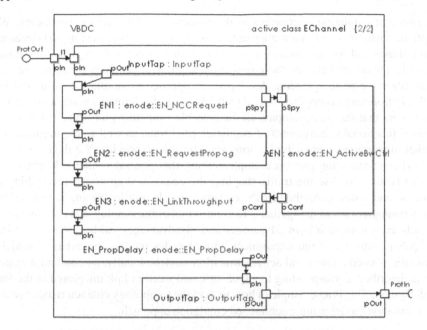

Fig. B.8. On-demand access classes experimentation channel

- The second ENode emulates the propagation delay from the ST to the NCC of the capacity requests and their processing time. A constant delay is applied with a possible delay variation introduced by request processing.
- The third ENode emulates the emission rate of data on the air link by the ST. This ENode has a communication port and applies bandwidth impairments, depending on information received from the emulation controller (the active ENode). This is based on real-time traffic measurements (volume or rate) by spying traffic on the first ENode. The Active ENode spies on the traffic packets and computes the actual input rate in real time. The configuration of the rate is calculated when packets reach the first ENode, but needs to be applied when requests come back. As a result, there is a delay introduced between the calculated rate and the time it is applied at the third ENode. The emulated rate can be limited by the SLA limitations as well as emulation of cross-traffic and the satellite system. This ENode also applies the buffer limitations.
- The fourth ENode emulates the delay encountered by the traffic to cross the satellite link. A constant delay is applied corresponding to propagation delay (250 ms).

B.3 Conclusions

Emulation is a widely used approach to experiment with real protocols or applications in order to meet user or QoS requirements. In this chapter, we proposed an overview of emulation approaches in the context of networking experiments. We explained why this emulation approach is useful for research, design and development phases and we compared it to simulation or real network experiments. Emulation is a trade-off between these two approaches, as it provides a way to test real applications or protocols being developed (as opposed to simulation) in a controllable environment (as opposed to real technologies). We defined a general emulation framework that should encompass all the possible emulation platforms. For this, we defined functional requirements of emulation platforms, as well as requirements on packet impairments that such platforms shall be able to provide. We then described the existing emulation platforms implementing this general framework, classified in two types to realise the traffic shaping: the centralised approach (everything is done on one system) and the distributed approach (the traffic shaping is realised by many computers working together). To control this traffic shaping, a set of emulation models exist with their own advantages and disadvantages: ad-hoc models setting up QoS parameters of the impairment, virtual nodes models, trace-based models, simulation-based models and active-emulation models. Finally, an emulation example is described, corresponding to a QoS-oriented satellite link integrated in the EuQoS System. This is an example of how to map the technology characteristics toward the emulation model using a centralised emulation approach.

References

1. R. Steinmetz and K. Nahrstedt, *Multimedia Fundamentals: Medai Coding and Content Processing*, 2nd ed. Prentice-Hall PTR, 2002, vol. 1.
2. R. Steinmetz and K. Nahrstedt, *Multimedia Systems*, 1st ed. Berlin, Germany: Springer Verlag, 2004.
3. S. Floyd, "Connections with multiple congested gateways in packet-switched networks part 1: One-way traffic," *Computer Communications Review*, vol. 21, no. 5, pp. 30–47, October 1991.
4. M. Mathis, J. Semke, and J. Mahdavi, "The macroscopic behavior of the tcp congestion avoidance algorithm," *SIGCOMM Comput. Commun. Rev.*, vol. 27, no. 3, pp. 67–82, 1997.
5. ITU-T, "Itu t recommendation g.114: One-way transmission time." 2003.
6. ITU-T, "Itu t recommendation g.1010: End-user multimedia qos categories." 2001.
7. T. Szigeti and C. Hattingh, *End-to-End QoS Network Design: Quality of Service in LANs, WANs, and VPNs (Networking Technology)*. CISCO Press, 2005.
8. S. Keshav, *An Engineering Approach to Computer Networking*. Addison Wesley, 1997.
9. R. Braden, D. Clark, and S. Shenker, "Integrated services in the internet architecture: an overview," RFC 1633, June 1994.
10. S. Shenker and J. Wroclawski, "General characterization parameters for integrated service network elements," RFC 2215, September 1997.
11. J. Wroclawski, "Specification of the Controlled-Load Network Element Service," RFC 2211 (Proposed Standard), September 1997. [Online]. Available: http://www.ietf.org/rfc/rfc2211.txt
12. S. Shenker, C. Partridge, and R. Guerin, "Specification of Guaranteed Quality of Service," RFC 2212 (Proposed Standard), September 1997. [Online]. Available: http://www.ietf.org/rfc/rfc2212.txt
13. J. Solomon, "Applicability Statement for IP Mobility Support," RFC 2005 (Proposed Standard), Oktober 1996. [Online]. Available: http://www.ietf.org/rfc/rfc2005.txt
14. S. Blake, D. Black, M. Carlson, E. Davies, Z. Wang, and W. Weiss, "An Architecture for Differentiated Service," RFC 2475 (Informational), Dezember 1998, updated by RFC 3260. [Online]. Available: http://www.ietf.org/rfc/rfc2475.txt
15. K. Nichols, S. Blake, F. Baker, and D. Black, "Definition of the Differentiated Services Field (DS Field) in the IPv4 and IPv6 Headers," RFC 2474 (Proposed Standard), December 1998, updated by RFCs 3168, 3260. [Online]. Available: http://www.ietf.org/rfc/rfc2474.txt

16. K. Nichols and B. Carpenter, "Definition of Differentiated Services Per Domain Behaviors and Rules for their Specification," RFC 3086 (Informational), April 2001. [Online]. Available: http://www.ietf.org/rfc/rfc3086.txt

17. K. Nichols, V. Jacobson, and K. Poduri, "A per-domain behavior for circuit emulation in ip networks," *SIGCOMM Comput. Commun. Rev.*, vol. 34, no. 2, pp. 71–83, 2004.

18. B. Davie, A. Charny, J. Bennet, K. Benson, J. L. Boudec, W. Courtney, S. Davari, V. Firoiu, and D. Stiliadis, "An Expedited Forwarding PHB (Per-Hop Behavior)," RFC 3246 (Proposed Standard), March 2002. [Online]. Available: http://www.ietf.org/rfc/rfc3246.txt

19. J. Heinanen, F. Baker, W. Weiss, and J. Wroclawski, "Assured Forwarding PHB Group," RFC 2597 (Proposed Standard), June 1999, updated by RFC 3260. [Online]. Available: http://www.ietf.org/rfc/rfc2597.txt

20. J. Babiarz, K. Chan, and F. Baker, "Configuration Guidelines for DiffServ Service Classes," RFC 4594 (Informational), August 2006. [Online]. Available: http://www.ietf.org/rfc/rfc4594.txt

21. L. Breslau, E. W. Knightly, S. Shenker, I. Stoica, and H. Zhang, "Endpoint admission control: architectural issues and performance," in *SIGCOMM '00: Proceedings of the conference on Applications, Technologies, Architectures, and Protocols for Computer Communication.* New York, NY, USA: ACM, 2000, pp. 57–69.

22. K. Ramakrishnan and S. Floyd, "A Proposal to add Explicit Congestion Notification (ECN) to IP," RFC 2481 (Experimental), January 1999, obsoleted by RFC 3168. [Online]. Available: http://www.ietf.org/rfc/rfc2481.txt

23. C. Cetinkaya, V. Kanodia, and E. W. Knightly, "Scalable services via egress admission control," *IEEE Transactions on Multimedia*, vol. 3, no. 1, pp. 69–81, 2001. [Online]. Available: citeseer.ist.psu.edu/cetinkaya01scalable.html

24. S. McCanne, V. Jacobson, and M. Vetterli, "Receiver-driven layered multicast," in *ACM SIGCOMM*, vol. 26, no. 4. New York: ACM Press, Aug. 1996, pp. 117–130.

25. V. Paxson, "Strategies for Sound Internet Measurement," in *4th Internet Measurements Conference*, 2004.

26. V. Paxson, G. Almes, J. Mahdavi, and M. Mathis, "Framework for IP Performance Metrics," RFC 2330, May 1998.

27. J. Mahdavi and V. Paxson, "IPPM Metrics for Measuring Connectivity," RFC 2678, Sept. 1999.

28. G. Almes, S. Kalidindi, and M. Zekauskas, "A One-way Delay Metric for IPPM," RFC 2679, Sept. 1999.

29. I.-T. R. Y.1541, "Network Performance Objectives fo IP-based Services," Review Jan. 2005.

30. G. Almes, S. Kalidindi, and M. Zekauskas, "A Round-trip Delay Metric for IPPM," RFC 2681, Sept. 1999.

31. G. Almes, S. Kalidindi, and M. Zekauskas, "A One-way Packet Loss Metric for IPPM," RFC 2680, Sept. 1999.

32. C. Demichelis and P. Chimento, "IP Packet Delay Variation Metric for IP Performance Metrics (IPPM)," RFC 3393, Nov. 2002.

33. M. Mathis and M. Allman, "A Framework for Defining Empirical Bulk Transfer Capacity Metrics," RFC 3148, July 2001.

34. I.-T. R. P.800.1, "Mean Opinion Score (MOS) terminology," 2003.

35. A. Takahashi, H. Yoshino, and N. Kitawaki, "Perceptual qos assessment technologies for voip," *IEEE/Comm. Mag.*, vol. 42, no. 7, pp. 28–34, 2004.

36. I.-T. R. G.107, "The E-model, a computational model for use in transmission planning," 2003.

37. I.-T. R. P.910, "Subjective video quality assessment methods for multimedia applications," 1999.
38. I.-T. R. P.862, "Perceptual evaluation of speech quality (PESQ): An objective method for end-to-end speech quality assessment of narrow-band telephone networks and speech codecs," 2001.
39. D. L. Mills, "Network Time Protocol (Version 3) Specification, Implementation and Analysis," RFC 1305, Mar. 1992.
40. D. Veitch, S. Babu, and A. Pàsztor, "Robust synchronization of software clocks across the internet," in *Internet Measurement Conference (IMC '04)*, 2004.
41. N. Duffeld, "Sampling for passive internet measurement: A review," *Statistical Science*, vol. 19, no. 3, pp. 472–498, 2004.
42. J. Quittek, T. Zseby, B. Claise, and S. Zander, "Requirements for IP Flow Information Export (IPFIX)," RFC 3917, Oct. 2004.
43. M. Crovella and B. Krishnamurthy, *Internet Measurement. Infrastructure, Traffic, and Applications*. John Wiley & Sons, Ltd, 2006.
44. D. Harrington, R. Presuhn, and B. Wijnen, "An architecture for describing simple network management protocol (snmp) management frameworks," RFC 3411, Dec. 2002.
45. "Lobster – Large-scale Monitoring of Broadband Internet Infrastructures," http://www.ist-lobster.org.
46. N. G. Duffield and M. Grossglauser, "Trajectory sampling for direct traffic observation," *IEEE/ACM Trans. Netw.*, vol. 9, no. 3, pp. 280–292, 2001.
47. T. Zseby, S. Zander, and G. Carle, "Evaluation of Building Blocks for Passive One-Way-Delay Measurements," in *Passive and Active Measurements Conference*, 2001.
48. S. B. Moon, "Measurement and Analysis of End-to-end Delay and Loss in the Internet," Ph.D. dissertation, University of Massachusetts, 2000.
49. J. Strauss, D. Katabi, and F. Kaashoek, "A measurement study of available bandwidth estimation tools," in *Internet Measurement Conference (IMC)*, 2003.
50. L. Lao, C. Dovrolis, and M. Y. Sanadidi, "The probe gap model can underestimate the available bandwidth of multihop paths," *SIGCOMM Comput. Commun. Rev.*, vol. 36, no. 5, pp. 29–34, 2006.
51. B. Melander, M. Bjorkman, and P. Gunningberg, "A New End-to-End Probing and Analysis Method for Estimating Bandwidth Bottlenecks," in *IEEE Globecom Global Internet Symposium*, 2000.
52. Q. Liu and J.-N. Hwang, "End-to-end available bandwidth estimation and time measurement adjustment for multimedia qos," in *ICME '03: Proceedings of the 2003 International Conference on Multimedia and Expo – Volume 3 (ICME '03)*. Washington, DC, USA: IEEE Computer Society, 2003, pp. 373–376.
53. A. Pásztor and D. Veitch, "Active Probing using Packet Quartets," in *Internet Measurement Workshop*, 2002.
54. R. Jain and S. A. Routhier, "Packet Trains-Measurements and a New Model for Computer Network Traffic," *IEEE Journal of Selected Areas in Communications*, vol. SAC-4, no. 6, pp. 986–995, 1986.
55. C. Dovrolis, P. Ramanathan, and D. Moore, "Packet-dispersion techniques and a capacity-estimation methodology," *IEEE/ACM Trans. Netw.*, vol. 12, no. 6, pp. 963–977, 2004.
56. "PlanetLab: An open platform for developing, deploying, and accessing planetary-scale services," http://www.planet-lab.org/.
57. "Cooperative Association for Internet Data Analysis (CAIDA)," http://www.caida.org/.
58. "Active Measurement Project (AMP)," http://amp.nlanr.net/.

59. F. Georgatos, F. Gruber, D. Karrenberg, M. Santcroos, A. Sanj, H. Uijterwaal, and R. Wilhem, "Providing Active Measurements as a Regular Service for ISP's," in *Proceedings of Passive and Active Measurement*, 2001.

60. "Evergrow Traffic Observatory Measurement InfrastruCture," http://www.etomic.org/.

61. "DIMES (Distributed Internet MEasurements & Simulations)," http://www.netdimes.org/.

62. "Ever-growing global scale-free networks, their provisioning, repair and unique functions," http://www.evergrow.org/.

63. S. Shalunov, B. Teitelbaum, A. Karp, J. W. Boote, and M. J. Zekauskas, "One-Way Active Measurements Protocol," RFC 4656, Sept. 2006.

64. S. McCanne and V. Jacobson, "The BSD Packet Filter: A New Architecture for User-level Packet Capture," in *USENIX Winter*, 1993.

65. "perfSONAR – PERFormance Service-Oriented Network monitoring ARchitecture," http://www.perfsonar.net.

66. I. Miloucheva, P. Gutierrez, D. Hetzer, A. Nassri, and M. Beoni, "Intermon architecture for complex QoS analysis in inter-domain environment based on discovery of topology and traffic impact," in *Inter-domain Performance and Simulation Workshop, Budapest*, March 2004.

67. "Passive Measurement and Analysis (PMA)," http://pma.nlanr.net/.

68. D. Awduche, J. Malcolm, J. Agogbua, M. O'Dell, and J. McManus, "Requirements for Traffic Engineering Over MPLS," RFC 2702 (Informational), Sept. 1999. [Online]. Available: http://www.ietf.org/rfc/rfc2702.txt

69. E. Rosen, D. Tappan, G. Fedorkow, Y. Rekhter, D. Farinacci, T. Li, and A. Conta, "MPLS Label Stack Encoding," RFC 3032 (Proposed Standard), Jan. 2001, updated by RFCs 3443, 4182. [Online]. Available: http://www.ietf.org/rfc/rfc3032.txt

70. L. Andersson, P. Doolan, N. Feldman, A. Fredette, and B. Thomas, "LDP Specification," RFC 3036 (Proposed Standard), Jan. 2001. [Online]. Available: http://www.ietf.org/rfc/rfc3036.txt

71. H. Smit and T. Li, "Intermediate System to Intermediate System (IS-IS) Extensions for Traffic Engineering (TE)," RFC 3784 (Informational), June 2004, updated by RFC 4205. [Online]. Available: http://www.ietf.org/rfc/rfc3784.txt

72. D. Katz, K. Kompella, and D. Yeung, "Traffic Engineering (TE) Extensions to OSPF Version 2," RFC 3630 (Proposed Standard), Sept. 2003, updated by RFC 4203. [Online]. Available: http://www.ietf.org/rfc/rfc3630.txt

73. R. Braden, L. Zhang, S. Berson, S. Herzog, and S. Jamin, "Resource ReSerVation Protocol (RSVP) – Version 1 Functional Specification," RFC 2205 (Proposed Standard), Sept. 1997, updated by RFCs 2750, 3936, 4495. [Online]. Available: http://www.ietf.org/rfc/rfc2205.txt

74. D. Awduche, L. Berger, D. Gan, T. Li, V. Srinivasan, and G. Swallow, "RSVP-TE: Extensions to RSVP for LSP Tunnels," RFC 3209 (Proposed Standard), Dec. 2001, updated by RFCs 3936, 4420, 4874. [Online]. Available: http://www.ietf.org/rfc/rfc3209.txt

75. B. Jamoussi, L. Andersson, R. Callon, R. Dantu, L. Wu, P. Doolan, T. Worster, N. Feldman, A. Fredette, M. Girish, E. Gray, J. Heinanen, T. Kilty, and A. Malis, "Constraint-Based LSP Setup using LDP," RFC 3212 (Proposed Standard), Jan. 2002, updated by RFC 3468. [Online]. Available: http://www.ietf.org/rfc/rfc3212.txt

76. D. Grossman, "New Terminology and Clarifications for Diffserv," RFC 3260 (Informational), Apr. 2002. [Online]. Available: http://www.ietf.org/rfc/rfc3260.txt

77. F. Le Faucheur, L. Wu, B. Davie, S. Davari, P. Vaananen, R. Krishnan, P. Cheval, and J. Heinanen, "Multi-Protocol Label Switching (MPLS) Support of Differentiated Services," RFC 3270 (Proposed Standard), May 2002. [Online]. Available: http://www.ietf.org/rfc/rfc3270.txt

78. F. L. Faucheur and W. Lai, "Requirements for Support of Differentiated Services-aware MPLS Traffic Engineering," RFC 3564 (Informational), July 2003. [Online]. Available: http://www.ietf.org/rfc/rfc3564.txt

79. F. Le Faucheur and W. Lai, "Maximum Allocation Bandwidth Constraints Model for Diffserv-aware MPLS Traffic Engineering," RFC 4125 (Experimental), June 2005. [Online]. Available: http://www.ietf.org/rfc/rfc4125.txt

80. F. Le Faucheur, "Russian Dolls Bandwidth Constraints Model for Diffserv-aware MPLS Traffic Engineering," RFC 4127 (Experimental), June 2005. [Online]. Available: http://www.ietf.org/rfc/rfc4127.txt

81. W. Lai, "Bandwidth Constraints Models for Differentiated Services (Diffserv)-aware MPLS Traffic Engineering: Performance Evaluation," RFC 4128 (Informational), June 2005. [Online]. Available: http://www.ietf.org/rfc/rfc4128.txt

82. F. Le Faucheur, "Protocol Extensions for Support of Diffserv-aware MPLS Traffic Engineering," RFC 4124 (Proposed Standard), June 2005. [Online]. Available: http://www.ietf.org/rfc/rfc4124.txt

83. H. Schulzrinne and R. Hancock, "General Internet Messaging Protocol for Signaling," IETF, Tech. Rep., 2006.

84. J. Manner, G. Karagiannis, and A. McDonald, S.V. den Bosch, "NSLP for Quality-of-Service Signaling," IETF, Tech. Rep., 2005.

85. M. Stiemerling, "Loose End Message Routing Method for NATFW NSLP," IETF, Tech. Rep., 2005.

86. R. Stewart, Q. Xie, K. Morneault, and H. Schwarzbauer, "Stream Control Transmission Protocol," IETF, Tech. Rep. 2960, 2000.

87. T. Dierks and C. Allen, "The TLS Protocol," IETF, Tech. Rep. 2246, 1999.

88. D. Katz, "Router Alert Option," IETF, Tech. Rep. 2113, 1997.

89. M. Stiemerling, H. Tschofenig, C. Aoun, and E. Davies, "Nat/firewall nsis signaling layer protocol (nslp)," IETF, internet draft, 2006.

90. D. Durham, J. Boyle, R. Cohen, S. Herzog, R. Rajan, and A. Sastry, "The COPS (Common Open Policy Service) Protocol," IETF, Tech. Rep. 2748, 2000.

91. isox214, "ITU-T recommendation X. 214 (11/95) information technology," Nov. 1995.

92. J. Postel, "Transmission control protocol: DARPA internet program protocol specification," IETF, Request For Comments 793, 1981.

93. J. Postel, "User datagram protocol (UDP)," IETF, Request For Comments 768, Aug. 1980.

94. H. Schulzrinne, S. Casner, R. Frederic, and V. Jacobson, "An extension to the Selective Acknowledgment (SACK) Options for TCP," IETF, Task Force 3550, 2003.

95. V. Jacobson and R. Braden, "TCP extensions for long-delay paths," IETF, Request for Comments 1072, Oct. 1988.

96. V. Jacobson, R. Braden, and D. Borman, "Tcp extensions for high performance," IETF, Request for Comments 1323, 1992.

97. L. S. Brakno and L. L. Peterson, "TCP Vegas: End to End congestion Avoidance on a Global Internet," *IEEE Journal on Selected Areas in Communications*, vol. 13, pp. 1465–1480, 1995.

98. S. Floyd, T. Henderson, and A. Gurtov, "The newreno modification to tcp's fast recovery algorithm," IETF, Request for Comments 3782, Apr. 2004.

99. S. Floyd, J. Mahdavi, M. Mathis, and M. Podolsky, "An extension to the selective acknowledgement (SACK) option for TCP," IETF, Request for Comments 2883, July 2000.

100. O. Ait-Hellal and E. Altman, "Analysis of tcp-vegas and tcp-reno," in *Proc. of the IEEE International Conference on Communications – ICC*, 1997, pp. 495–499.

101. V. Jacobson, L. Peterson, L. Brakmo, and S. Floyd, "Problems with arizona's vegas," mailing list, end2end-tf, Tech. Rep., 1994, ftp://ftp.ee.lbl.gov/email/vanj.94mar14.txt.

102. L. Xu, K. Harfoush, and I. Rhee, "Binary increase congestion control for fast long-distance networks," in *Proc. of IEEE INFOCOM*, Mar. 2004, pp. 2514–2524.

103. S. Floyd, "Highspeed tcp for large congestion windows," IETF, Request for Comments 3649, Dec. 2003.

104. D. Katabi, M. Handley, and C. Rohrs, "Congestion control for high bandwidth-delay product networks," in *Proc. of ACM SIGCOMM*, 2002.

105. Y. Xia, L. Subramanian, I. Stoica, and S. Kalyanaraman, "One more bit is enough," in *Proc. of ACM SIGCOMM*, 2005.

106. K. Ramakrishnan, S. Floyd, and D. Black, "The addition of explicit congestion notification (ECN) to ip," IETF, Request for Comments 3168, Sept. 2001.

107. P. Sinha, T. Nandagopal, N. Venkitaraman, R. Sivakumar, and V. Bharghavan, "WTCP: A reliable transport protocol for wireless wide-area networks," *Wireless Networks*, vol. 8, no. 2–3, pp. 301–316, 2002.

108. M. Gerla, M. Y. Sanadidi, R. Wang, A. Zanella, C. Casetti, and S. Mascolo, "Tcp westwood: congestion window control using bandwidth estimation," in *Proc. of IEEE GLOBECOM*, 2001, pp. 1698–1702.

109. C. P. Fu and S. C. Liew, "Tcp veno: Tcp enhancement for transmission over wireless access networks," *IEEE Journal on Selected Areas in Communications*, vol. 21, no. 2, pp. 216–229, Feb. 2003.

110. R. Stewart, Q. Xie, L. Yarroll, J. Wood, K. Poon, K. Fujita, and M. Tuexen, "Sockets API extensions for stream control transmission protocol (SCTP)," IETF, Internet Draft draft-ietf-tsvwg-sctpsocket-06.txt, Mar. 2003.

111. E. Kohler, M. Handley, and S. Floyd, "Datagram congestion control protocol (DCCP)," IETF, Request for Comments 4340, Mar. 2006.

112. S. Floyd and E. Kohler, "Profile for DCCP Congestion Control ID 2: TCP-like Congestion Control," IETF, Request for Comments 4341, Mar. 2006.

113. S. Floyd, E. Kohler, and J. Padhye, "Profile for DCCP congestion control ID 3: TRFC congestion control," IETF, Request for Comments 4342, Mar. 2006.

114. M. Handley, S. Floyd, J. Pahdye, and J. Widmer, "Tcp-friendly rate control (TFRC): Protocol specification," IETF, Request for Comments 3448, Jan. 2003.

115. S. Iren, P. D. Amer, and P. T. Conrad, "The transport layer: tutorial and survey," *ACM Computer Survey*, vol. 31, no. 4, pp. 360–404, 1999.

116. S. Floyd, "Congestion control principles," IETF, Request for Comments 2914, Sept. 2000.

117. Y.-Q. Z. D. Wu and T. Hou, "Transporting real-time video over the internet: Challenges and approaches," *Proc. of the IEEE*, vol. 88, no. 12, Dec. 2000, pp. 1855–1875.

118. V. Jacobson, "Congestion avoidance and control," in *Proc. of ACM SIGCOMM*, Stanford, CA, Aug. 1988, pp. 314–329.

119. R. Talluri, "Error-resilience video coding in the ISO MPEG-4 standard," *IEEE Communications Magazine*, pp. 112–119, June 1998.

120. Y. Wang and Q.-F. Zhu, "Error control and concealment for video communication: A review," *Proc. of the IEEE*, vol. 86, no. 5, May 1998, pp. 974–997.

121. M. Mathis, J. Mahdavi, S. Floyd, and A. Romanow, "TCP selective acknowledgment options," IETF, Request For Comments 2018, Oct. 1996.

122. J. Widmer, "Equation-based congestion control," Diploma Thesis, University of Mannheim, Germany, Feb. 2000.

123. S. Floyd and K. Fall, "Promoting the use of end-to-end congestion control in the internet," *IEEE/ACM Transactions on Networking*, vol. 7, no. 4, pp. 458–472, 1999.

124. P. Amer, C. Chassot, C. Connolly, P. Conrad, and M. Diaz, "Partial order transport service for MM and other application," *IEEE/ACM Transactions on Networking*, vol. 2, no. 5, 1994.

125. L. Rojas-Cardenas, E. Chaput, L. Dairaine, P. Snac, and M. Diaz, "Video transport over partial order connections," *Computer Networks*, vol. 31, no. 7, pp. 709–725, Apr. 1999.

126. J.-P. V. A. Farrel, J. Ash, "A Path Computation Element (PCE)-Based Architecture," The Internet Society, Request for Comments 4655, Aug. 2006.

127. J. Enríquez, M. A. Callejo, and et al., "EuQoS Architecture Deliverable D122," 2007.

128. A. Beben, "EQ-BGP: an efficient inter-domain QoS routing protocol," in *AINA '06: Proceedings of the 20th IEEE International Conference on Advanced Information Networking and Applications*. Los Alamitos, CA, United States: IEEE Computer Society, Apr. 2006, pp. 560–564.

129. X. Masip-Bruin, M. Yannuzzi, R. Serral-Gracia, J. Domingo-Pascual, J. Enriquez-Gabeiras, M. Callejo, M. Diaz, F. Racaru, G. Stea, E. Mingozzi, A. Beben, W. Burakowski, E. Monteiro, and L. Cordeiro, "The EuQoS System: A solution for QoS Routing in Heterogeneous Networks," *IEEE Communications Magazine*, vol. 45, no. 2, Feb. 2007.

130. Y. Rekhter, T. Li, and S. Hares, "A Border Gateway Protocol 4 (BGP-4)," The Internet Society, Request For Comments 4271, Jan. 2006.

131. L. Baresse and et al., "Integrated EuQoS system Software architecture for application use cases and API for application driving Deliverable D421."

132. P. Krawiec and W. Burakowski, "Resource allocation strategies for new connections in qos multi-domain networks with signaling capabilities," in *Proceedings of Australian Telecommunication Networks and Applications Conference 2007 (ATNAC 2007)*, Christchurch, New Zealand, Dec. 2007, pp. 337–342.

133. A. Beben and et al., "Definition of measurement and monitoring system for Phase 2 Deliverable D222."

134. A. Bak, W. Burakowski, F. Ricciato, S. Salsano, and H. Tarasiuk, "A framework for providing differentiated QoS guarantees in IP-based network," *Computer Communications*, vol. 26, no. 4, pp. 327–337, 2003.

135. C. Brandauer, W. Burakowski, M. Dabrowski, B. Koch, and H. Tarasiuk, "AC algorithms in AQUILA QoS IP network," *European Transactions on Telecommunications*, vol. 16, no. 3, pp. 225–232, 2005.

136. M. Dabrowski, G. Eichler, M. Fudala, D. Katzengruber, T. Kilkanen, N. Miettinen, H. Tarasiuk, and M. Titze, "Evaluation of the AQUILA Architecture: Trial Results for Signalling Performance, Network Services and User Acceptance," in *Art-QoS*, 2003, pp. 218–233.

137. K. Chan, J. Babiarz, and F. Baker, "Aggregation of DiffServ Service Classes," Transport Area Working Group," Internet-Draft, Nov. 2007.

138. "Nexuiz project," www.alientrap.org/nexuiz/.

139. J. M. Batalla and R. Janowski, "Provisioning dedicated class of service for reliable transfer of signaling traffic," in *International Teletraffic Congress*, ser. Lecture Notes in Computer Science, L. Mason, T. Drwiega, and J. Yan, Eds., vol. 4516. Springer, 2007, pp. 853–864.

140. "Medigraf," http://www.medigraf.pt/.

141. J. W. Roberts, U. Mocci, and J. T. Virtamo, Eds., *Broadband Network Teletraffic – Performance Evaluation and Design of Broadband Multiservice Networks: Final Report of Action COST 242*, ser. Lecture Notes in Computer Science, vol. 1155. Springer, 1996.

142. L. Kleinrock, *Queueing Systems, Volume 2, Computer Applications*. John Wiley & Sons Inc, 1976.

143. H. Tarasiuk, R. Janowski, and W. Burakowski, "Admissible traffic load of real time class of service for inter-domain peers," in *Proceedings of Joint International Conference on Autonomic and Autonomous Systems and International Conference on Networking and Services (ICAS/ICNS 2005)*. Papeete, Tahiti, French Polynesia: IEEE Computer Society, Oct. 2005.

144. H. Tarasiuk, R. Janowski, and W. Burakowski, "Application of Admission Control and Traffic Shaping for providing TCP Throughput Guarantees," in *Proceedings of International Workshop To-QoS'2006 in conjunction with IFIP 2006 Networking Conference* (ed. W. Burakowski), Coimbra, Portugal, May 2006, pp. 163–172.

145. "IEEE standards for local and metropolitan area networks. Virtual bridged local area networks," *IEEE Std 802.1Q, 2003 Edition (Incorporates IEEE Std 802.1Q-1998, IEEE Std 802.1u-2001, IEEE Std 802.1v-2001, and IEEE Std 802.1s-2002)*, 2003.

146. "IEEE Standard for Local and metropolitan area networks Media Access Control (MAC) Bridges," *IEEE Std 802.1D-2004 (Revision of IEEE Std 802.1D-1998)*, 2004.

147. M. Carmo, J. S. Silva, E. Monteiro, P. Simões, and F. Boavida, "Ethernet QoS Modeling in Emerging Scenarios," in *Proceedings of 3rd International Workshop on Internet Performance, Simulation, Monitoring and Measurement (IPS-MoMe 2005)*. Warsaw, Poland: IST MoMe Cluster, Mar. 2005, pp. 90–96.

148. M. Carmo, B. Carvalho, J. S. Silva, E. Monteiro, P. Simões, M. Curado, and F. Boavida, "NSIS-based Quality of Service and Resource Allocation in Ethernet Networks," in *Proceedings of 4th International Conference on Wired/Wireless Internet Communications 2006*, 2006.

149. M. Carmo, J. S. Silva, and E. Monteiro, "EuQoS approach for Resource Allocation in Ethernet Networks," *International Journal of Network Management*, vol. 17, no. 5, pp. 373–388, Sept./Oct. 2007.

150. "Wireless LAN Medium Access Control (MAC) and Physical Layer (PHY) specifications: Amendment 8: Medium Access Control (MAC) Quality of Service Enhancements," *IEEE Std 802.11e-2005*, 2005.

151. E. Lochin, L. D. A. Jourjon, "gtfrc, a tcp friendly qos-aware rate control for diffserv assured service," *Springer Telecommunication Systems*, doi:10.1007/s11235-006-9004-2, ISSN: 1018-4864 (Print) 1572-9451 (Online), September 2006.

152. E. Exposito, P. Sénac, and M. Diaz, "Compositional architecture pattern for qos-oriented communication mechanisms," in *MMM*, Y.-P. P. Chen, Ed. IEEE Computer Society, 2005, pp. 413–420.

153. B. Quinn and K. Almeroth, "Ip multicast applications: Challenges and solutions," The Internet Society, Request for Comments 3170, Sept. 2001.

154. Z. Albanna, K. Almeroth, D. Meyer, and M. Schipper, "Iana guidelines for ipv4 multicast address assignments," The Internet Society, Request for Comments 3171, Aug. 2001.

155. R. Hinden and S. Deering, "Internet protocol version 6 (ipv6) addressing architecture," The Internet Society, Request for Comments 3513, Apr. 2003.

156. B. Cain, S. Deering, I. Kouvelas, B. Fenner, and A. Thyagarajan, "Internet group management protocol, version 3," The Internet Society, Request for Comments 3376, Oct. 2002.

157. A. Adams, J. Nicholas, and W. Siadak, "Protocol independent multicast – dense mode (pim-dm): Protocol specification (revised)," The Internet Society, Request for Comments 3973, Jan. 2005.

158. B. Fenner, M. Handley, H. Holbrook, and I. Kouvelas, "Protocol independent multicast – sparse mode (pim-sm): Protocol specification (revised)," The Internet Society, Request for Comments 4601, Aug. 2006.

159. D. Waitzman, C. Partridge, and S. Deering, "Distance vector multicast routing protocol," Network Working Group, Request for Comments 1075, Nov. 1988.

160. J. Moy, "Multicast extensions to ospf," Network Working Group, Request for Comments 1584, Mar. 1994.

161. K. Savetz, N. Randall, and Y. Lepage, *MBONE: Multicasting Tomorrow's Internet*. John Wiley & Sons Inc, 1996.

162. R. Zhang and Y. C. Hu, "Borg: A hybrid protocol for scalable application-level multicast in peer-to-peer networks," in *NOSSDAV '03: Proceedings of the 13th international workshop on Network and operating systems support for digital audio and video*. New York, NY, USA: ACM Press, June 2003, pp. 172–179.

163. A. Sobeih, W. Yurcik, and J. C. Hou, "Vring: A case for building application-layer multicast rings (rather than trees)," in *MASCOTS '04: Proceedings of the The IEEE Computer Society's 12th Annual International Symposium on Modeling, Analysis, and Simulation of Computer and Telecommunications Systems (MASCOTS'04)*. Washington, DC, USA: IEEE Computer Society, 2004, pp. 437–446.

164. S. Q. Zhuang, B. Y. Zhao, A. D. Joseph, R. H. Katz, and J. D. Kubiatowicz, "Bayeux: An architecture for scalable and fault-tolerant wide-area data dissemination," in *NOSSDAV '01: Proceedings of the 11th international workshop on Network and operating systems support for digital audio and video*. Port Jefferson, New York, United States: ACM Press, 2001, pp. 11–20.

165. M. Castro, P. Druschel, A.-M. Kermarrec, A. Nandi, A. Rowstron, and A. Singh, "Splitstream: High-bandwidth multicast in a cooperative environment," in *19th ACM Symposium on Operating Systems Principles (SOSP'03)*, Bolton Landing, New York, USA, Oct. 2003.

166. A. Rowstron and P. Druschel, "Pastry: Scalable, distributed object location and routing for large-scale peer-to-peer systems," in *IFIP/ACM International Conference on Distributed Systems Platforms (Middleware)*, Heidelberg, Germany, Nov. 2001, pp. 329–350

167. M. Castro, P. Druschel, A.-M. Kermarrec, and A. Rowstron, "Scribe: A large-scale and decentralized application-level multicast infrastructure," *IEEE Journal on Selected Areas in Communication (JSAC)*, vol. 20, no. 8, Oct. 2002.

168. M. Brogle, D. Milic, and T. Braun, "Qos enabled multicast for structured p2p networks," in *4th IEEE Consumer Communications and Networking Conference*, Las Vegas, NV, USA, Jan. 2007.

169. D. Milic, M. Brogle, and T. Braun, "Video broadcasting using overlay multicast," in *Seventh IEEE International Symposium on Multimedia (ISM 2005)*, Irvine, CA, USA, Dec. 2005, pp. 515–522.

170. A. Sulistio, C. S. Yeo, and R. Buyya, "A taxonomy of computer-based simulations and its mapping to parallel and distributed systems simulation tools," *Softw. Pract. Exper.*, vol. 34, no. 7, pp. 653–673, 2004.

171. N. Metropolis, A. W. Rosenbluth, M. N. Rosenbluth, A. H. Teller, and E. Teller, "Equation of state calculations by fast computing machines," *The Journal of Chemical Physics*, vol. 21, pp. 1087–1092, 1953.

172. T. Yung, J. Martin, M. Takai, and R. Bagrodia, "Integration of fluidbased analytical model with packet-level simulation for analysis of computer networks," 2001.

173. C. Kiddle, R. Simmonds, C. Williamson, and B. Unger, "Hybrid packet/fluid flow network simulation," in *PADS '03: Proceedings of the seventeenth workshop on parallel and distributed simulation*. Washington, DC, USA: IEEE Computer Society, 2003, p. 143.

174. J. Incera, R. Marie, D. Ros, and G. Rubino, "Fluidsim: a tool to simulate fluid models of high-speed networks," *Perform. Eval.*, vol. 44, no. 1–4, pp. 25–49, 2001.

175. B. Liu, D. R. Figueiredo, Y. Guo, J. F. Kurose, and D. F. Towsley, "A study of networks simulation efficiency: Fluid simulation vs. packet-level simulation," in *INFOCOM*, 2001, pp. 1244–1253.
176. "Glomosim," http://pcl.cs.ucla.edu/projects/glomosim/.
177. "Qualnet," http://www.scalable-networks.com/.
178. "Swans," http://jist.ece.cornell.edu/.
179. "Ssfnet," http://www.ssfnet.org/homePage.html.
180. "Omnet++," http://www.omnetpp.org/.
181. "ns-2," http://www.isi.edu/nsnam/ns/index.html.
182. "Vint – virtual internetwork testbed project," http://www.isi.edu/nsnam/vint/index.html.
183. K. Fall and K. Varadhan, "The ns manual (formerly ns notes and documentation)," 2002.
184. F. J. Ros and P. M. Ruiz, "Implementing a new manet unicast routing protocol in ns2," Dept. of Information and Communications Engineering University of Murcia, Tech. Rep., 2004.
185. "Vmware software (virtual machine)," http://www.vmware.com, 2005.
186. V. J. Easton and J. H. McColl, "Statistics glossary v1.1," http://www.cas.lancs.ac.uk/glossaryv1.1/main.html. vol. 2005, 2005.
187. M. Allman, A. Caldwell, and S. Ostermann, "One: The ohio network emulator," *TR-19972*, 1997.
188. L. Rizzo, "Dummynet: a simple approach to the evaluation of protocols," *ACM Computer Communication Review*, 1997.
189. M. Carson and D. Santay, "Nist net: A linux-based network emulation tool," *ACM Computer Communication Review*, 2003.
190. S. Hemminger, "Netem, network emulator," http://developer.osdl.org/shemminger/netem/, 2005.
191. P. Zheng and L. M. Nil, "Empower: A network emulator for wireline and wireless networks," in *IEEE Infocom*, San Francisco, California, USA, 2003.
192. R. Buyya, D. Abramson, and J. Giddy, "A case for economy grid architecture for service oriented grid computing," in *10th IEEE International Heterogeneous Computing Workshop*, San Francisco, California, USA, 2001.
193. B. White, J. Lepreau, L. Stoller, R. Ricci, S. Guruprasad, M. Newbold, M. Hibler, C. Barb, and A. Joglekar, "An integrated experimental environment for distributed systems and networks," in *5th symposium on Operating systems design and implementation*, Boston, USA, 2002.
194. CNRS, "Grid 5000," http://www.grid5000.org, 2003.
195. L. Peterson, T. Anderson, D. Culler, and T. Roscoe, "A blueprint for introducing disruptive technology into the internet," in *First Workshop on Hot Topics in Networking (HotNets-I)*, Princeton, New Jersey, USA, 2002.
196. D. Herrscher and K. Rothermel, "A dynamic network scenario emulation tool," in *11th International Conference on computer communications and networks*, Florida, USA, 2002.
197. "Network node emulation and method of node emulation," *European patent*, 2002.
198. S. Dawson and F. Jahanian, "Probing and fault injection of distributed protocols implementations," in *International Conference on Distributed Computer Systems*, 1995.
199. M. Zec and M. Mikuc, "Operating system support for integrated network emulation in imunes," in *First Workshop on Operating System and Architectural Support for the on demand IT InfraStructure*, Boston, USA, 2004.
200. X. W. Huang, R. Sharma, and S. Keshav, "The entrapid protocol development environment," in *IEEE Infocom*, Boston, USA, 1999.

201. E. Savage and D. Wethereall, "Alpine, a user level infrastructure for network development environment," in *IEEE Infocom*, Boston, USA, 1999.
202. F. Baumgertner, T. Braun, and B. Bhargava, "Virtual routers: a tool for emulating ip routers," in *27th Annual IEEE Conference on Local Computer Networks*, 2002.
203. B. Noble, M. Satyanarayanan, D. Narayanan, J. E. Tilton, J. Flinn, and K. R. Walker, "Trace-based mobile network emulation," in *ACM SIGCOMM*, Cannes, France, 1997.
204. NS-Group, "The network simulator – ns-2," http://www.isi.edu/nsnam/ns, 1989.
205. K. Fall, "Network emulation in the vint/ns simulator," in *Fourth IEEE Symposium on Computers and Communications*, 1999.
206. C. Kiddle, R. Simmonds, and B. Unger, "Improving scalability of network emulation through parallelism and abstraction," in *38th Annual Simulation Symposium (ANSS'05)*, 2005.
207. M. Gineste, H. Thalmensy, L. Dairaine, P. Senac, and M. Diaz, "Active emulation of a dvb-rcs satellite link in an end-to-end qos-oriented heterogeneous network," in *23rd AIAA International Communication Satellite Systems (ICSSC)*, Rome, Italy, 2005.
208. ETSI, "Dvb-rcs: Digital video broadcasting (dvb); interaction channel for satellite distribution systems," vol. EN 301 790, 2003.
209. ETSI, "Digital video broadcasting (dvb); dvb specification for data broadcasting," vol. EN 301 192, 1999.
210. ISO/IEC, "Information technology – generic coding of moving pictures and associated audio: Systems," vol. 13818-1, 1994.
211. ISO/IEC, "Information technology – generic coding of moving pictures and associated audio information – part 6: Extensions for dsm-cc," vol. 13818-6, 1998.
212. S. Kota and M. Marchese, "Quality of service for satellite ip networks: a survey," *International Journal of Satellite Communications and Networking*, vol. 21, pp. 303–349, 2003.
213. ETSI, "Satellite earth stations and systems (ses); broadband satellite multimedia (bsm) services and architectures: Qos functional architecture," vol. TS 102 462, 2006.

Index